Players 1st

BILL DOOLEY

PLAYERS

1ST

**COMPLETE SOCCER COACH'S
GUIDE TO DEVELOPING
EXTRAORDINARY PLAYERS**

AGES 7-14

Meyer & Meyer Sport

British Library Cataloguing in Publication Data
A catalogue record for this book is available from the British Library

Players 1st
Maidenhead: Meyer & Meyer Sport (UK) Ltd., 2018
ISBN: 978-1-78255-131-7

© 2018 by Meyer & Meyer Sport (UK) Ltd.
Aachen, Auckland, Berit, Cairo, Cape Town, Dubai, Hägendorf, Hong Kong, Indianapolis, Manila, New Delhi, Singapore, Sydney, Tehran, Vienna

 Member of the World Sports Publishers' Association (WSPA)
Printed by Print Consult, GmbH, Munich, Germany

ISBN: 978-1-78255-131-7
Email: info@m-m-sports.com
www.m-m-sports.com

CONTENTS

Contents

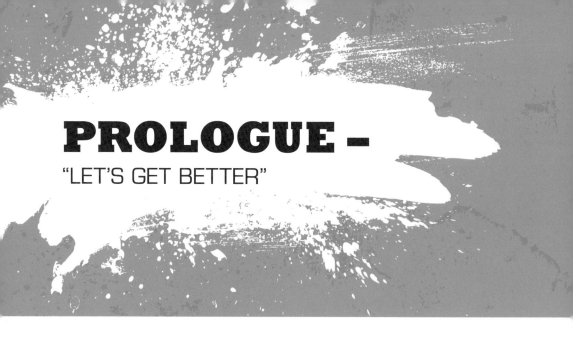

PROLOGUE –
"LET'S GET BETTER"

"You owe it to yourself and to your teammates to do everything you can and give everything you have toward your goal of Being the Best"

–Tracey Bates Leone, World Champion, 1991 US Women's National Team

JOURNEYS

Too many years ago I shared coaching duties with a fellow teacher—let's call him Brian—at a small private school on the East Coast. He coached the varsity soccer team, his first coaching job. I coached the JV and a middle school team in addition to my duties, at age 27, as the school's athletic director. Together, and with even less of a clue, we coached the school's girls' varsity basketball team. (The highest qualifications for that assignment were our limited experiences in faculty pick-up games. But that's another story.) We were the proverbial teachers one textbook page ahead of the students—except we had no textbook.

In time, both of us moved on to other places and other responsibilities. Decades later we continue to coach. Every few years we trade notes, and somewhere in those conversations, we always ask ourselves: *Don't you wish we could go back and coach those kids again, knowing what we know now?* The discussion that follows usually includes some declaration of how we would have just *crushed* the teams from the Big-School-Down-The-Road.

Just a few years earlier my first coaching duty was with the school's fifth and sixth grade soccer team. The team went 9-0-0, with coaching that was, looking back, woefully inadequate. It was a classic example of "coaching as you had been coached." Practices were dedicated to organizing the team on the field in the same W-M formation I'd played in high school. Skill work? Small-sided games? Preparing the players as people for the psychological demands of the game and beyond? You must be kidding! But those 10- to 12-year-olds did get fit.

Brian would discover how little they learned when coaching many of those same players on his varsity team six years later. At the time, though, their lack of success was puzzling.

Learning by doing was how we managed our early coaching assignments. It wasn't completely useless. The best part of experiential learning, and there were some spectacular learning experiences, is that you usually learn more from getting it wrong than getting it right. Fortunately, there were enough of the opposite, those very satisfying moments that kept you thinking you were figuring it out, getting better at it, eventually getting pretty good. But no matter how interesting that journey was personally, the fact remains that the kids in those early years didn't learn what they could have if "we knew then what we know now."

Coaching rarely allows mulligans. The kids you're coaching won't be waiting around for you to figure it out.

That's the idea behind this book. For the dad or mom who has just become coach of a group of 8-year-olds because "we don't have a coach and nobody leaves the room until we get one," these pages are designed to get you through. *You can do it. It's really not that difficult.* But *Players 1st* is also a roadmap for the more experienced coach, be it one who is returning to coaching after a break and looking for something new or one who has a group of young athletes headed for bigger things and is willing to indulge his or her (and their) **Teachable Spirit**.

The program you will find here is simple and efficient. It adapts to the differing experience levels of players and coaches. Despite an atypical approach to how some things are more frequently done, *it works* at all those different levels. And when you do it again with a second group, the results will be even better.

THEN AND NOW

Since that earlier time there has been an explosive growth in youth sports, with youth soccer very much in the vanguard. The most significant difference is that youth sports, including youth soccer, have become Big Business. That change has been accompanied by several unintended and unwelcome consequences.

First among them is that the fundamental purpose of youth sports—developing better kids, *"stronger, more responsible and confident individuals who will be successful in life"*[1] in the words of Positive Coaching Alliance (PCA) founder Jim Thompson—is too often

---

[1] Thompson, J. 2003. *The Double-Goal Coach*. William Morrow Paperbacks, p. 246.

ignored. Words in the mission statements of youth sports organizations about personal development and building character are rarely accompanied by substantive plans to make that happen. Of greater concern is a growing trend in mission statements to exclude even the words.

Another significant difference is an ever-increasing emphasis on winning at ever-younger ages. Driven by a mix of economic influences—notably revenue and market share battles among soccer clubs—and abetted by parental pressure a) to have Monday morning content for the water cooler, b) to shield their kids from the supposedly damaging impact of failure on "self-esteem," c) to chase college scholarships, or d) all of the above, much of the youth sports culture has become adult-centered and adult-driven for adult purposes.

Here's a question to consider: What possible personal or athletic benefit (to use one of the more ridiculous examples) accrues to a child who wins a "World Championship" in 3v3 soccer at age 8? Yet tremendous resources are devoted to just that end.

TOWARD A DIFFERENT MODEL

There's an adage that says, *"There are those who know, those who don't know, and those who don't know that they don't know."* Many youth coaches, especially the draftees, fall into the second group; a disturbing number get mired in the third. The best youth coaches, though, know they don't know and sometimes even *what* they don't know. These coaches are constantly adapting, chipping away at their deficiencies, trying to get better. It's a Sisyphean task, of course. You always discover that there's something more after that. But it becomes a boulder that is fascinating to push.

ON THE FIELD

The changes in youth sports and the excesses that accompany them (early selection, overtraining, the emphasis on tactics and strategy over technical development) impede the realization of the two fundamental soccer purposes at issue in preparing players: lifelong enjoyment of the Game and continuing success at higher levels of play.

Given a group of 10-year-olds and a mandate to win a game in two weeks, quite a few coaches could get it done. (The formula: organize things to get the ball as quickly as possible to the biggest/fastest/strongest kids up front.) But the process of preparing for a similar outcome would be—or at least should be—very different if the mandate is to prepare them to win consistently at age 16.

The pursuit of the immediate result presents a number of problems. It leads to team selection at the younger ages based on advantages of size, strength, and athleticism that often vanish once all have reached puberty. This consigns those not selected to lesser opportunities which, of course, produce "lesser" players. The early selection becomes the ultimate self-fulfilling prophecy. Meanwhile, many of the selectees reach the high school age lacking the fundamental skills to go much further. As one coach has put it: *"Players who do not get a thorough grounding in the game's essential skills at the younger ages are being cheated out of their futures in the game."* Another has put it more simply: *"Teach skills and they will play for a lifetime."* A third, Dr. Jay Martin, editor of the United Soccer Coaches' (formerly the National Soccer Coaches Association of America [NSCAA]) *Soccer Journal*, sees the ultimate result of too much focus on winning and too little on developing players: *"We are creating a nation of kids who can win but cannot play the game."*[2]

This book promotes a longer-term view. It outlines a process that pursues three basic objectives: **1.** *better kids* **2.** *who will play for a lifetime* **3.** *at the highest level their interests and efforts will allow.* It leads to a style of play that is as fun to play as it is enjoyable to watch. And should that process somehow result in teams that win a lot of games including a healthy dose of upsets against your own version of the Big-School-Down-The-Road (spoiler alert: it does), that's a nice bonus.

The fundamental philosophy of the Players 1st approach has been in place for a while. In a nutshell, it says that coaches of younger players (ages 7 to 14) should use the time with their teams to prioritize development of the individual players, with particular attention to their soccer skills. For a time, attention to tactical development and team play is limited to only what is necessary to avoid total chaos on game day.

This is not the way things are commonly done in youth soccer. If anything, there has been a declining emphasis on technical development in recent years. In part, this happens because *teaching* skills is itself a talent that many coaches do not have, even though they may possess the skills themselves.

A greater impediment to skills instruction, though, is related to the pressures associated with that push to win more and more, earlier and earlier. It takes considerably more time, patience, and perseverance to develop skillful players who will win in the long run than it does to teach team organization that will "succeed" at this Saturday's game.

BEYOND THE GAME

Stumbling along in *learn-by-doing mode* in those earlier years of blissful ignorance, many things went surprisingly and even spectacularly well on the field. With hindsight, we

---

[2] Martin, Jay. 2006. Perspective check. Soccer Journal. National Soccer Coaches Association of America.

began to figure out why. More was involved than soccer ability. Those athletes were developing qualities as people that gave them confidence, drive, and determination. This was equally—or more—critical to their success than anything they were learning about soccer. It appeared to be a fortunate (if unintended) outcome of soccer training that was a good fit for the school's core values. So the next question became, "What would have happened if we had really *planned* to develop those character traits alongside the soccer?" We suspected that the players would have been even better sooner. This then led to the most challenging question: "How in the world do you plan for that?"

Fortunately this was an area getting increasing attention at very higher levels of *the Game*. Soccer in the United States in the 90s was fortunate to have the U.S. Women's National Team. So many of the team members were (and remain) terrific role models for our kids—as players and as people. More important to our story is how the WNT coaches—notably Anson Dorrance, Tony DiCicco, Lauren Gregg, April Heinrichs, and Colleen Hacker—were (and remain) so incredibly willing and eager to share everything they were doing with any coach who wanted to learn. This included information about the character strengths of the team's players and how the WNT program worked to develop and enhance those qualities. Both coaches and athletes regularly spoke about how strength of character was a fundamental ingredient in the team's success.

Attention to the role of character in sports came from other directions as well. The programs of the Positive Coaching Alliance had begun. PCA promoted a **Double Goal** model for youth sports (see chapter 4.1). That model pursued winning, not through chasing "the Result" but as a logical consequence of relentlessly seeking to learn and improve in environments where failure is not feared. PCA also recognized a second goal: using sports to teach positive life lessons and life skills that would endure long after the cleats had been retired.

Bruce Brown, then with the Champions of Character Program of the National Association of Intercollegiate Athletics (NAIA), was also pioneering work about the development of strong personal values in college athletes. Materials from that program adapt quite well for use with much younger players. At the professional level Bill Beswick, a psychologist then working with Manchester United, became a regular presenter at the NSCAA's (now the United Soccer Coaches) annual convention on matters dealing with developing personal character traits and effective team cultures.

PUTTING IT TOGETHER

This book is written from a perspective that reflects a blend of those early experiences with what has been learned since. It is meant to provide the foundation and framing for an unconventional approach to developing soccer players from ages 7 to 14. Much of it is based on the premise that kids have until about their 13th birthday to develop a solid base of soccer skills and that their futures in *the Game* will be compromised if they do not. It addresses the importance of character development in young athletes, both for immediate use on the field and as preparation for later life off the field. And it provides alternatives to many of the practices in youth soccer that do not necessarily benefit players personally or athletically.

This book has three main sections. The first, **Foundation**, starts with ways to develop team and club cultures that maximize opportunity for both personal and soccer development. Then it turns to the topic of growing talent to achieve excellence. This section includes several stand-alone essays and handouts that you can download from www.PlayersFirst.com for use with your players and parents, team, and club.

Next comes **Framing**, the "on the field" part, mostly in the form of fundamental exercises that can be used to develop players with exceptional skill. Most contain variations to enrich the activity or make it useful with a variety of topics. There are video downloads for some of these activities on the website, www.PlayersFirst.com, though the videos may not show all the options.

The exercises progress from "one-with-a-ball" activities to play in 2s, 3s, and 4s. They are effective and they are fun. Each has been extensively tested over the past decade with players 7 to 16 years old who, if given the opportunity, would play them forever.

The focus throughout is on developing players' skills, poise, confidence, and even creativity with the ball. A chapter breaks down ball control, another the elements of striking a ball with power and accuracy, a third the role of **Vision**. (These three elements combine over time to allow athletes to play faster and smarter; see chapter 14.1.) Two chapters examine ways to train the skills and tactics of the 1v1 situation, so often a determining factor in games. Then come activities using those basic skills in the small group situations from 2v1 to 3v3 that are the building blocks of team play. Finally there are activities that teams with strong technical and tactical fundamentals can use in preparing and organizing for the full-sided game.

Within those activities you will find an emphasis on *ideas*—a word or phrase here, a paragraph there. Not just what to do but *why*. To make your players think. To make *you* think. And to help grow your athletes, not just as players but as people so that their sports experience helps to make them the kind of *"stronger, more responsible and confident adults"* PCA's Jim Thompson describes.

Occasionally in these first two sections, where there are known obstacles, you will also find clues to prepare you for **WCPGW** (What Could Possibly Go Wrong).

The final section, **Finishing Touches**, addresses some of the collateral issues involved in youth soccer such as travel, tryouts and player selection, and the coach–parent dynamic. Again, there are some downloadable materials (which explains why some things appear more than once within the book.) This section also includes a selection of books and links for further study.

YOUR JOURNEY

We make no claims that our approach is the only way. Just that it is one way that works for all players without regard to their ability or to the soccer level of their particular team. The Players 1st method has regularly led to teams that have reached a high level of success, and over two dozen future All-Americans and Youth National Team players have worked on their fundamentals within the framework. But it is equally suitable for players and teams with a more relaxed attitude toward *the Game*.

We also make no claims that there are a lot of original ideas here about developing young players. What is different is how things are connected. We'll see later how creativity is largely a function of making such connections in different ways, and that's what we hope that this book will inspire in you.

NOW WHAT?

There's a lot of information in these chapters. Please take your time. Chapters 1 through 9 have the background information. But if you've got a training session looming, feel free to jump ahead to the "on the field" portions of the book, beginning with chapter 10 which includes ideas about structuring your training program.

Get the players working on foot skills and conduct the first weekly **Juggling** test (see chapter 12.3). Introduce some ball moves (see chapter 15.3) and two or three of the activities where they'll get used (see chapter 16.4). Start teaching the **Seven Words** process for striking a ball (see chapter 13). Get *"heads up"* and *"on a swivel"* (see chapter 14); there is no more important habit. Make a first attempt at **3v1 in a Box** keep-away (see chapter 20, activity 56) (if only to create a memory, and perhaps a video, of how badly it goes!).

Off the field, establish the initial elements of your team culture (see chapter 5), not the least of which will involve setting out the character traits you hope your athletes will develop in their time with the team (see chapters 3 and 4).

You'll get at least a couple of weeks of training out of those basic elements of the program, enough time to become familiar with all the ideas found in the earlier chapters.

With that said, *"Let's Get Better."*

FOUNDATION:

**THE
PLAYERS 1ST
CULTURE**

1 START WITH THE END IN MIND

Any instructional program for a youth soccer player must meet the athlete's needs in two basic respects:

1. The player must have the opportunity to learn *the Game* in a manner that enables continued enjoyment of soccer for as long as he or she wishes to play. This includes a) developing a solid foundation in the game's skills, b) learning to recognize and solve the small group situations that are the basic components of team play, and c) acquiring a repertoire of effective soccer habits

2. The program must also focus, perhaps more so, on the additional benefits of participation in sports. These personal and social rewards follow from what athletes learn about character traits such as commitment, dedication and discipline, fair play and sportsmanship, integrity, facing challenges, perseverance and resilience, accepting responsibility, pursuing excellence, and developing an appreciation of the competitive process.

The obligation in those two areas, to the player and the person, is as important for the athlete whose future in soccer lies with youth and adult recreational teams as it is for the potential National Team member.

In a Players 1st program, the development of the skills, habits, and character of the individual player comes first. Until that is done, attention to team play is limited to basic offensive and defensive organization.

Many programs talk about the importance of individual player development. Yet too often the commitment to that principle disappears under pressures tied to wins and losses. The development of creative and skillful individual players can be at some initial cost to team "success," especially when judged only by the numbers on the scoreboard. We know, though, that teams developed using the Players 1st philosophy quickly become surprisingly "successful"—not because they are better teams, but because of the superior skill of the players. That skill forms a rock-solid foundation for the development of creative, attractive, and effective team play that is successful by any definition.

The Players 1st program is designed to develop:

- A Dynamic First Touch—the skill and vision to place the ball with the first touch with either foot to a spot where it can be played again quickly and productively. This training is found in every session.

- Accuracy and Power when striking a ball, and the ability to use several surfaces of both feet.

- Superior 1v1 Skills—the ability and confidence to take on and beat an opponent in a one-on-one situation, together with the poise to keep possession of the ball when under strong defensive pressure. Players can expect some sort of one-on-one activity at every session.

- Mastery of the Small Group Situations (2v1, 3v1, 3v2, etc.) that are the building blocks of team play.

- Mastery of the Great Soccer Habits, the little things great players do that make a big difference on the field and form the basis for a player's Sense of the Game (a.k.a., "game smarts.")

- An Appreciation of the Competitive Process—learning to make the maximum effort at practice as well as in games, both to make yourself better and to challenge your teammates to be their best.

By the end of the Under-14 year, players will be exceptionally skilled. They will be poised, confident, creative, and bold with the ball and will make excellent use of the fundamental elements of team play. They will *"see the game"* and regularly anticipate the coming movements of players and the ball. They will demonstrate the ability to make good decisions about the mix of individualism (*"I can beat you myself"*) and team play (*"or with the help of my teammates"*). And they will demonstrate the **Qualities of Great Athletes** on the field and in all other aspects of their lives.

2 PLAYERS 1ST

"It's about being comfortable on the ball."

–Pia Sundhage, Former Coach, U.S. Women's National Team,
2008 & 2012 Olympic Gold Medalists

The call came one day to a state youth soccer office. It was the coach of a State Cup winner in the Under-14 age group. He complained that none of the players he was coaching had been selected for the state's Olympic Development Team.

On and on he went about his team, until finally the person on the receiving end interrupted. "I've never seen your team play, but I can describe it for you. They are well organized on the field. They are always moving to get open. They pass brilliantly. They use the give and go, back passes, long passes to change the point of attack ..." "Absolutely," says the coach, who then resumes with how his *team* does this, his *team* does that, all the time emphasizing the passing and teamwork.

The coach of another team took those players to the State Cup semi-finals at Under-12— where they lost. When you watched that team play the ball moved like this: win the ball (beating the first defender with the first touch), dribble and beat a second opponent, pass, pass, beat someone, beat another, pass, back pass, pass, beat another, shot.

Both teams won lots of games, most in fact at their age level. One came up short as a team this time, but our bets were on them for the long term. The reason: The coach of one team had only a team. It was built for today. The second team, though younger, had *players* already well prepared for their tomorrows in *the Game*.

2.1   JUST WHAT IS A PLAYER?

Successful soccer play requires more than knowing how to pass, move, and work together. A *player*, in our definition, is first an individual with a dynamic first touch. She is poised and creative with a ball, confident in the ability to hold it under pressure, and will, when needed, take on and beat an opponent in a one-on-one situation.

Facing a defender, a player always has this choice: *"I can beat you myself or I can beat you using a teammate."* He's a double-edged sword, while his one-dimensional peer can only pass. Over time defending against a team of one-way players becomes increasingly easy. Defending against a team of players, however, will forever make you crazy.

2.2 "I THOUGHT THIS WAS A TEAM SPORT"

It is. And to those who grew up playing other team sports, an emphasis on individualism and creativity seems almost "un-American." (Wasn't "ball hog" among the worst names you and your friends used?) Please understand, we do not advocate kids playing 1v7 (or 9 or 11.) But we do want to develop players who *could* play "One versus Many" (and might be inclined to try!) yet who also recognize when a pass is the better choice. This, though, is critical: *the player must have both the skills and confidence to allow that choice.*

2.3 WHY "PLAYERS 1ST?"

Skillful players first, then team is here a conscious choice. That choice can and should be made for several reasons:

- Team play is essentially impossible without the ability to control the ball. (Just keep track of the high percentage of one-touch balls that are just given to the opponents in the next youth game you watch.) Conversely, a team of skilled players will match up well from their first full-field game together against an established team where skill development is not the primary focus.

- Developmentally, children at the younger ages are more inclined toward individual than team play. Teamwork is more natural when athletes reach an age where the peer group becomes important.

- Developing individual skills is tougher for older kids. It can be done, but requires hours and hours of very basic practice and repetition that can try the patience of older athletes. By starting younger such practice is spread over a longer time.

- In our experience, it is far easier to teach the dribbler to pass than to teach the passer to take someone on. It's difficult to retrofit a 12-year-old who has only experienced the passing side of the Game and whose other skills are underdeveloped. Even then, it is rare for an athlete to reach the level of technical or tactical proficiency in the 1v1 situation that he would have gained from strong and ongoing skills training beginning at age eight or nine.

- Strong skills allow every player to be in control of the game. It has been said that in soccer every player is a quarterback. Any player who can control the ball and play with poise and confidence in 1v1 match-ups is truly in command when the ball is at her feet.

● It works. Teams and clubs that have adopted this philosophy of player development (mandating, for example, that 75% of training through U14 be centered around skill development) have seen huge increases both in the number of players chosen for Olympic Development Teams and in team success in league and tournament play.

2.4 INDIVIDUALISM ENABLES TEAMWORK

Individual creative play is the key to great teamwork in soccer. The player who takes on and beats an opponent now continues to goal with a numerical advantage. The next defender, suddenly outnumbered, immediately faces two options. Challenge the dribbler: the pass is open. Deny the pass: the dribbler continues to carry the ball forward.

It's called *"forcing the defender to make the wrong choice,"* where either choice is wrong! Skillful, creative Players use the **individual option** to put defenders into positions where they continually face those no-win decisions.

2.5 WALKING THE WALK

It's easy to talk about the importance of individual player development. Too often, though, the commitment to that principle disappears under the ever-increasing pressures tied to wins and losses—now seen at younger and younger ages. The development of creative and skillful individual players can be at some initial cost to team "success," especially if measured just by the scoreboard. *It's faster and easier to "win on the cheap"* by emphasizing team organization over the development of the players.

What we've learned, however, is that teams developed using the Players 1st philosophy quickly become surprisingly successful. Not too long ago, three of the five U9 winners in a state recreational tournament were teams trained with a primary focus on player development. None were the better teams, nor were they teams "stacked" with the best athletes. *They won because, player for player, they had developed skills superior to those of their opponents.* Such skills form a rock-solid foundation for further development of creative, attractive, and effective team play that will be successful by any definition. More importantly, those players are already acquiring the tools to allow them life-long enjoyment of *the Game.*

2.6   BE PATIENT. BE PERSISTENT.

And be happy when your players show poise, show confidence, show creativity, and show some flair with the ball. Create an environment of fearlessness where attacking one-on-one is *"always allowed, is usually encouraged, and is frequently demanded."* When your players dribble too much at first—as some will—suppress the *"pass the ball"* responses from your sidelines. Once they have the **take-on mentality** you can begin to develop their options involving teammates.

Like the second of those teams mentioned previously, your teamwork may come up short at first. In time, your players will learn to recognize and make the better choices. Then the team becomes unstoppable.

The coach of that second team placed five players on her state's youngest Olympic Development Team. She had developed players built for tomorrow with the abilities and characteristics that would allow them to go anywhere and play well for anyone. The team's moment came two years later in a State Cup final where skill and poise with the ball prevailed over size, strength, and speed for the first of several state championships.

This essay, Players First, can be downloaded from the website www.PlayersFirst.com.

3 THE BEST KIND OF OWNERSHIP

"I play to be happy, not to win titles."

–Andrés Iniesta, FC Barcelona

For many of us youth sports before junior high or high school consisted of neighborhood games of hide-and-seek, sardines, capture the flag, and seasonal variations on the major sports—touch football, h-o-r-s-e, stickball, runners-up. Every aspect of those endeavors was ours to control—each of us commissioner, owner, coach, player, umpire, and fan.

Along the way we usually learned something about whatever game we were playing. But mostly we were learning about life: choosing how much physical, social, and emotional investment we would make to be first to kick-the-can, working through issues of fair play and sportsmanship on a close play in a kickball game, deciding whether or not to cheat at Marco Polo. In the end those games, whether we knew it or not, had quite an impact in terms of shaping who we would be as adults.

Is that impact disappearing as sports for kids become increasingly organized and adult directed? It doesn't have to. That wonderful phrase from Positive Coaching Alliance founder Jim Thompson about developing *"stronger, more responsible, and confident individuals who will be successful in life"* describes what should be a fundamental and intentional purpose of *organized* youth sports. Just as it happened in the neighborhood's less-structured games.

The critical issues here involve matters of ownership and control. What follow are insights both about how to sort them out to the athletes' greatest and most permanent benefit and how coaches and parents can effectively help their children grow from the youth sports experience.

3.1 UNDERSTANDING EXPECTATIONS

For many years Bruce Brown directed the NAIA's Champions of Character Program. He recommends that each season parents consider the following questions: Why do I want my child playing? What will be a successful season for me as a parent? What are my goals for him? What do I hope he gains from the experience? What do I think his role will be on the team?[1]

---

[1] Brown, B. 2003. *Teaching Character Through Sport.* Coaches Choice Books, p. 124.

Once parents have done that, they will need to find a quiet time to discuss the same questions with their young athlete. Ideally the child's answers will be in sync with the parents'. If they are not, it's time to decide whose expectations the athlete will be asked to pursue.

Not all athletes on a team are likely to have the same goals. Some players may be dreaming of playing on a top college team. Others are there just to be with their friends. Each is OK. What matters is that a player's commitment to a team contains a complementary obligation to helping teammates attain their dreams.

With a little help, athletes figure this out early on. They then freely choose to make efforts that honor the goals and aspirations of their teammates—even where those goals are different from their own. It's important that parents honor and support this commitment as well, whether or not their son or daughter is one of those hoping to play at a Division I school or on the National Team.

3.2   IT'S HIS THING

Recognizing the athlete's commitment is the first step toward "releasing" the athlete to the game and the team. It's not always an easy thing to do. Dr. Brown:

One of the best "gifts" parents can give their children is to release them to their sport. As such, during the season, parents must share their child with the coach and the team. The earlier in their child's career they are able to do this, the better it is for their children's development and growth.

By releasing their young athlete, parents are telling their children that all successes are theirs, all failures are theirs, and all problems are theirs. There are not many places in a young person's life where parents can say, "This is your thing." This can't be done with friends, academics, decisions on weekends, or even movies; it can be done in athletics.[2]

University of North Carolina coach Anson Dorrance, citing the parents of future World Champions Julie Foudy, Michelle Akers, Mia Hamm, Tisha Venturini, and others, puts it a little differently:

In my experience, the best soccer parents more or less let their children do their own thing. These parents are not directly involved in their children's soccer, especially not as part of a "management team" [...] They are completely supportive of their players – win, lose or draw. The bottom line – they fulfill the parent's role and job, which is basically to love their children [...] Parents who learn to have faith in their children learn to let go of their desire to control and protect [...] I know it can be hard, but a player has to fight her

---

[2] Brown, B. 2003. *Teaching Character Through Sport*. Coaches Choice Books, p. 125.

own battles. If sports can have any value off the field, it is in the athletes dealing with these difficult, but ultimately empowering challenges on their own.

He goes on to advise the athlete:

The first step in a healthy soccer career is to become your own manager [...] The more you can do about your game on your own, the more you are playing for yourself. And the more you play for yourself, the less you will require of your parents and the more freedom you will have to pursue something you enjoy for its own sake. You want (your parents) to enjoy watching you be challenged and enjoying that world, but it is your world to manage.[3]

When an athlete feels in control of his sports experience, interesting things happen. The athlete takes ever-increasing responsibility for his own effort, learning, and improvement, will work harder, and stick to the task longer. Who wouldn't want that?

On teams where expectations are clear and athletes control their performance, ownership is vested where it belongs—with athletes making their personal investments in their team. They develop a "we play for each other" mentality that continually reinforces itself, and that may be the most important quality a team can enjoy.

Athletes who get ahold of their sport in this way enjoy "the best kind of ownership, and the most permanent."[4]

This essay, The Best Kind of Ownership, can be downloaded from the website www.PlayersFirst.com.

---

[3] Dorrance, A. 2005. *The Vision of a Champion*. Huron River Press, p. 115-122.
[4] Russell, T. 1967. *On the Loose*. Sierra Club Books, p. 37.

4 COACHING FOR CHARACTER

"We are what we repeatedly do. Excellence is not an act but a habit."

–Will Durant, describing the philosophy of Aristotle

Discussions of character in sports hinge on two sometimes competing beliefs. One holds that sports build character, the other that sports reveal it. A case can be made for both ideas.

Character is regularly revealed in the way that players, coaches, parents, and leaders of youth sports organizations (YSOs) conduct themselves on and off the field.

The "sports builds character" belief is a trickier proposition. Who is to question that participation in sports provides wonderful settings for the development of poise, confidence, determination, resilience, self-sacrifice, courage? The list goes on, and it is not a coincidence that a strong involvement in sports was an attribute shared by those who tried to retake Flight 93 over Pennsylvania on 9/11. Yet every Positive Life Skill associated with sports has an evil twin that can be learned equally well. And often more easily. If you can learn fair play and sportsmanship, you can also learn to cheat. If you can learn about commitment, you can also learn to quit on yourself and your teammates. Accountability and accepting responsibility: making excuses. Again, the list goes on.

Based on their own childhood experiences, many of the adults involved in sports simply assume that the positive side of those character traits will emerge. In fact, without a concerted and *intentional* effort to use sports to teach Positive Life Lessons, you might as well be flipping a coin.

4.1 DOUBLE GOAL COACHING

Attention to these issues is a major focus of *The Double-Goal Coach* by Jim Thompson. The author is founder and executive director of the Positive Coaching Alliance (www.positivecoach.org), an organization based at Stanford University that seeks "to transform the culture of youth sports so that sports can transform youth." Like many books on the state of youth sports, Thompson chronicles the excesses. What sets his book apart are solutions to these problems based on research in the fields of education and sports psychology as well as lessons in organizational culture drawn from the business world.

Theory is then turned into practice through the presentation of many simple tools for establishing and maintaining a positive culture for youth sports. Coaches, parents, and the leaders of YSOs will find things here that can be put to immediate use.

What is a **Double Goal Coach**? First, he or she is a coach who wants to win. Thompson makes clear that the Positive Coaching message is not anti-competitive or about "happy talk." This is not an invitation to go kick a ball around with the characters from *Sesame Street*. We've reached a time when real competition at Field Day has been reduced to (at most) a 50-yard dash. Seasonal trophies for participation are so widespread that they are mocked in television ads. Thompson sees the competitive sports experience as an increasingly important, and rare, opportunity for kids to develop positive character traits—the second and more important goal of the Double Goal Coach. After all, it's the character traits that will endure long after players hang up their boots.

There are three elements to Double Goal Coaching. The first seeks to redefine winning, changing the definition from one based only on results (the "win-at-all-costs" model) to "a mastery approach to performance" based on effort, learning, and a positive view of the value of mistakes. The goal is nothing more, or less, than doing the best you can. "Winners" in this definition are those who *"make the maximum effort, continue to learn and improve, don't let mistakes - or the fear of mistakes - stop them."*[1] The essential difference between the "w-a-a-c" and mastery approaches has to do with control. Results are very much in the control of others; with a mastery approach control belongs to the athlete. What's interesting, though, is that research shows that a mastery approach actually produces better performance (and results) than one where the focus is primarily on the scoreboard.

CoachNotes

As a child, Landon Donovan was so competitive that his mother felt the need to take some pressure off him. After every game she would ask Landon, "Did you try your best?" (Yes.) "Did you have fun?" (Yes.) "Good! Then you won. Now, what was the score?"

Guest CoachNotes

With young players, I would ask them to define a "winner;" however, they could not use certain words in the definition. Those words were: win, lose, loser, victor, defeat, score, point, beat. It forced them to think about why they played the game and what they wanted out of it. When I approached players in my club that I did not directly coach during practice, I asked, "How did you do last weekend?" Inevitably, they would start by saying, "We won" or "We lost," and I would stop them and say, "Now, how did YOU do last weekend?" Always got a better answer and a smile. –AFB

---

[1] Thompson, J. 2003. *The Double-Goal Coach*. William Morrow Paperbacks, p. 37.

Next comes the concept of Honoring the Game. This is largely a proactive view of sportsmanship issues based on what you *will* do rather than what you *won't* do. Honoring the Game involves developing and demonstrating respect for **R**ules, **O**pponents, **O**fficials, **T**eammates, and **S**elf (ROOTS).

The third element of the Double Goal model involves *"Filling the Emotional Tank,"* motivation through encouragement and positive reinforcement. Again, the book provides a number of useful tools for coaches.

There is also a section of the book for Sports Parents. Thompson promotes the notion of the Second Goal Parent, whose primary task is to be unconditionally supportive of their child, whose focus is on those Life Lessons and positive character traits, who recognizes that their child's participation in sports belongs to the child, and who leaves coaching to the coaches. (A more detailed look at this element of the PCA model is found in Thompson's *Positive Sports Parenting*.)

The Double Goal Coach will give the individual coach many ways create a more enjoyable environment for his or her team, and one where players are much more likely to reach their individual potential on and off the field. And it's no insignificant bonus that a Double Goal approach will be much more enjoyable and rewarding for the coach as well.[2]

The Double Goal model is particularly well suited to the Players 1st approach. Using the bulk of available training time to advance individual technical prowess means that you're not spending that time on team organization for the next game, and the scoreboard will, for a time, reflect that. Establishing an alternative measure of success based on personal effort, learning, and improvement will be useful in that time.

4.2 THE TEAM'S VALUES

Successful organizations are usually based on a set of core values. A Boy Scout, for instance, is to be *"trusted, loyal, friendly, and considerate"* and more. If you ask coaches and athletes in programs with perennial success, they will quickly speak of the values and character traits that underlie the program.

A particularly good set of qualities found in all the greatest athletes (Mia, Messi, Curry, Jordan, Gretzki, etc.) comes from *Teaching Character Through Sport* by Bruce Brown of Proactive Coaching.[3]

---

[2] **The Positive Coaching Alliance** provides a "systems approach" to developing positive cultures for youth sports through an integrated set of workshops for athletes, coaches, parents, and leaders of YSOs. Each of the workshops is two hours in length and is very much worth the time and effort to attend. If live workshops are not available, online versions can be found at *www.positivecoach.org*. You can also register there for several online newsletters.

[3] Brown, B. 2003. *Teaching Character Through Sport*. Coaches Choice Books, p. 48-60.

Qualities of a Great "Athlete"

-From Bruce Brown, www.proactivecoaching.info.

Having each of these qualities is at least as important *beyond* sports.

Confidence. An *athlete* displays a quiet inner **confidence based on preparation,** her own and that of her teammates. Confidence is a **belief based on your daily work habits and your constant progress.** This kind of confidence is **contagious** within a team, built as athletes subject themselves to **touch challenges and practices** and see the value in **hard work. These athletes develop a "go for it" mentality, become unafraid of failure,** and **remain confident in "rough waters." They prepare hard every day.** When success follows, athletes tell you it's because of the effort they put into preparation.

The *non-athlete* has a **false confidence, not built on preparation** but on factors she doesn't control. Maybe she is blessed with great athleticism. Maybe she thinks that the team will "carry" her. In either event, she does not put the same effort or attention into practices as do the athletes on the team. *Having true confidence is a choice.*

Teachable Spirit. *Athletes* **want to learn and improve. They bring an enthusiasm for continuous improvement every day.** They know that correction happens because a coach sees potential in them to get better. They have learned to take **correction as a compliment** and look at correction as an opportunity to improve. The athlete responds to correction with verbal and physical cues that she is listening and learning.

The *non-athlete* looks at any **correction as criticism** and **often responds with an excuse.** *Having a teachable spirit is a choice.*

Pride. The pride of an *athlete* is a shared one. It is found in **the "shared joy of the inner circle," a feeling among team members that no one on the outside can understand.** Shared pride involves a desire **to become as good as possible for yourself and for your group of teammates.** It involves unselfishness and accountability. Team pride is developed in parts of the game that require more effort than skill, where determination is more important than talent (**DIMITT**). An example: "optimistic recovery" by everyone when a ball is lost.

The pride of a *non-athlete* is **self-oriented, often selfish.** Such players often develop a **"sense of entitlement,"** where they think athletic skill should guarantee **special treatment.** *Developing the right kind of pride is a choice.*

Accountability. The *athlete* is **responsible** and demonstrates it when she **takes personal accountability for what happens to her**. When things are not going well, **she looks to herself first to see where she can act to make a difference**. She becomes a problem-solver, better able to cope with stress, and more likely to persevere when facing difficulties. She realizes that **"you are either getting better or you are getting worse,"** that if you are not making steady improvement, you are losing ground to those athletes who are.

The *non-athlete* **blames everyone but herself** when things do not go well. She often fixates on things she cannot control rather than those she can. *Being accountable is a choice.*

Competitive Perseverance. The *athlete* and great teams are not deterred by bumps in the road. Since she is committed to continuous improvement, she **can recover quickly from a mistake and refuse to remain discouraged**. Positive, competitive, persevering athletes are "mentally tough," a quality that allows an individual to remain confident, enthusiastic, and positive. *Athletes* who are mentally tough **simply cannot have their spirits broken**. They can lose to an opponent 10 times and look forward to the next rematch. **They welcome challenges and look forward to the toughest competitions as tests of themselves.**

The *non-athlete* is **easily discouraged and allows yesterday's failures and disappointments to interfere with today**. *Non-athletes* are unable to recover quickly from mistakes. *Perseverance and positive attitude are a choice.*

Discipline. This is nothing more than **focused attention and effort**. To be successful individually or collectively, sacrifices involving discipline ("focused attention and effort") are required. Great *athletes* not only accept discipline, they embrace it for the benefit of the team. They have the **strength of character** to overcome temptations and pressures and **will do what's right for their team** at the moment of truth. Discipline is exhibited by **attentiveness, enthusiasm, sportsmanship, respecting authority, and personal responsibility**. Because they display "athletic integrity," disciplined athletes are better teammates. They are **reliable and trustworthy and are always there for their teammates**. For a team, discipline can be *the* characteristic that sets them apart and gives them an edge.

The *non-athlete* chooses **self-indulgence** (I'll do what I want!") over self-control and only thinks of discipline in terms of punishment. *Accepting discipline ("focused attention and effort") is a positive form of teamwork and a choice.*

Team First. Teamwork is a **rare gift that allows ordinary people to attain extraordinary results**. The process of becoming a good teammate is a decision based on attitude, specifically the choice of **interdependence over independence**. The *athlete* **intentionally puts the needs of the team ahead of herself. She will never let her teammates down**. She understands that everyone on a team can have different roles that together make the team stronger. On a great team, all roles have equal value, and great teams are made up of athletes who have given up the quest for individual glory, who willingly and wholeheartedly commit themselves to the team effort. Sports provide many individually satisfying memories, but for the true *athlete*, **nothing can compare with the memories built from being part of something bigger than yourself.**

The *non-athlete* is a **selective participant, looking to satisfy her own needs first by being selfish with her effort, attention, or behavior.** *Putting the team first and not letting your teammates down in any situation is a choice.*

In Teaching Character Through Sport, *Dr. Brown has a similar list of the "Qualities of Great Teams." But you'll just have to buy the book to see it.*

Once you have identified and defined the qualities that will be emphasized, the next step is to make them real for the team. A good way is to focus on one a week. (With a list like Dr. Brown's, you'll get through it twice in a 14-week season.) Briefly discuss the quality at the beginning of the week. Have the athletes find examples at school where someone demonstrates—or clearly disrespects—one of the qualities. At the end of practice, have athletes "spotlight" (another Brown idea) teammates who have shown the quality that day.

The list, Qualities of a Great Athlete, can be download from www.PlayersFirst.com.

4.3   IMPRINTING

It had been a most uncommon season. Playing in a league where there would be promotion and relegation, the now U12 girls team had in the previous season missed promotion by the margin of scoring one more goal or conceding one less in any one of five of the season's 10 games. Then, days before training for the new season began, the only goalkeeper left to concentrate on golf. And yet, playing 11v11, the 13-player squad (each—sometimes much to the horror of her parents—playing in the goal at least once) managed what all seemed to agree was the impossible, nearly winning the league and getting promoted to the highest division, where the team would stick.

At the NSCAA convention following that season, Anson Dorrance, coach of the University of North Carolina's women's team, made a presentation about some of the things that set the spectacular 2003 Carolina team apart from some of the other champions he had trained.

He talked about an article from the *New York Times* concerning a professor of poetry at Columbia who required his graduate students to memorize and recite the poetry they were studying. Despite significant resistance the poems were learned. (One must, after all, get the grade.) In a short time for the students *"the poems they'd learned were now in their blood, beating with their hearts."* The students were demonstrating the values highlighted in the verses they had memorized.

Anson adopted something similar for his team. For each of the team's core values (e.g., work hard, don't whine), there is a quote that the players can recite by heart. (A sample, related to Carolina's "we don't whine" value: *"Be a force of fortune instead of a feverish, selfish little clod of ailments and grievances complaining that the world will not devote itself to making you happy."* –G. B. Shaw.) He believes these messages, too, are in his players' blood.[4]

Now that improbable season made sense: it was the T-shirts. Each season had begun with a new practice T-shirt containing an inspirational quote from a member of the U.S. Women's National Team that reflected a core value of the younger team. Though only into the fourth of what would become ten shirts, it became clear that the shirt quotes had been a far greater influence on the team's culture than realized. Wearing the quotes, seeing and hearing them daily in practice, committing them to memory, the words had not just been imprinted on their memories, but had found the way into the bloodstreams of these younger athletes as well.

In succeeding seasons, the "shirt quotes" usually reflected a "next step" for the team, sometimes much more than anticipated. In time, players picked a season's quote from a selection of choices.

The T-shirts started out as just an idea to acquaint the team with members of the Women's National Team and some of their ideas. They became and continue to be much more than that. To this day those players can recite those quotes and see them reflected in the way they live their lives.

---

[4] From www.carolmuskedukes.com/articles/2002_articles/NYTimesOPEDdec02.htm. Presentation: www.ncgsc.com/leadership%30convention.pdf.

4.4 "LET'S GET BETTER"

Many organizations base their entire cultures around those three words, and they make a great mantra for the start of a training session. The following paragraphs expand on that mantra, and apply just as well to off-the-field pursuits as on.

Great Teams, Great Athletes

All great teams and all great athletes know how to train. They know how to use time to gain a competitive advantage. They realize that *it isn't a matter of quantity but of quality of practice*. They know how to maximize the time they have, using it to perfect those parts of their game that need perfection or to improve on those parts of their game where there's room for improvement.

Essentially, *great athletes want to be better*. And, more importantly, they truly believe they *can* get better. They are never satisfied with where they are, and *they are constantly demanding higher levels of performance from themselves*. These players don't just get done with practice, they get *better* with practice. They have a vision of what they want for themselves, a vision that motivates them toward greater levels of achievement.

–Tony DiCicco, Coach of Olympic and World Cup Champions
From DiCicco, T. 2003. *Catch Them Being Good*. Penguin Books, p. 140.

---

5 YOUR CULTURE: IT'S THE LITTLE THINGS THAT MAKE A BIG DIFFERENCE

"Building bold hearts and strong character through outrageous fun, extraordinary friendships and lifelong values."

–From the Mission Statement of Adirondack Camp

Culture is defined by the Positive Coaching Alliance as "the way *we* do things *here*." Every team has a culture. So does every club. Some arise by accident, but it is preferable to design your culture intentionally around several things, large and small, that will set your program apart from any other.

What follows is an assortment of cultural icons culled from numerous teams, clubs, and camps. Some will seem goofy, but all have a soccer purpose. The common factor among them is that they are catalysts in creating challenging and fun learning environments, the kind that leave the athletes always wanting more. They have great takeaway value: Kids remember them and associate them with belonging to their program. They are *the little things that make a big difference.*

Cultural icons often take the form of *sticky quotes*, words and phrases that the team will hear over and over again and eventually begin to use. Examples are shown throughout this book in **"bold."** Components of a culture fall into several broad categories.

5.1 PROMOTING CORE VALUES

- "Let's get better." These are great words to use at the start every session. There should be a penalty if the players catch the coach not saying them. Variation: "Get uncomfortable; get intense; make mistakes, and let's get better."[1]

- Attitude—Three Things for Every Day: "Make the maximum effort. Continue to learn and improve. Always be bold and daring."

- Embrace the Growth Mindset. "I can accomplish anything, and I'm going to keep working at it until I do." –Kristine Lilly

---

[1] Practice starter: thetalentcode.com/2016/10/06/stop-warming-up-start-learning-up/.

- Cultivate Persistence, Adaptability, and Grit. "You can always find ways to get it done." –Kate Sobrero Markgraf

- "Mistakes are good; struggle makes you stronger." Players who are being bold will make mistakes ("Doers make mistakes" –John Wooden), and such mistakes are often the best way to get better. Develop a "Go-For-It"[2] mentality where there is no higher form of praise than "Great mistake!" (See chapter 8.2.)

- Practice Shirts. It's common for a practice shirt to contain an inspirational quote. Seeing it all the time will result in players demonstrating the quality the quote addresses. With an additional shirt given each season (make the first ones too big), in a few seasons the team will be reminded of the team's most important values at every practice. (See chapter 4.3.)

- Celebrate Your Culture. "What you learn and do here makes you different from other players. Use that difference to make a difference, not just here but in all your soccer play and in your lives."

5.2 ADDRESSING CHARACTER

- Identify, Model, and Teach. What personal qualities and Positive Life Skills do you think players should develop? Whatever they are, teach them, recognize players who demonstrate them, and get the players to recognize them in themselves and others.

- Make the Fundamentals Clear. "Members of the team are expected at all times to be polite, well mannered, cooperative, good sports, and respectful and considerate of others."

- Embrace the Dual Commitment of Team Sports. Players are there to make themselves better and to make their teammates better. "You owe it to yourself and your teammates to do everything you can and give everything you have toward your goal of being the best." –Tracey Bates Leone

- Honoring the Game. All participants are expected to demonstrate respect for the Rules, Opponents, Officials, Teammates, and Selves (ROOTS). Remind the athletes that demands for intensity do not give permission for hard fouls or hard words.[3]

- Message Bombardment. Advertisers know you must see an ad seven times before you remember it. And there's no such thing as too often.

---

[2] Go-For-It: thetalentcode.com/2013/03/20/how-to-overcome-fear-of-mistakes-one-coachs-story/.
[3] Thompson, J. 2003. *The Double-Goal Coach*. William Morrow Paperbacks, p. 101.

5.3 CONNECTING

- Greetings. Greet every player by name as they arrive for training and games. Better yet, connect twice with each before things begin. Have players doing the same.

- Use Players' Names Constantly. There's no better form of affirmation. (In a camp or clinic situation, make sure everyone knows everyone else's name.)

- Be Relentlessly Positive and Enthusiastic. Technical training requires lots of corrections. This can drain the athletes emotionally unless it is balanced with continual recognition of effort and progress. For maximum impact, all feedback needs to be not a "Good job," but "truthful, specific, and using the player's name." False or empty praise quickly diminishes a coach's credibility.

- "Correction is a compliment," an affirmation of the coach's belief in the player's ability.[4]

- "Ask rather than tell" whenever you can (especially when making corrections). Players can usually put an answer in words.

- Check for Understanding (CFU).[5] A self-reporting "yes" answer to "Do you understand?" does not guarantee understanding. The better question is something like, "What are you going to do now?" CFU is an incredibly powerful teaching tool.

- "Soccer voices." Create conditions, even artificial ones, where players must communicate in a loud voice. This helps players, especially the shy ones, to be more vocal on the field. When reviewing ball moves, always have players count out how many they are doing. Use other opportunities to encourage "talk" on the field. But you may need to remind players that using the voice can needlessly attract a defender's attention. Sometimes it's best to "call for the ball with your movement."

- Keep Score Out Loud. This is great way to develop "soccer voices" (also to help girls play hard against their friends and to minimize disputes among the boys).

- "Olé!" Involve players in recognizing great play. Get players to give an "Olé!" when it happens, especially if "boldness" or "daring" is involved. Note that even unsuccessful efforts that are bold and daring can qualify for an "Olé!"

---

[4] Brown, B. 2003. Teaching Character Through Sport. Coaches Choice Books, p. 51.
[5] Lemov, D. 2014. Teach Like a Champion 2.0. Jossey-Bass, p. 24.

5.4   PROVIDING STRUCTURE

- Preparation. Confidence, both for players and coaches, is rooted in preparation. For coaches, preparation includes planning for things that could go wrong (starting with the player who always arrives for training after an argument in the car with mom). It can also include planning for things that you intend to go wrong.[6]

- Attendance. Avoid issues by having clear expectations. Here's what they were for a higher level U13 team: "Players will be expected to be at every practice, game, and tournament unless excused in advance for reasons of illness, injury, family emergency, religious observance, or the occasional school function. (The player is expected to notify the coach, by phone if possible, about an absence as soon as he/she knows it's going to happen, and to find out afterward what was missed. [Note: This works as young as U11.] Players missing practice will not start that week's games ahead of players who were there.) While other requests for excused absences might have individual merit, their collective effect on a team can be devastating."

- "We start on time. We end on time." This shows respect for the time of the athletes, their chauffeurs (chauffeuses), and the coaches. Start even if only a few players are present. When players arrive late, they emerge from the car with cleats and shin guards on and run to join the team.

- Practice killers. The three Ls: lines, laps, and lectures.

- Maintaining Tempo. Players jog to their water on breaks and jog back. Remind them that coaches always notice who's back first (and last). Where lines are unavoidable, try to maintain a work-to-rest ratio between 1:2 and 1:3.

- Positive Recovery. Have extra soccer balls around the perimeter of an exercise so play can resume quickly. Alternately, have players sprint after balls that go out of bounds. "You want the ball." You may even want to use a "who gets it gets it" challenge (a good opportunity to explain the meaning of "touchline").

- Mistake Rituals. Adopt rituals which allow athletes to quickly put mistakes behind them, so that "one doesn't become two."

- Team Names. When you divide the squad for a game, have each group pick a name for itself—either a national team or a professional club team. Give a bonus point when a team chooses the best Team of the Day, (e.g., Iceland). This activity ("Galatasaray") will also increase players' soccer literacy.

---

[6] Lemov, D. 2014. *Teach Like a Champion 2.0*. Jossey-Bass, p. 60.

- "Positive Conditioning." Why associate losing or punishment with a physical activity? Have the winners of an activity do 20 sit-ups. ("You've earned the right to get stronger.") This is highly counterintuitive, but athletes will eventually reach the point where they must take ownership of their fitness level. This idea promotes a positive view of fitness work.[7]

- Two-Minute Rule. When starting an activity, let it go for two minutes or more before stopping to make any corrections. Some of the problems you'll see will take care of themselves in that time. Also allow uninterrupted time at the end. (Hint: Look for a great moment to end things.)

- Grid Size. Size matters when creating the "just-right challenge." As a rule, "if it's not working, the space is too small" for the current skills of the players. With too large a space the game becomes too easy or turns into more of a fitness exercise than intended.

- Halftime: Three Things. "What do you think?" This is a great way to start a team's halftime conversation. Work the responses into no more than "three things for the second half." That's all that most players will be able to process.

- Spotlighting is an end-of-the-practice/game activity where players recognize teammates' best efforts, accomplishments and displays of character that day. There are many formats, but it usually starts with, "Who wants to spotlight somebody?"[8]

- Closing Ceremonies. This five-minute ritual should summarize the session's key points, "homework" and other announcements, and spotlight the day's best moments. When it's all done, players should look satisfied with what they've experienced and leave with smiles and happy chatter. So should the coach.

- Post-Game. This should be a slightly extended version of the team's Closing Ceremony ritual, 7 to 10 minutes at most, adding a few "What do you think?" questions to highlight mostly good things from the game and one or two items for future work. Coaches and players need time to process the game. Save any extensive post-mortem for the next training session. Some teams invite the parents to watch. (Let the players decide.)

---

[7] Brown, B. 2003. *Teaching Character Through Sport*. Coaches Choice Books, p. 99.
[8] Brown, B. 2003. *Teaching Character Through Sport*. Coaches Choice Books, p. 71.

5.5   CUSTOMS AND TRADITIONS

All teams develop rituals. Many are planned, but sometimes an unplanned moment evolves into a wonderful tradition. Before a practice with a newly formed team of 10-year-olds, the coach was talking about an old-time summer camp song. The players wanted to hear it. Instead, the coach promised to sing the song on the condition that everyone else would pick a song to solo as well. This would happen at the end of the week as part of the final practice before the team's first-ever game.

That Songfest was an incredible team-building moment. The activity set a tone for how the team would deal with failure; for most of the players nothing that happened on the field afterward would be more embarrassing. (The only regret was the lack of a video camera.)

An instant tradition, the event was repeated at the start of each subsequent fall and spring season. It included on one occasion an unfortunately unforgettable rendition of the theme from *Annie*. The guilty party has been known by that name since that day.

- Freaky Friday. On these days, players are not required to wear the regular practice uniforms. It can be instructive to see which players take full advantage. One pre-Halloween edition featured two players who showed up in inflatable sumo-wrestler kits. A more reserved teammate's interpretation of "freaky" came as one blue sock and one grey sock.

- Player of the Game. Many teams have a traveling award bestowed after each game. A women's professional team in Sweden passes along a teddy bear to the game's best player. Another team awarded a small ceramic statuette that bore a troubling resemblance to the Bride of Chucky for the game's "baddest" (in the good sense) performance.

- The Hooded Warriors. The players in one high school program have for decades paraded onto the pitch in black hooded warm-ups that evoke the Grim Reaper.

- Winners Circle. Although this is a lengthy activity—order pizza for a halftime break—it can be an incredibly powerful end-of-season activity for a team. Players sit in a circle. Each in turn will be addressed by the three to five teammates to the right, plus any others who really want to do so. They will briefly say what it is that they most appreciate about the teammate. The coach also provides a summary comment. While the comments are designed to be positive, some roasting ("Although Annie will NEVER be able to sing...") is to be expected.

5.6 TIPS FOR TEACHING TECHNIQUE

- Imitatsiya. Have players perform a ball skill with an imaginary ball, one of the best teaching techniques. Imitatsita in slow or super-slow motion adds to the effectiveness.[9]

- "Getaway Touches." (Words matter; use "touches," not "steps.") A ball move is not properly done unless the player has exploded away at speed with two Getaway Touches on the ball. It must become a habit.

- Ball Move "Challenges." 1. Do "something" with the ball (Ronaldo Ball; see chapter 15.4, activity 22) before you can pass. 2. Must "do a move" before passing. 3. Must "use a move" (against a defender). When possible, set challenges that reward those who take the "individual option." As a rule, do not require a move before a shot in any scrimmage situation (2v2 up).

- Juggling. Have a Juggling Progression and a weekly test. A lemon drop awarded every time a player sets a new personal best will acquire the status of a Gold Medal. In a camp or multiple team setting, have players Ring the Bell when they complete a level of the progression. It inspires everyone. "Juggling makes every touch better." (See chapter 12.3.)

- Teach to the Weaker Foot. It forces players to slow down and concentrate on technique. You can always allow use of the stronger foot in the last two to three reps for dessert. (See chapter 13.1.)

- Shooting. Shooting exercises and games should always be preceded by a few minutes of hard skills technical work on striking the ball.

- No Weak Feet. Have players look for every opportunity to use the weaker foot more than their stronger: a) when practicing ball moves, b) for passes and dribbling during warm-ups, and c) in shooting activities.

- The Dakota Rule. A partial or total ban on using the dominant foot—for use with a talented but severely one-footed player.

- Futsal Balls are unforgiving of poor technique and therefore great for refining passing and shooting technique.

- Pirate Eye Patches, covering the dominant eye, make players slow down to focus on their technique, especially when working on striking a ball.

---

[9] Coyle, D. 2009. *The Talent Code*. Bantam, p. 82.

5.7   BASIC GAME RULES

These items should in time become "automatic," where players don't even ask if they are in effect. Note that with younger players, "rule overload" can distract from the topic at hand and should be avoided.

- Enforcement. As soon as possible, make the players responsible for calling infractions.

- "Pink Cone Rule." In many games, especially 1v1, use pink cones set 5 to 7 yards from the goal to establish shooting zones. Shots must be from inside those zones. Players on the opposite team must call the infraction. (Note that the cones are always "pink," no matter their color.)

- "Minus One." In games, a shot that misses a totally open goal costs the shooting team a point. (Just as missing a "sitter" in a real game is like giving the opposing team a goal.) Players call the infraction.

- THE RULE "You must look before receiving." (For girls, this results in flying "Ponytails.") There is no more essential soccer habit. The standard penalty for an infraction ("Didn't look!") is loss of possession or temporary removal from the activity. (For more, including a particularly diabolical means of enforcement that will get heads moving, see chapter 14.2.)

- "Giveaway." A totally unforced error that just gives the ball to the other team. The offending player leaves the game until either team scores. (This creates useful man-up and man-down situations, especially in 3v3 and 4v4 play.)

- "OH!"–Outrageous Soccer. This challenge encourages bold and daring play. Award an extra point for something that makes you go "Oh!", two for something that makes you go "Oh!!!", and three for an "OH MY!!!!!". Do not neglect to reward unsuccessful effort. (This combines well with "Olé!")

- The "Step" Rule. In any activity involving shooting and scoring, a player must "STEP" ("finish forward") at the end of a shot for a goal to count. Have players on the opposing side call the infraction; it makes them pay attention.

5.8   ADVANCED CHALLENGES

These add intensity, but can also lead to "rule overload" if too many are in force at once.

- "Two-Second Standard." Scouts, including college coaches watching prospective recruits, will often focus on what a player does in the first two seconds of possession. A "Look" before receiving in effect adds time. (Note, though, that you can touch the ball 5 times in 2 seconds and not do anything.) Have an assistant keep track of whether players' first two seconds of possession are highly effective, effective, or relatively useless. In time, expand the Standard to include what players away from the ball do in the 2 seconds after the team wins or loses possession. (See chapter 12.1.)

- "Six-Second Challenge." When possession is lost, they try to regain it in under 6 seconds. Award a bonus point, two if a goal results. (Hat tip: FC Barcelona.)

- Pass the Steal. Winning the ball and (intentionally) passing it to a teammate in a single touch usually puts the opposition in such difficulty that it can be worth a bonus point in practice, three if it becomes the first pass in a wall pass, even more— maybe a "Game Over" (see following)—if a goal results. (Hat tip: Brazil National Team, 1994 World Cup.)

- Wall Pass Challenges. A wall pass requires vision and anticipation from several players at once. Any wall pass that is part of a goal-scoring buildup is worth a bonus point. On the other hand, getting the footwork wrong at the wall when there's time to do it right might cost a team a point (see chapter 19, activity 46).

- Negative Passes. This is where players are not allowed to pass backwards. It is particularly useful in developing the "Go-For-It" mentality (see chapter 8.6).

- Silent Running. In scrimmage situations of 3v3 or more, players are not allowed to speak. This is a great condition to promote Vision and combines well with the Where's Waldo activity (see chapter 14, activity 8).

- "Game Over." This is a Golden Goal moment that immediately wins a game. Examples could include scoring three consecutive goals in the Breakout Game (see chapter 20, activity 65) without the opposition touching the ball, or completing either form of a Double Wall Pass (see chapter 19, activity 49) or breaking an ankle (making an opponent fall down) with a ball move.

- Must Mark. Here each player on one team may only mark a designated player on the other. This gives the attacker time and space to "Do a Move" or "Use a Move." (Usually a player will be paired with an opponent, but it can be interesting to have each team choose which players each team member will mark.) This is a good challenge for providing risk–reward decision-making (e.g., "Should I really try to get free to be part of the attack?").

- Big Five Moments. An unusual percentage of goals are scored in the first and last five minutes of a half, in the five minutes after a goal has been scored, and in the five minutes after a critical game moment (e.g., penalty kick, player ejection.) Many teams will have all the players raise hands with the five fingers extended whenever the team is entering one of these intervals.

- Pizza Goal. This is a goal scored in the first minute of either half and results in pizza for the team at a subsequent practice. It could be expanded to include other Big Five moments.

5.9   COACHING AND CULTURE

On a website for coaches, a long and spirited discussion led to the following list of "20 Questions" (plus 5 more for Game Day) drawn from the habits of highly effective coaches. (Some items will seem familiar.) Imagine how a coach's answers will impact a team's culture.[10]

1. *How are players greeted*? Is it warm, positive, confident?

2. How *engaged* is the coach throughout the session?

3. How much time are players *doing*, rather than stopped and listening?

4. Is *everyone* on the team being coached? Is there coaching that appears directed to increase individual player strengths, not just eliminate weaknesses? Does the coaching seem to *inspire* players?

5. *"Correction is a compliment."* Is correction given in a positive manner that conveys the message both that "I want you to get better" and "I believe you can?"

6. "What gets rewarded gets repeated." How much *recognition, using players' names,* is given to positive moments?

7. Does effort and boldness receive positive recognition (and encouragement), or does that go only to the outcomes that succeed?

8. *"Doers make mistakes."* Mistakes can make you better. (*"Mistakes are good. Struggle makes you stronger."*) Are those kinds of mistakes praised or criticized?

9. Do sessions seem *well prepared*? Are activities set up before the session starts? Are players moving with a ball at the designated starting time? Is there good flow from one activity to the next? Does the session end on time?

10. How many soccer balls are in play? At younger ages, a fair amount of time should be spent "everyone with a ball" or "a ball for two."

11. What percent of sessions includes some form of 1v1 play? (All should.)

12. If working on shooting, does it include working on technique or is it just shooting games?

---

[10] andagain.websitetoolbox.com/post?id=5138477&trail=.

13. Overall, does the session seem to be focused more on developing better players or organizing the team for the next game?

14. *"Juggling makes every other touch better."* Does it appear that learning to juggle is encouraged (or required)?

15. Is there any emphasis on exterminating "Useless Weak Foot Syndrome?"

16. A clue to player engagement: is the practice noisy or is the only voice that of the coach? Do the players appear to be enjoying their time together?

17. Watch players' faces. Do they seem to be enjoying it? Better, do they have that scrunched-up-face look that comes with total focus and involvement?

18. What's the tone of the end-of-the-session (or end of day) summary? Does it efficiently sum up what was done and why?

19. When it's all done, do the players look satisfied with what they've experienced? Do they leave with smiles and happy chatter?

20. Does the coach leave the same way?

On Game Day

1. Whose game is it? Games should largely belong to the players. Does the coach largely *"Train and Trust"* the players, letting them think and make decisions? Or is there a constant stream of instructions that micromanages play on the field?

2. Is the positive–negative environment of the team the same as at practice, regardless of the score?

3. Even if you can't hear what the coach is saying pre-game, during half-time, and at the end, how would you describe the tone or body language?

4. What are parents saying or doing on the sideline? It's amazing how much parental sidelines reflect the influence of and respect for the coach.

5. Is the post-game summary "quick and done?" It takes everyone, including players, time to process a game, so the in-depth stuff should wait until the next practice. *(A timely reminder here that one of the things players most dread is the PGA—Post-Game Analysis—which happens most frequently on the CRH, the Car Ride Home.)* Does the coach's summary end on a positive?

This list of questions can be downloaded from www.PlayersFirst.com.

GROWING TALENT:

A NEW LOOK

6 THE CULTIVATION OF EXCELLENCE

"Greatness Isn't Born. It's Grown."

–Daniel Coyle, *The Talent Code*

6.1 "START WITH THE END IN MIND"

Talent is a result of purposeful effort over time. Innate ability has a role, but it appears to be less important that commonly thought. Rather, effort and repetition grow the brain in ways that allow performance that is increasingly fast, strong, and accurate. Maximum growth happens in environments where every effort is a stretch for what is just out of reach and where mistakes and failure, painful as they may be, are valued as guideposts on the way to better performance.

Opportunity plays an important role in talent development, particularly when it comes to the critical moments that ignite the passion required to endure a path to greatness filled with challenge and difficulty. Also important is the opportunity at a young age to have solid coaching that is knowledgeable and maintains high standards in a nurturing environment while also messaging and modeling a belief in human potential for development.

The best training environments are built on **deliberate practice** within a culture that values and promotes **discipline** ("focused attention and effort"), **perseverance**, and **resilience** ("grit"), having a **teachable spirit**, and **accountability** (assuming ever more personal responsibility for one's performance). All are Positive Life Skills with significance that goes well beyond the value of anything learned about a particular sport.

Among the most frequent comments heard in youth sports are those related to the talent of players. These remarks reflect common assumptions about innate ability and are colored by beliefs about the boundaries of human potential. If questioned about the source a player's talent, significant emphasis is given either to being "born with it" or at least born with a special potential to become so talented. Further questioning often reveals a belief that such potential has, no matter the talent, some limit that is fixed as much by genetics as by any other factor.

Recently, such views about talent and potential have been challenged by those who study the learning process as well as journalists who have helped popularize an alternative narrative. This chapter and the next two look at the books of five of those authors. The intent—until you can carve out the time to read these books in whole—is to weave a single narrative that you can use both to explore the latest thinking about talent and talent development and to provide optimal environments for nurturing great performance.

Malcolm Gladwell's *Outliers* (2007) became a number one bestseller. In his book, he examines individuals and clusters of individuals who achieved massive success in ways that defy the "born to greatness" model of talent development. Most of his subjects displayed little early on that would have predicted future greatness. Instead their successes shared many common factors totally removed from genetics, most notably the role played by opportunity and the vast amount of time devoted to their particular endeavors. It was Gladwell who popularized the notion that 10,000 hours of preparation was a pre-requisite to world-class achievement in any field.

Geoff Colvin's *Talent Is Overrated* (2008) examines the 10,000 hour proposition, explaining that superior performance arises not due to the quantity of time involved so much as the quality of the work done in that time together with the opportunistic impact of teachers and coaches. He also examines the elements of the deliberate (or "deep") practice that is the key to optimal learning.[1]

Mathew Syed had firsthand experience with unusual opportunity. An Olympian with a number 1 national ranking, he was among a cluster of national and international table tennis champions who came from the same middle-class neighborhood in England. *Bounce* (2010) details his experience and makes the argument that most people can achieve high levels of performance with the right mix of opportunity and dedication.

Syed also touches on advances in scientific understanding of the learning process, the focus of *The Talent Code* by Daniel Coyle. Coyle's work began with a study of "talent hotbeds," those clusters of high performance that seem to appear out of the blue (e.g., Syed's neighborhood). His inquiry then took him to those researching the neuroscience of learning and the role of myelin in developing skill. He shows how deep practice amplifies the process of adding myelin to the brain. (Coyle's follow-up work, *The Little Book of Talent* (2012), provides a number of tips for maximizing the learning process. His blog at www.thetalentcode.com gives many more.)

While acknowledging that genetic make-up has some role in talent development (e.g., LeBron James could never have been a jockey), these books make a compelling case that *"Greatness isn't born; it's grown"* and that a surprisingly large portion of the population could approach the level of great talent.

---

[1] Researcher Anders Ericsson coined the term *deep practice*. An in-depth look at the concept (and the fascinating research on which it is based) is found in his book, *Peak*.

So why doesn't such greatness happen more frequently? The authors would identify lack of opportunity as a primary cause. Equally important, though, is the *Mindset* (Carol Dweck, 2006) of both teachers and learners. Dweck posits that people operate along a continuum of belief. At the one end is the Fixed Mindset, which holds that one's talent will be significantly limited, if not determined, by genetic inheritance. At the other end is the Growth Mindset, grounded in the belief that an individual can achieve pretty much anything by purposeful work and application. Few people sit fully at one end or the other of that scale, but where one sits has a profound impact on one's belief about the ability of people, including self, to grow or change. And belief informs action. (Find a simple Mindset Test mindtestonline.com.)

The following chapters bring together the most important elements of these books. The focus is often on great performers and how they got there, but the same principles and ideas that explain exceptional success can be applied to developing talent at much younger ages.

7 UNDERSTANDING THE LEARNING PROCESS

"What any person in the world can learn, almost all persons can learn, if provided with the appropriate prior and current conditions of learning."

–Dr. Benjamin Bloom

7.1 THE SCIENCE

Much of the new research about talent revolves around the brain, specifically a substance called myelin.

Myelin is an insulator (you might recall the term *myelin sheath* from biology class). This refers to its function of wrapping the wires of our brain in the same way that electrical tape wraps around an electrical wire: It makes the signal move faster and prevents it from leaking out. For the past hundred years or so, scientists considered myelin and its associated cells to be inert. After all, it looked like insulation, and it didn't appear to react to anything.

Except the early scientists were wrong. It turns out that myelin does react—it grows in response to electrical activity (i.e., practice). In fact, studies show that myelin grows in proportion to the hours spent in practice. It's a simple system and can be thought of this way: Every time you perform a rep, your brain adds another layer of myelin to those particular wires. The more you practice, the more layers of myelin you earn, the more quickly and accurately the signal travels, and the more skill you acquire.

Studies have linked practice to myelin growth and improved performance in such diverse skills as reading, vocabulary, music, and sports. The research is still in its early phases but is threatening to rewrite the old saying. Practice doesn't make perfect. Practice makes myelin, and myelin makes perfect.[1] For more information, read *The Talent Code*.

---

[1] Coyle, D. 2012. *The Little Book of Talent*. Bantam, p. 117-119.

CoachNotes

For coaches, the implication is immediate. Practice that requires a skill to be performed correctly sets the stage for the next repetitions of that skill to be done better (i.e., with great speed, power, and precision). It follows that when a skill is done incorrectly, the stage is also set for the next repetition to be done with greater speed, power, and precision—only incorrectly.

Precision is particularly important when practicing the **hard skills**. These are actions that need to be repeated the same way every time, while **soft skills** tend to be broader, less specialized, and often requiring recognition of patterns in the stimuli. In soccer, a driven instep kick is a hard skill while finishing is a soft skill that often includes that particular hard skill. Ball moves are primarily hard skills; one-on-one attacking blends those skills with various soft-skill elements that make the use of a ball move effective. Developing **vision** (see chapter 14.1) demands first the hard skill of constantly moving the head to see the field and then developing the soft skills necessary to understand and react with increasing speed and precision to all the things that *"having a look"* allows the brain to take in.

Most performance is a mixture of hard and soft skills. But the hard skills are the foundation. They must come first. "Precision first [...] build the basic pathways [...] the key investment."[2] Less obvious to many is the importance of continuing to revisit and hone basic skills. The NFL's Peyton Manning began every training session by working on sets of footwork skills he learned in his college years. Stephen Curry's pre-game routine is so amazing that NBA arenas open their doors early because people want to see it (search online for a video of the routine). Yet it's rare, for example, for youth soccer teams to work on the technical elements of striking a ball beyond age 12. Coaches seem to forget that fundamentals never stop being fundamental. And they can always be sharpened.

Finally, fix the bad stuff but capitalize on the good stuff. One thing that set apart the early U.S. Women's National Team (the Akers, Foudy, Hamm, Lilly group) was that each player was the best in the world in some aspect of *the Game*. While always at work on what they couldn't do (yet), they were also encouraged to improve their best quality, what made them (in coach speak) **personality players**.

---

[2] Coyle, D. 2012. *The Little Book of Talent*. Bantam, p. 22.

7.2   THE TRAINING: DELIBERATE PRACTICE

Each of the books we're examining recognizes that those who demonstrate superior talent are consistently those who put more time into the proper sort of preparation than those who demonstrate less talent. The beliefs, motivation, and character of the individual are important here, and we'll deal with that later on. For now, let's look at what *proper preparation* is, particularly in terms of practice.

The most effective practice has come to be known as **deliberate practice**. Psychologist Anders Ericsson, who first coined the term and identified its characteristics, says:

(This) practice is different. It entails considerable, specific and sustained efforts to do something you can't do well – or even at all. Research across domains shows that it is only by working at what you can't do that you turn into the expert you want to become.[3]

Deep practice involves an ongoing series of sequences that reach–reflect–refine–repeat. Reaching, or *stretching*, can be described like this: *"Go to the very edge of what you can almost do, then step beyond."* Once you've done that, it's time to evaluate what happened, successful or not. Then repeat, using the reflection to fix what didn't work and confirm or refine what did.

Let's use training the instep drive (see chapter 13.4) as an example.

- Chunking. Almost every method of striking a soccer ball can be divided into three segments: the preparation, the strike, and the follow-though. Breaking something down this way is called "chunking," and players learn most effectively chunk by chunk. When chunking, the first thing to do is provide the "big picture," in this instance demonstrating the skill whole by striking a stationary ball, so that the players can "start with the end in mind." Next subdivide the "preparation" chunk into three parts: the final step, the "backswing," and locking the ankle for the shot. Now break down the elements of only that "final step." Start with just the placement of the foot, 3 to 5 inches away from the ball, anklebone square with the center of the ball, foot pointed in the direction you'll want the ball to go. (Three mini-chunks!) Do this first with the foot beside the ball, then from a step away, then two.

- Reflect, Refine, Repeat. Once the placement can be done with precision, add emphasis to the quality of that final step. It should be aggressive, a "hop" that carries momentum forward as opposed to a "plant" that directs the energy downward. With each repetition comes an evaluation. The coach or another player might do it, but most often it's a self-evaluation. "Was it correct?" If not, "What needs to be fixed,

---

[3] Syed, M. 2011. *Bounce*. Harper Perennial, p. 80.

and how?" If a repetition is successful, "freeze perfection,"[4] stopping for a moment to "describe what was right" or "describe what it felt like." Now repeat to "fix it" if that's what's needed, alternately with an attempt to go a little faster, harder, or with more precision if the previous repetition was good. Whether to correct or to enhance that next repetition involves yet another reach. Refinement often produces breakdowns in the quality of collateral elements of the skill. It's not uncommon to have to switch back and forth between chunks and groups of chunks when working toward assembly of the whole. With each repetition, the myelin winds. With lots of correct repetition the skill becomes automatic. When working on hard skills, this is what most call muscle memory. But it is really neuromuscular memory with the brain trained to fire the muscles.[5] The more training, the more quick, powerful, and accurate will be the response.

7.3 CATALYSTS

By now you're probably getting the idea that this is not a simple process—for the teacher or the learner. It *is* hard, and creating deep practice progressions that are both productive and engaging is perhaps the essential skill of youth coaching. Here are some things that help:

- In the Beginning. Have players exaggerate, both when working on the chunks and assembling them. Use vivid language to help players remember concepts. When performing repetitions in slow motion, for instance, go to "suuuuuperrrrrr-slooooowww" motion to illustrate the idea of "Do it right, then do it fast." Combine slow motion and exaggeration when performing the repetition with an imaginary ball—what the Russians call imitatsiya.[6] As performance improves, asking for multiple repetitions against a time limit works, too. All these variants demand additional focus and concentration on the part of the player, increasing the chances of a correct response (while highlighting the incorrect parts).

- Size matters. Another important soft skill, especially for new coaches, is learning to manage spatial limitations. As a rule, "If at first it's not working, the space is too small." But once it is working, shrinking the space adds to the challenge. Limits on time can serve the same purpose.

---

[4] Coyle, D. 2012. *The Little Book of Talent.* Bantam, p. 66.
[5] Coyle, D. 2009. *The Talent Code.* Bantam, p. 82.
[6] Coyle, D. 2009. *The Talent Code.* Bantam, p. 82.

> **Guest CoachNotes**
> Even at young ages, I would tell players that when they were doing well, I would **"shrink the grid."** When they needed more focus, I would **"expand the grid."** I could reward play without ever making a comment or seeming to criticize a player directly. –AFB

- Speed kills. There's no rush to get it done. "When we do things at a slower pace [...] we get through a lot more. There's a lot more retention, better understanding of the material."[7] Legendary basketball coach John Wooden adds, "By applying yourself to the task of becoming a little better each and every day over a period of time, you will become a lot better,"[8] and famously, "Be quick, but don't hurry."

- Except when it doesn't. There comes a time, especially in the development of hard skills, when it can be useful to push the tempo of repetitions to the point where technique fails. This will identify the chunk(s) that are weakest and need additional refinement. If the fix is the right one, the next trial will allow a higher tempo before failure. This tactic is sometimes referred to as Mistake Based Training. (See chapter 8.5.)

> **CoachNotes**
> Deep practice can lead to extraordinary gains in performance in a very short time, especially with younger players. This tempts the coach to go faster (e.g., to abandon technical work on striking the ball in favor of shooting games or finishing exercises), when in fact it is more beneficial to go deeper (introducing activities which refine the technique itself).

- Make It a Game. If you can count something, you can make a game out of it.

- Kids Can "Get It." They not only can understand the basic ideas of myelin growth, they'll be fascinated by the idea that with repetition "you can build a better brain."

- "Less is more." The ski patrol will tell you how often a skier's last run of the day ("I think I'll take just one more") finishes on the toboggan. "Fatigue slows brains. It triggers errors, lessens concentration and leads to shortcuts that create bad habits."[9] This is not embraceable failure. Deliberate practice is physically and mentally demanding,

---

[7] Gladwell, M. 2011. *Outliers*. Back Bay Books, p. 262.
[8] Dweck, C. 2011. *Mindset*. Ballantine Books, p. 207.
[9] Coyle, D. 2012. *The Little Book of Talent*. Bantam, p. 81.

and the ability to sustain it grows over time. With younger players, just a few intense minutes at a time will be a reach. At the other end, a practice session for the North Carolina women's soccer team, which is structured to be a full-out onslaught of deep practice, lasts 90 minutes—the length of a game. (That's a good guide to how long training sessions should be at different ages.) Within that time, coaches must learn when to end an activity. This is particularly difficult when it's "gone magical." But since actions performed correctly grow the brain in ways that set the stage for the next repetition to be done even better, ending with success provides not only an ideal stopping point, it also leaves the players wanting more.

- Corrections need to be concise and accurate. Develop key words as "sticky note" shortcuts that describe whole ideas.

7.4 THE WILD CARD

A player's every action is a blend of hard and soft skills. Those whose actions are more successful than others' are usually viewed as more "talented." But what has really happened is that these players have performed the actions—and their precursors—more frequently and with more attention to detail. Their practice has been different and better.

In terms of talent development, **opportunity** is the wild card. Outstanding performers are commonly

beneficiaries of unusual circumstances, hidden advantages, extraordinary opportunities, and cultural legacies that allow them to learn and work hard and make sense of the world that others cannot.[10]

Opportunity's role is most telling in two areas:

1. Lighting the Fire.
   The 10,000 hour rule seems to hold with all top performers. *"No one has yet found a case in which true world-class expertise was accomplished in less time."*[11] Just the time alone is staggering, requiring an uncommon level of dedication and **discipline** ("focused attention and effort").

   Researchers have found that such traits in an athlete have a common factor: a spark that sets the player off. This is called **ignition**. For Syed it was, among other things, a table tennis table in the garage and growing up in a neighborhood with many other very good table tennis players. For a young boy or girl, it can be something as simple as discovering you have the same birthday as Lionel Messi or Alex Morgan.

---

[10] Syed, M. 2011. *Bounce*. Harper Perennial, p. 9.
[11] Gladwell, M. 2011. *Outliers*. Back Bay Books, p. 40.

An 8-year-old Jackie Evancho saw a performance of *Phantom of the Opera*, and then had her parents buy the CD so she could sing along. More top players are the youngest child in their families rather than the oldest: Julie Foudy's description of being pummeled by her older brothers in backyard soccer games is a classic, and both Mia Hamm and Kristine Lilly talk about playing with and against older brothers. Syed had an older brother who also became an international for England's table tennis team.

Ignition takes the form of *"brief powerful encounters that spark motivation by linking your identity to a high performing person or group" and allows the creation of "a view of one's future self."*[12] Teachers and coaches are a ready a source of ignition; they *"get the learner involved, captivated, hooked and get the learner to need and want more information and expertise."*[13] Coaches can also be catalysts for ignition by bringing in older players as assistants and giving information about games and players to watch (especially in person) or camps to attend where there will be models with whom kids can connect.

Ignition is a powerful motivational jolt that results in a transition between external and internal motivation. It brings heightened passion, greater personal responsibility for preparation and performance, and a greater reliance on intrinsic reward. One of the best indicators of ignition is that a player engages in solo practice *"when no one else is watching."* Not because a coach or parent expects it but because *the player* wants to do so.

2. Quality Early Instruction.

Syed's neighborhood also had an outstanding coach in Peter Charters, the local school's gym teacher, who not only identified potential table tennis champions, but also provided them with superior early instruction and a rundown, "one-table hut" that was available all year, 24/7 to his students.[14] The equally ramshackle Spartak Tennis Club near Moscow has produced multiple world-class players under the direction of Larisa Preobrazhenskaya.[15]Master teachers know what to teach and how to teach it—a primary emphasis on hard skills, ongoing repetition and refinement, constantly challenging players, reinforcing the effort and strength of character needed to reach, reflect, refine, and reach again.

Such master teachers have high standards and something more. Benjamin Bloom's *Developing Talent In Young People* is the masterwork on the subject. In his study of

---

[12] Coyle, D. 2012. *The Little Book of Talent*. Bantam, p. 3.
[13] Coyle, D. 2009. *The Talent Code*. Bantam, p. 175.
[14] Syed, M. 2011. *Bounce*. Harper Perennial, p. 7.
[15] Coyle, D. 2009. *The Talent Code*. Bantam, p. 82.

the upbringing of top performers, Bloom emphasizes the nurturing role of their early teachers:

Perhaps the major quality of these teachers was that they made the initial learning very pleasant and rewarding. Much of the introduction to the field was playful activity, and the learning at the beginning of this stage was much like a game. Those teachers gave much positive reinforcement and only rarely were critical of the child. However, they did set standards and expected the child to make progress, although this was largely done with approval and praise.[16]

Charters and Preobrazhenskaya are outliers, of course. But every coach can learn from their model and apply the same principles when working with young athletes.

7.5   LET'S GET BETTER

What's here is only a start, enough to get you going. If it has ignited your interest in learning more, buy the books and get out your highlighter. Coaching is mostly soft skills. (This explains why those who have spectacular abilities often struggle when trying to teach them to others.) Putting any of these ideas into practice will involve the same reach–reflect–refine–repeat process, easily as equally challenging as that the athletes you are coaching will experience. Done with focus, an attention to detail, and, of course, continual of stretching, you'll get better over time. Now let's look at the most powerful element in learning and achieving excellence: **failure**.

---

[16] Coyle, D. 2009. *The Talent Code*. Bantam, p. 176.

8 FAILING WELL: "MISTAKES ARE GREAT"

"There are very few activities in life that can teach you how to handle adversity without having to experience actual, tragic adversity. Sport is one of them. Soccer is one of them."

–Dan Blank, www.soccerpoet.com

8.1 "DOERS MAKE MISTAKES"

Widely regarded as the greatest basketball player of all time, Michael Jordan often talks about all his game-winning shots that missed. Fellow GOAT, hockey's Wayne Gretsky, amazed his coaches and teammates with his skating routines before practice—because he fell so often.[1]

Obviously, Gretzky was not a klutz. What his observers were seeing was someone who was repeatedly reaching or stretching for a level of skating skill that was just out of range. Similarly, it is estimated that Shizuka Arakawa landed on the ice over 20,000 times on her path to an Olympic Gold Medal in figure skating.[2]

One of the great ironies of our time is that society increasingly seeks to shield children from mistakes and failure while at the same time discovering how important both are to optimal learning. When players are asked to reach and to be spontaneous and daring, a hefty portion of their efforts will end unsuccessfully. But that doesn't make the outcome a failure. You can learn far more from getting it wrong than by getting it right, especially if the training environment is one where *"it's OK to make a mistake."* In fact, you will find that such an approach leads to a decrease in anxiety among your players and an increase in their ability to work harder and stay on task longer.

8.2 EMBRACING STRUGGLE

"Mistakes are good; struggle makes you smarter and stronger." Inventor Thomas Edison said, *"If I find 10,000 ways something won't work, I haven't failed. I am not discouraged, because every wrong attempt discarded is another step forward."* Gretzky and Arakawa

---

[1] Coyle, D. 2012. *The Little Book of Talent.* Bantam, p. 13
[2] Colvin, G. 2010. *Talent Is Overrated.* Portfolio, p. 187.

did not interpret falling down as failure. Armed with a growth mindset, they interpreted falling down not merely as a means of improving, but as *evidence* that they were improving. Failure was not something that sapped energy and vitality, but something that provided opportunity to learn, develop, and adapt. Excellence is about striving for what is just out of reach and not quite making it; it is about grappling with tasks beyond current limitations and falling short again and again. The paradox of excellence is that it is built upon the foundations of necessary failure.[3]

Building a culture that embraces failure in this manner is a formidable challenge for coaches. Pushing beyond the comfort zone is, by definition, uncomfortable. Just the notion of risking failure is daunting enough for lots of people, and failing is rarely, if ever, enjoyable.

The Elephant in the Room

For all the talk about embracing challenges and valuing failures, the fact remains that kids are often shielded from the latter by dumbing down the former. Megan McCardle, who writes about the notion of **"failing well"** nails the problem:

The metaphor for our age is the disappearance of high monkey bars from playgrounds across the country. We have made it impossible for children to fall very far - and in so doing, we have robbed them of the joys of climbing high.[4]

Other common manifestations of society's failure phobia include grade inflation and social promotion in schools and "helicopter parenting" (and its extension to the "bulldozer" variety) at the family level. In both settings discussions about the qualities needed to excel tend to understate or sugarcoat the difficulty of achieving great performance. Dweck laments how *"lowering standards just leads to poorly educated students who feel entitled to easy work and lavish praise."*[5] Bruce Brown of Proactive Coaching addresses both the problem and the solution:

The dilemma for most adults is that it is easy for them to see "solutions" in athletic situations and too painful for adults to let their children find their own solutions. On the other hand, it is both necessary and helpful to allow children to work their own ways out of troubling dilemmas. No downside exists for allowing a young athlete to take a risk and fail in a game or practice. **If young athletes are going to develop into intelligent, instinctive individuals, it is critical that they are given the opportunity to solve their own problems** [...] [This gives them] an enhanced chance to grow in a meaningful way.[6]

---

[3] Syed, M. 2011. *Bounce*. Harper Perennial, p. 127-129.
[4] McArdle, M. 2014. *The Up Side of Down*. Penguin Books, p. xiii.
[5] Dweck, C. 2011. *Mindset*. Ballantine Books, p. 193.
[6] Brown, B. 2003. *Teaching Character Through Sport*. Coaches Choice Books, p. 126.

Combatting these influences is one of the most common and difficult obstacles for a coach. Anson Dorrance, who has coached the University of North Carolina women's soccer team to twenty-one national championships, says this:

Getting your team to **transcend ordinary effort** is the challenge in every training session and every match. To get this effort, you as a coach are regularly dealing with the emotional strain of not accepting the lower standard of performance and effort. Your strength in coaching is having the combative courage to constantly deal with the athletes that unconsciously try to take things a bit easier and to fight the human tendency to be comfortably mediocre.[7]

Coaches who work to impart in players the value of effort and embracing challenge must also make sure the athletes' parents understand what's being done and why. Those parents who value the same things will appreciate the reinforcement. Those who don't (yet) might learn something, though they could also decide to look for something less demanding. (For the coach, at least, any of the three parental outcomes can be an acceptable outcome.)

8.3   BELIEF AND CHARACTER

For most players, the life skills and lessons learned through athletics will be more lasting and, ultimately, more important than anything learned about a specific sport. A growth-centered approach to learning and personal development can be a fertile breeding ground for many positive life skills.

Personal Growth Through Deep Practice

The Positive Coaching Alliance (PCA) has a three-part definition of a "winner." The first two describe athletes who *"make the maximum effort, continue to learn and improve."*[8] The third element is addressed on page 72. **Deep** or **deliberate practice**, described in detail in the previous chapter, is a training regimen of systematic, focused, and persistent reaching in order to move beyond what you can currently do. It accustoms players to stepping out of their comfort zones and making the kind of effort that leads to maximal learning, improvement, and, over time, well-earned success. No matter the final level of play one attains, the model provides a platform for athletes to become lifelong learners and "to do great things" in *the Game* and beyond.

Grit. Deep practice is also associated with a critical character trait found in top performers. It's called "grit"—*"that mix of passion, perseverance, and self-discipline that*

---

[7] Dorrance, A. 1997. From speech given at NSCAA convention.
[8] Thompson, J. 2003. *The Double-Goal Coach*. William Morrow Paperbacks, p. 37.

keeps us moving forward in spite of obstacles."[9] Gladwell gives a vivid example: *"Success is a function of persistence and doggedness and the willingness to work hard for twenty-two minutes to make sense of something that most people would give up on after thirty seconds."*[10]

Grit is related to self-control. Angela Duckworth, the leading researcher on the role of grit in performance, defines grit along a time continuum:

Grit equips individuals to pursue especially challenging aims over years and even decades. Self-control, in contrast, operates at a more molecular timescale, in the battle against [...] the hourly temptations – among whose modern incarnations I would nominate Facebook, Angry Birds, Krispy Kreme donuts, and other pursuits which bring pleasure in the moment but are immediately regretted.[11]

Grit is measurable and seems to be the catalyst in attaining success at high levels. (There are several questionnaires that provide a "grit score." A basic Grit Test is found at sasupenn.qualtrics.com.) In one commonly cited example, the Grit Test scores provided the single best predictor of how incoming cadets would fare during "Beast Barracks," the basic training regimen for incoming plebes (freshmen) at West Point.

Grit kicks in as tasks become more difficult, and is particularly important when responding to adversity. *"Exceptional people seem to have a special talent for converting life's setbacks into future successes."*[12]

Grit appears to be a product of a growth mindset. That mindset is based on a belief that for most people the potential for achievement is immense. It's a belief supported by educational research:

Benjamin Bloom studied 120 outstanding achievers. They were concert pianists, sculptors, Olympic swimmers, world-class tennis players, mathematicians, and research neurologists. Most were not that remarkable as children and didn't show clear talent before their training began in earnest. Even by early adolescence, you usually couldn't predict their future accomplishment from their current ability. Only their continued motivation and commitment, along with their network of support, took them to the top.

Bloom concludes, "After forty years of intensive research on school learning in the United States as well as abroad, my major conclusion is: What any person in the world can learn, almost all persons can learn, if provided with the appropriate prior and current conditions

---

[9] Coyle, D. 2012. *The Little Book of Talent.* Bantam, p. 110.

[10] Gladwell, M. 2011. *Outliers.* Back Bay Books, p. 246.

[11] www.theatlantic.com/education/archive/2013/09/we-need-to-be-gritty-about-getting-our-kids-grittier/279992/.

[12] Dweck, C. 2011. *Mindset.* Ballantine Books, p. 13.

of learning (e.g., motivation, commitment, support)." He's not counting the 2 to 3 percent of children who have severe impairments, and he's not counting the top 1 to 2 percent of children at the other extreme. He is counting everybody else.[13]

Anders Ericsson first studied the limits of memory. This led to further study of, in his words, *"the remarkable potential of 'ordinary' adults and their amazing capacity for change with practice."*[14] His innovative research gave rise to the concept that he named **deliberate practice**. Syed summarized what Ericsson found and would continue to find.

As Ericsson puts it, "There are apparently no limits to improvements in memory skill with practice."

Think about that for a moment, for it is a revolutionary statement. Its subversive element is not its specific claim about memory but its promise that *anybody* can achieve the same results with opportunity and dedication. Ericsson has spent the last thirty years uncovering the same groundbreaking logic in fields as diverse as sports, chess, music education, and business.[15]

Grit is and can be grown. Conquering a challenge reinforces the perseverance and resilience that grit allows. As effort is rewarded, a person can develop an approach to learning and improving that doesn't just seek challenge, but thrives on it, where the cycle of **"hard work and more hard work"**[16] required to constantly learn and improve actually becomes enjoyable.

It's here that coaches are so important as "allies in learning."[17] Young athletes need help to grow into this cycle. As players move along the pathways to becoming responsible for their own learning, they need to be provided with an ongoing series of activities designed to require reaching and stretching. They will require environments that encourage persistence and occasionally provide the nudge that helps them find ways to overcome obstacles. They should learn that *"if it were easy, everyone could do it,"* that getting better requires *"an effort of focus and concentration [that is] not inherently fun"*[18] but can become so.

The ultimate affirmation of a great learning environment is, **"This is hard! This is fun!"** (A good article on developing grit, *The Power of Defeat*, can be read at www.scholastic. com/parents/resources.) Of course, a coach can do all those things and still it won't stick for some players. The rewards of deep practice are not always immediate, so the costs in

---

[13] Dweck, C. 2011. *Mindset*. Ballantine Books, p. 65-66.
[14] Colvin, G. 2010. *Talent Is Overrated*. Portfolio, p. 39.
[15] Syed, M. 2011. *Bounce*. Harper Perennial, p. 23.
[16] Dweck, C. 2011. *Mindset*. Ballantine Books, p. 198.
[17] Dweck, C. 2011. *Mindset*. Ballantine Books, p. 67.
[18] Colvin, G. 2010. *Talent Is Overrated*. Portfolio, p. 70-71.

terms of time and effort are more than they are willing to invest. Fear of failure locked in by a fixed mindset does not allow a belief in the ability to change. It happens. Sometimes the best you can do is to wish them well and move on with the rest.

Grit involves an unconventional relationship with failure. To quote Winston Churchill: *"Success consists of going from failure to failure without loss of enthusiasm."*

Mistake Rituals. The player who goes over the ball and crashes while trying a new ball move experiences the physical pain of the crash and often the nervous laughter of teammates who are secretly relieved not to be the one on the ground. The third element of PCA's definition of "winners" identifies individuals who *"never let failure or the fear of failure get in their way."* These people often use "mistake rituals" to deal with errors and failure.[19] One of the best is one of the simplest, where the player gets back up, throws the arms victoriously in the air, and proclaims **"Ta-Da!"** thereby demonstrating the *"willingness to be stupid"*[20] and make mistakes in the pursuit of progress. Coaches can use the words **"Great Mistake!"** to indicate appreciation and support of efforts "at the edge" that didn't work.

Recovery. The U.S. Women's National Team used a three-part mistake ritual introduced by team psychologist Colleen Hacker called the Three Fs. Mistakes elicited **"Fudge"** (or something that sounded similar.) Next came the **"Fix-it"** moment, so it would be less likely to happen again. Finally, **"Focus"** to return to the immediate task at hand. This ritual is a wonderful tool for coaches. Rather than providing a solution, by asking **"Fix it"** a coach gets *the player* to verbalize a potential solution. Then, with a comment like, *"Great idea. Now focus,"* the coach affirms the response and directs the player to move past the mistake.

This particular mistake ritual reinforces the importance of the **reflect** element in the learning process. Merely trying harder won't always fix it. It's usually more important to examine factors besides effort that may need to be changed to get a better result the next time. That turns failure into failing well.

The WNT mantra also illustrates a characteristic of great performers. They will instantly analyze a mistake rather than ignoring it or putting it off for a later time.[21]

---

[19] Thompson, J. 2003. *The Double-Goal Coach.* William Morrow Paperbacks, p. 51.
[20] Coyle, D. 2012. *The Little Book of Talent.* Bantam, p. 13.
[21] Coyle, D. 2012. *The Little Book of Talent.* Bantam, p. 57.

8.4   WORDS MATTER

Outstanding performers understand that effort, persistence, and resilience are necessary to advance. Young players won't have that understanding. They'll have to grow it like everything else related to their personal and athletic development. And like those other elements, that best happens in environments that are stimulating, structured and supportive.

Messaging is a key part of that support. Bloom's research found that in environments that grew excellence, *"to excel, to do one's best, to work hard and to spend one's time constructively were emphasized over and over again."*[22] Realistic acknowledgement of the difficulty in overcoming obstacles, incessant reinforcement of the necessity of failure, and promoting a **"Go-For-It"** mentality are examples of messaging that cannot be sent too often. The use of a **"sticky quote"** mantra like **"Let's Get Better"** to mark the start of every training session has real impact over time. Inspirational quotes on practice T-shirts (see chapter 4.3) have a way of producing the behaviors the quotes spotlight. Modeling effort, perseverance, resilience, and a commitment to lifelong learning and improvement—a **teachable spirit**—sends powerful messages as well.

Feedback. *"What gets rewarded gets done."* Both praise and correction can be used to improve performance, and both can be rewarding. The Positive Coaching Alliance advises that praise be a) truthful—a shot into the hands of the goalkeeper is rarely a "good shot"—and b) specific—*"you really stepped into that shot aggressively"* as opposed to "good shot" or the even more generic "good job." Then c) use the player's name to further personalize the reinforcement. PCA also encourages praising effort, particularly effort that does not succeed.[23]

Correction also needs to be *"truthful, specific, and use the player's name."* It will be best received within a culture which holds that *"correction is a compliment,"*[24] an affirmation of the coach's belief that the player can and will improve. Using the **"fix it"** question is also a great method of correction. Players will usually come up with a good answer, frequently a better one than the coach had in mind! Also, when making corrections pronouns are important; there's a big difference between *"We need to..."* and *"You need to..."*

PCA also talks about the magic ratio of praise to correction. They say that 5:1 is optimally effective.[25] Remember, though, that a single statement can carry the impact of many. It's best to think of the magic ratio in terms of overall weight. Dweck points out the perils

---

[22] Colvin, G. 2010. *Talent Is Overrated*. Portfolio, p. 172.

[23] Thompson, J. 2003. *The Double-Goal Coach*. William Morrow Paperbacks, p. 64.

[24] Brown, B. 2003. *Teaching Character Through Sport*. Coaches Choice Books, p. 51.

[25] Thompson, J. 2003. *The Double-Goal Coach*. William Morrow Paperbacks, p. 70.

of praising ability.[26] Her research indicates that praising "talent" or intelligence (fixed mindset constructs) can foster player doubt about having those qualities when there's a failure and may cause the player to seek easier and safer performance next time.

More Bad Language. The *"c-word"* is "can't," and it is bad unless accompanied by the most important word in a growth mindset universe: *"yet."* Players who are struggling can be helped to get back on track by statements that connect a positive character trait with the task at hand. The Positive Coaching Alliance teaches starting such statements with the phrase *"You seem like the kind of person who..."*[27]

Connecting. One of the most quoted of John Wooden's sayings is, *"People don't care how much you know until they know how much you care."* Not every player will be equally likable, but each deserves equal attention. Coach Wooden was known for his ability to give to all players equally.[28] This requires connecting with each athlete as an individual. It can be simply done by greeting each player at the start of every practice (and having a word at the end as well) and by regularly using the athlete's name. Questions like, *"What would you like to work on?"* can be used to reinforce that coach and athlete are allies in learning. Once players get to an age where they can begin to become managers of their own careers, around age 11 or 12, simple self-evaluation questionnaires become terrific starting points for detailed discussion about process and progress.

And if you're fortunate enough to have players thank you for the training session, always remember to reply, **"Thank you for learning."**

8.5   MISTAKE-BASED TRAINING

Skills need to be done slowly at first, then faster—**"Do it right, then do it fast."** But be sure to ask players to *"now go faster."* Build up the speed—have players do five to six reps of the skill as quickly as possible until the technique breaks down. Back off the speed a level or two, then start to build up the speed again. You should see that the next breaking point is at a faster speed than before.

That's the general idea behind **Mistake-Based Training**[29] Deliberate practice is done at the edge of one's ability, and MBT is a powerful and very effective technique to use when dancing around that precipice. Use it with foot skills, ball moves, 1v1 games, shooting technique, and maybe even juggling.

---

[26] Dweck, C. 2011. *Mindset*. Ballantine Books, p. 73. See also pages 174-183 for more about words that work in praise and correction.

[27] Thompson, J. 2003. *The Double-Goal Coach*. William Morrow Paperbacks, p. 259-261.

[28] Dweck, C. 2011. *Mindset*. Ballantine Books, p. 208.

[29] Coined by Mike Giuliano, Greater Atlanta Christian School.

8.6   THE "GO-FOR-IT" MENTALITY

It was said of the U.S. Women's National Soccer Team in the early 1990s that they would rather lose 5-4 than win 1-0. That team displayed an all-out **"Go-For-It"** mentality that was wildly entertaining and very successful. Current leadership favors a more "sophisticated" style of play, and one can understand a more cautious approach when World Championships and Olympic Medals are on the line. Until that level of play, there's much to be said for following the earlier model. One coach marvelously calls it "wantitude." *"When there is hard work and students are not afraid to take a risk, they are bound to be successful."*[30]

"The team that makes the most mistakes usually wins, because doers make mistakes." –John Wooden[31]

---

[30] Lemov, D. 2016. Teachlikeachampion.com.
[31] Wooden, J. 1997. *Wooden*. Contemporary Books, p. 73.

9 WHEN LESS IS MORE

"So if a four month season of one's sport of choice is good, then six months is better. Ten months is better yet. And twelve months: optimum. Except that it's not."

–James Sokolove, *Warrior Girls*

Each October on the weekend when the state recreational tournament is held, no games are scheduled for teams in Colorado's "competitive" (select) soccer leagues. Nonetheless, during that weekend tournaments have sprung up for those teams. There are ODP tryouts. Some teams even hold training sessions. On both days.

Meanwhile, we take calls from concerned parents (all of players younger than U13) whose kids' teams had taken no significant time off since *January*. And when we conducted a survey of participants in one of our programs, it revealed athletes at U10 who had soccer activities up to 22 days a month—in the month of February! In Colorado! It snows in Colorado!

We have also noted how rare it is for fall State Cup winners (that's when this competition happens for the older girls' teams) to advance to the next year's finals. Many (most in some years) are eliminated no later than their first round of knockout games.

9.1   REST IS A WEAPON

Athletes need time off for rest, for recovery, as a balance to the intensity of the time on, and to allow opportunities for other sports, interests, activities, and friendships that bring texture and equilibrium to their lives.

That's not happening for far too many youth soccer players. The concept of "off-season," which once in youth soccer were from the last game in November until three to four weeks before the first league game in the spring and from the final June game into August, has largely disappeared.

The endless season has an increasing role in the overuse injuries, mental as well as physical, that are significant contributors to kids' decisions to leave *the Game*. To remedy this, a 2007 article in *Pediatrics*, the journal of the American Academy of Pediatrics, included a number of recommendations. Among them: *"Encourage the athlete to take two to three months away from a specific sport during the year,"* and, *"Encourage athletes to strive to have at least one to two days off a week from competitive athletics, sport specific training, and competitive practice to allow them to recover both physically and psychologically [...] [with] longer scheduled breaks from training and competition every 2 to 3 months."* The article also noted: *"Young athletes who participate in a variety of sports have fewer injuries and play sports longer than those who specialize before puberty."*[1]

Not that we would expect—or want—young athletes to settle in for a lengthy stretch of pizza and pop in front of a video game console. Active kids want and need to be active. But they can actually get better at their sport of choice by, in the words of the article, *"focusing on other activities and cross training to prevent loss of skill or level of conditioning."* Athletes will also learn valuable athletic competencies from other sports, notably in the areas of strategies and tactics. It's conceivable that the best way to become a better soccer player during the winter is through swimming or skiing or playing basketball.

Off-Season Guidelines

We know that getting away from the game completely during off-season periods is a difficult option. So here are four ideas about what soccer should be during those intervals:

1. **Different** from the normal routines of team and club. Different coaching, different mixes of players, different versions of *the Game* (e.g., futsal; see chapter 25). Use non-soccer activities (e.g., holiday events, trips to a corn maze) to allow teammates to maintain contact.

2. **Low Key**, particularly where games are involved (futsal, indoor leagues, etc.). Let those activities belong totally to the athletes. Make them opportunities to develop spontaneity and daring in their play. If they need "coaching," your club should be able to find some older players who'd love to provide light guidance.

3. **Limited**, with the maximum number of soccer activities per month between one-half and two-thirds of the player's age (e.g., 5-7 for a 10-year-old). And never more than one a day.

4. **Voluntary**, truly voluntary—as opposed to "voluntary (wink, wink)" with the implied threat that without participation a place on the team could become at risk. Athletes and their parents need to *clearly* understand which definition of "voluntary" is in play.

We've seen great success with teams whose schedules provided regular breaks in the routine, who would turn that Saturday off in the fall into a full week off the field, with a similar break during the spring season. Team cultures can be constructed so that kids return from longer breaks with good fitness levels and skills that need minimal sharpening—things the athletes do on their own (while learning to take responsibility for

---

[1] pediatrics.aappublications.org/content/119/6/1242.full.

their own training) and which they will willingly do in return for the freedom to do other things and to "just be kids."

Players in such "less is more" environments return to training (and largely stay) refreshed, excited, and motivated to continue their soccer journeys. It even becomes a decisive competitive advantage—a secret weapon—as opponents who often do much more wear down from the volume and monotony of their activities.

This essay, When Less Is More, first appeared—and gets repeated—in the *Coerver Minute,* the newsletter of the Coerver Coaching of Colorado. It can also be downloaded from www.PlayersFirst.com.

FRAMING:

THE
PLAYERS 1ST
SYLLABUS

10 SKILLFUL SOCCER, WINNING SOCCER

"With the overemphasis on winning in this country, we are creating a nation of kids who can win but cannot play the game"

–Dr. Jay Martin, United Soccer Coaches

10.1 THE STATE OF THE GAME

Dr. Martin's quote is taken from an article in the *Soccer Journal* following the 2006 World Cup. That article seemed prophetic while watching the U.S. Women's National Team during the following year's Women's World Cup in China. The team's third-place finish was disappointing, as was seeing other teams display greater skill, poise, and ability to possess the ball under pressure. The WNT had begun to forfeit its technical advantage, a trend that has only accelerated since.

Even more troubling was the (then) U.S. coach defending the team's new, more-direct style as simply a matter of "greater sophistication," adapting to changes in the game and improvements in other teams. Dunga, coach of Brazil's men's team, ignited controversy there in the next few years with similar statements and a similar attempt to fundamentally transform Brazil's distinctive style of play.

Neither program has really recovered from those changes. We believe that both coaches were wrong in their assessment of *the Game* and its future. Creative, attractive soccer and winning soccer are not incompatible.

10.2 THE 75% SOLUTION

"Players who don't get a thorough grounding in soccer's essential skills at the younger ages are being cheated out of their futures in The Game."

–Marcelo "Chelo" Curi, Coerver Coaching of Colorado

Our opening chapters addressed the benefits of developing players and teams with strong skills and a philosophy of player development aimed at creating skillful Players 1st.

Two things stand in the way of widespread implementation of that philosophy. First, as a nation we lack the ability to teach skills well. Not even the various Coaching Education programs address skills teaching in sufficient depth. The other impediment is related to pressures associated with wins and losses. It is faster, and easier, to win games at the younger ages by allocating training time to team organization. Winning because the team's players are skillful and comfortable with the ball at their feet requires a patience and perseverance that is not always in abundant supply—with coaches or parents.

Skillful soccer is fun to watch, more fun to play. But to achieve both objectives requires a different use of a team's time on the field. We would encourage you take the longer view that training players for U14 and younger needs to be based on what we call **the 75% Solution**. That is, at least 75% of training time should be centered on developing new skills while improving the speed and proficient use of existing ones, where every session contains significant time that players are "one with a ball" and limited time where it's more than four to six players to each ball in use.

CoachNotes

The coaching education programs of US Soccer and the United Soccer Coaches (USC) provide useful sequential guidance in areas such as child developmental abilities, structure of training programs, and age-appropriate technical and tactical training. In clubs requiring coach certification, those requirements normally use US Soccer's licensing program (for more, visit www.ussoccer.com). The introductory US Soccer "F" course is completed online. The 18-hour "E" and 36- to 40-hour "D" courses focus on coaching players ages 9 through 12 and 13 through 14, respectively. (To be able to **"start with the end in mind,"** coaches should complete the course that's structured for the next older level.) The USC program (www.nscaa.com) features a series of one- and two-day diplomas. Both programs are long on coaching theory, and participants will be required to demonstrate the ability to organize training sessions in the "approved" structure. US Soccer programs tend to be more formulaic, the USC's more holistic, but both will make you a better coach.[1]

[1] Coaching courses provide lots of information about developmental stages, and the best teaching methods for each. They remain, however, very short on details about the skills being taught. A recent "E" course participant reported that there was nothing in that entry level course about the details involved in striking a ball correctly. "How are coaches supposed to learn that stuff?" she asked.

The Players 1st approach does not always lend itself to the formula of structuring a training session to develop a single theme on a given day. (Particularly, it consigns most full-team play to the weekly games.) Rather it is designed to create pieces of a puzzle that reveal a larger picture as they are joined together.

The 75% Solution focuses on creating five types of puzzle parts:

1.   1v1. (See chapters 15 and 16.) *"The team that wins the majority of the 1v1 duels in a game will win the majority of those games."* Players should participate in some sort of 1v1 activity *every time they're together*, pregame warm-ups included. The cumulative impact of such regular 1v1 play provides the first step in developing exceptional poise, creativity, and confidence under pressure with a ball at one's feet.

2.   **Juggling.** (See chapter 12.3.) Players who can juggle well with both feet develop amazing ball control. While this is most evident in their "first touch," *juggling makes every touch better. Weekly testing* (and rewarding players' progress) will, in time, get it done. But it will take patience and perseverance.

3.   **Striking the Ball.** (See chapter 13.) Players should also do some sort of *technical work each week* on striking the ball: getting the technique right, using the different surfaces of both feet. *Teaching exclusively to the weaker foot* will develop power and accuracy in both.

4.   **Possession.** As soon as passing and receiving skills allow, begin to do possession activities *at least once a week*. The basic progression for this starts in a 12-by-12 grid with 3v1 keep-away, progressing in a year or two to where players can keep possession 3v2 in a 10-by-10 grid where they must touch the ball at least five times before passing. Along the way, this progression develops ever-increasing poise, creativity, and confidence in small-group settings to match the same in 1v1 competence. Teams whose players can play *"3v2, 5 touch"* do not get the ball taken away from them.

5.   **Exterminating the "Weaker Foot."** This is a matter of using *every opportunity* to get it done over time. It will be mostly lots and lots of little things. You'll find many ways in warm-ups, when working on foot skills and ball moves, and in exercises involving passing or receiving and shooting technique. One simple idea is to establish situations where the weaker foot is to be used two or three times for every repetition with the dominant foot.

For more athletes to reach higher levels of play, those five elements need to be a *much* greater part of all soccer training for players through age 14 than is currently the norm.

10.3 ORGANIZING THE TRAINING PROGRAM

At higher levels of the game, much of the training time has a week-to-week focus, notably fixing what went wrong in the last game and preparing for the upcoming opponent. With a longer-term goal of developing "players for tomorrow," that method makes little sense. Instead training should be driven by a vision of the long-term product (see chapter 1) and then by specific goals and objectives for the season.

CoachNotes

It is always a good idea at the end of one season to preview with the team what's ahead in the next.

The coach of an Under-12 was planning to switch from a stopper-sweeper defensive scheme to a flat-back zonal system. The change was introduced in the week between the last spring-season game and the team's one early summer tournament. Needless to say, the first two games of the tournament were an extended barrage of breakaways aimed at the team's goalkeeper. The parents were less than thrilled. By the third game, though, the players were getting the hang of it—enough that the team scraped through to the semi-finals. Improbably, the tournament was won, although more by individual player skill than the team's newly minted tactical brilliance.

What was most interesting was that after an extensive summer break (**"rest is a weapon"**), the team's first game in the fall featured far better defensive organization in that zonal system than was seen in any of those five tournament games.

When you provide a preview, new ideas introduced at the end of a season will percolate in the players' heads over the break. Those athletes weren't consciously thinking about zonal defending during the break, but the minds were still at work. Subsequent experiments with introducing new ideas at season's end yielded similar results.

Once priorities have been established, create an outline for a three- or four-week block of training sessions. During a 12- to 15-week season, plan to repeat that schedule four or five times. Consider the length of your sessions and the frequency per week, then fill in warm-ups (every session), 1v1 activities (every session), shooting (at least weekly), possession (at least weekly), and the juggling test (weekly).

The advantages repeating a three- to four-week block are many. Among them, you will spend far less time explaining new activities. (Most of the activities which follow come with enough variations that even an activity that appears more than once in a block can stay fresh.) The players will also benefit as you become better at teaching and managing the activity with each repetition.

10.4 TRAINING AND GAMES

For U6 players, U.S. Youth Soccer recommends one 40- to 60-minute training session per week plus a game. For U8s, two sessions at 60 minutes plus a game. U10s, 60 to 75 minutes plus a game. At U12 and U14, a schedule of eight sessions every three weeks works well (Tuesdays and Thursdays with some Mondays and Fridays—never before or after a multiple game weekend). If sessions are properly intense, 90 minutes will be more than sufficient.

Games and tournaments are fun for players and their parents. But their place in the player development process needs to be thoughtfully considered, beginning with the ratio of training sessions to games.

In the United States, it is rarely better than 4:1 and often dips below 2:1. Contrast that with European youth teams, where ratios of 6:1 (Ajax) to 8:1 (Barcelona) are common. Then factor in the difference in number of touches per minute per player in a training session as compared to in a game. Typically, game touches are between 1/20th and 1/100th of practice touches.

Tournaments are even more problematic. By U14, games on back-to-back days are not productive in terms of player development. Games on three or more consecutive days, or twice on any day, are more likely to be *counterproductive* in addition to increasing the risk of injury. The soccer purpose can be as well served, at considerably less expense, by getting four teams together for a single-day round-robin of shortened games.

10.5 THE GOALKEEPER

If goalkeepers are the Cinderella-esque stepchildren on your team, don't feel too guilty. They are here as well as goalkeeper training is not within the purview of this book. Still, keepers are a necessity, involving specialty technical training that not only helps them to be effective, but also keeps them safe. So here are a few ideas that might help.

At the younger ages, goalkeepers should be learning all the same skills as the other players. At higher levels of play, keepers are increasingly asked to use their feet, with many playing as much as an extra defender as a shot stopper. Prepare them for this.

CoachNotes

Even if you don't know much about training a goalkeeper, you can make yours better by discussing each goal conceded. What was the game situation? What happened? Then, what might you have done to prevent the goal? There's usually something, although it often happens well before the shot. The ball has to get by 10 teammates before it's the keeper's turn, and direction from the goalie can help prevent that from happening. This process should also examine the keeper's best moments, using a similar set of questions. Tracking these moments over time will reveal patterns.

The technical training of a goalkeeper is a coaching specialty. Many clubs have a coach to do this, and the best of them will provide ways to integrate the keepers into your other training activities. With teams U12 and under, having this trainer do a few sessions for the entire team is worthwhile. It gives the field players an appreciation of the position, and often produces players who would like to give the role a try.

Where that's not available, there are some options. The NSCAA Goalkeeping Level 1 Diploma is a six-hour course designed for a team coach. Failing that, head for the videos. For straight-up technical basics, *"Dr. Joe Machnik's Goalkeeping Complete Video Series"* is terrific. On DVD, Tony Dicicco's *Goalkeeping: The DiCicco Method* provides a better blend of the technical, tactical, and psychological components of goalkeeper training.

At U12 and above, a team will need either a pair of goalkeepers or a designated keeper with a pair of capable backups. Younger than that, most teams will rotate several or even all the players through the position. When you do this have the keepers play a whole half, but give them the full other half on the field without substitution.

10.6 PERMISSION TO PLAY

Soccer is a game where every player controls the game any time he or she has the ball. In an instant, the player must choose to pass, dribble, or shoot; choose whether to combine play with teammates or take the "individual option;" and choose whether to play for possession or to risk losing the ball with a more daring or aggressive play toward the goal.

For young athletes, it's a moment of uncommon freedom. Unfortunately, as one coach has lamented, this doesn't happen enough. *"Decision making is being taken away from the athletes – on and off the field – by coaches and other adults in their lives."*

A few years ago, we watched a defender try to dribble out of a 1v2 situation just outside the corner of the penalty area. It didn't work, and the ball was lost. But the opponents now lost the ball, and it was cleared away. No harm was done, yet this was followed immediately by the coach yelling across the field, addressing the player *by name*, saying: *"I don't ever want to see you do that again!"* A minute later the coach, again loudly addressing the player by name, yelled, *"Do you understand what I said?"*

Needless to say, that defender will never again choose "the individual option" in that situation. Nor will she, we suspect, when placed in the midfield. Or up front. The response from that coach produces that sort of a result in the kid when the player is 11 years old.

The Game is most enjoyable when players are allowed to make their own decisions—when they are given **Permission to Play**. That begins with the following mantra: **"You are always allowed to take on opponents. Often you will be encouraged to. Sometimes you must."** That response affirms a coach's confidence in the players' abilities. It has an enormously empowering impact on young athletes.

It's not easy to turn that mantra into reality. First, the players must be trained in the 1v1 skills needed to succeed in those moments. This takes patience and dogged perseverance over countless repetitions.

Then there's Game Day. When players fear what will happen if a move doesn't work, they're not going to try one. Coaches must create a culture of fearlessness, an acceptance of the mistakes that will happen as players learn to train and play at the edge of their game. As legendary basketball coach John Wooden said, *"I want players to make mistakes. Doers make mistakes."* Learning from those mistakes and **failing well** is a great way to get better.

Finally comes the decision-making. When permission to play is given, some horrible decisions will follow. If it happens too often, players should be asked what other choices they saw, and then what might have happened if those options were chosen. But always with an affirmation of the permission to use the individual option. Over time this helps athletes become "two-way players," equally capable and confident both individually and "with the help of my teammates."

Those players are unstoppable.

"I am not a believer in burn out. I do believe, however, that many leave the sport because we have failed to give them the tools to succeed. I have met many players who thought they were playing soccer only to find when they reached high school that they had been misled. They leave the game because they cannot compete. They could have competed if trained right from day one. Teach skills and they will play a lifetime."

–Alan Blinzler, Kansas City United Youth Soccer Club

11 GREAT SOCCER HABITS

Defining a style of play.

It was essentially a pick-up squad. The players, U16s, came from many teams and several clubs. They were talented individually but would need to blend their abilities on the field in four tournaments during a European soccer tour.

That they did, finishing second at U19 in Austria then winning in England and Denmark (twice). More notable was that it was very attractive soccer, a wonderfully unpredictable mix of individualism and team play. At the **Dana Cup**, an early game in a central venue drew onlookers who then followed the team throughout the tournament, including to the semi-final game that was well outside of town. "We have groupies!" exclaimed one of the players.

Only afterward did the coaches write down the ideas that had become the underpinning of the team's distinctive style of play. Many of the ideas (e.g., **"Look before receiving"**) reflected effective soccer habits seen in top players everywhere. Others (e.g., **"Play balls on the ground"**) were matters of choice. Ideas about the **individual option** spoke to the permission and encouragement players received to **"Use your 1v1 skills."**

The list has seen many forms over the years but remains rooted in the original 18 ideas. It has taken on the **Soccer Habits** name but is really a set of interconnected ideas that define a style of play, a whole that becomes much greater than the sum of its parts.

The list is presented here in three forms. The **Great Soccer Habits** (following page) contains 13 ideas for the baseline for players 11 through 14. There is also a **Starter Edition** of 8 ideas (numbered in red on the 13 habits list) that is useful for players ages 8 to 10. Finally, the **25 Great Ideas** version is one team's expansion of the collection to further define elements of its style of play. You can download all three from www.PlayersFirst.com.

Each list is self-explanatory, but two of the items merit additional comment.

Take Two. The next time you go to a youth game as a spectator, take a pen and paper. Choose a team and tally two things: a) balls played "one touch" (circle the ones that go to a teammate) and b) balls played after two or more touches (circle the successful ones, too). What you will find is that a far greater percentage of the one-touch balls result in possession lost. More than that, very often the percentage of one-touch balls lost will closely match the percentage of balls retained when the pass comes after two touches or more.

The Great Soccer Habits

1. *"Make Yourself Available" Keep moving all the time* to get open for a pass from a teammate. There's a big difference between getting "open" and getting **"OPEN"**. *Don't "hide"*. Always *"Give the Dribbler a Path to the Goal."* If you're in the way, *"Get Lost"* to get open!

2. *"Call for the Ball With Your Movement"* if you are in the vision of the player with the ball. Avoid "name calling": communicate by giving *"instructions"* using a *"soccer voice"*.

3. *"Go to the Ball"* when receiving a pass or making a steal. If you wait for the ball, it won't always get to you. Learn to get away from a defender with a *"check run"*.
   "Check back at an angle" to be able to receive the ball *"sideways on"*.
   "Receive across the body." Open up your body to receive the ball with the foot away from the ball. This allows you to see more of the field.

4. *"Look" Both Ways Before Receiving*: to create a _productive_ 1st touch and a chance to *"Think Ahead."* (*"Look, then think." – Xavi*)
   "Ponytails" should be flying because of all the turning heads. (Sorry, guys!)

5. *"Change The Pressure" When You Win a Ball:* In *"two seconds or less"*. Either an _explosive_ first touch – *immediate* transaition to the attack to put the other team under instant pressure. Or pass to take the pressure off us, then your teammates's first touch will put the other team under pressure.
   "Pass the Steal!" if your challenge is contested.
   "Eat up Space" if you win it free and clear.

6. *"Play in the Direction you're Facing"* if receiving a ball with your back to goal.
   Or *"dribble square"* toward the middle of the field.
   Turn to goal only in the attacking third (*and only if you have that skill*.)

7. *Every Touch on the Ball Must Have a Purpose.*
   Dribble, pass, shoot, clear. Never just kick.
   "Pass to what you can see", not to what you just hear. *"No blind passes."*
   Every first touch must be _productive and explosive_. *"Prepare"* the ball for the next touch.
   Killing a ball dead at your feet must be a last choice.

When is One Touch OK?
1. Back Passes
2. Wall Passes
3. Many Shots
4. "Killer Pass"
5. "Pass the Steal"
6. Clearing the Ball
NO FLICK-ON PASSES

8. *"Take Two"* Touches or More.

9. *Use Your One-on-One Skills:*
   Attack the defender who tries to contain.
   Attack full speed before the 1v1 opportunity disappers.
   "Beat one, draw the next, then pass."
   Then *"stay in the play."* Especially defenders.

10. *"Beat 'em and Leave 'em."* Use your arms to help put the definder behind you.
    Never cut a ball back once you've gained the advantage.

11. *The Carolina Rule:* **"If you have one player to beat to either shoot or cross, you have to beat that player."** Take responsibility. The only excuse for not beating the players is if your pass results in a first-time shot on goal from a better angle. *"No 'buck passes'."*

12. *Play Balls "ON THE GROUND."* Make it easy for your teammates to receive your passes.

13. *Everybody Plays the Accordian* (everbody attacks, spreading out, getting **"OPEN"**; everybody defends, closing on the ball; but mostly, everybody attacks – *all the time!!!*)
    "Push up" hard and fast on offense, *especially on punt by your keeper, cleared corner kicks*.
    In today's game, defenders are expected to provide goals and assists.
    "Chase" back hard *immediately* when possession is lost, harder still of _you_ lost the ball"
    "Defend as a team" to win ball back. Lots of talk on defense helps to organize the team and can intimidate an opponent.

Make *"take two"* the default position. There are times, though, when a player's **vision** will indicate that one-touch play makes sense (green box in figure). Two are "only choice" situations, where time and pressure makes it a *necessity* (some shots, but less often than you might think, and when clearing the ball, but much less often than you see it done).

There are also times when one-touch play can be a good *choice*. A back pass to *"playing in the direction you're facing"* or *"to change the pressure"* is a good example. One touch at the "wall" of a "give-and-go" will be more effective than taking two to beat the defender. Then there are the bold choices, where a one-touch ball can immediately make things tough for a defense: the **killer pass** and **pass the steal**. Those six situations aside, one-touch play for younger players is best confined to the practice field as one of the better tools for developing players' vision. Until players have that vision, great touch, poise under pressure, and the ability to use either foot, one-touch play will be at best ineffective on Game Day. For the time being, work to make the first touch dynamic (explosive and productive) where that touch moves the ball away from defensive pressure to a place it where the next touch(es) can be most useful. Train those skills, and a team's two-touch play can become nearly as fast as one-touch.

Play the Accordion. What do you see when watching 6-year-olds-play? Most often it's a swarm or cluster of players around the ball. The 4v4 game commonly resembles a 1v7 contest. The challenge for coaches of these players is to get them to *"spread out."*

There's a growing tendency that sees 6-year-old soccer returning to the mix at about age 12. It appears to be a trickledown effect of the high pressure defending found at the professional level. This starts with a misapplication of the idea popularized by FC Barcelona to try to regain a possession lost in *6 seconds or less*. Ignored is the second reason for Barcelona's immediate pressure—to contain and delay the opposition so that the other players can begin to organize defensively in the event that the immediate attempt fails and the ball escapes the pressure. After six seconds, Barcelona is much more patient about regaining possession.

Combine extended, high-pressure defending with a tendency of attacking players to drift toward the ball and you end up with the common picture of all 22 players on one side of the field. Any semblance of **width** (see chapter 18) disappears, and any player who does win the ball must deal not only with nearby opponents but also with teammates who are only in the way!

High-pressure defending can work at the youth level where players lack the skills to keep the ball under duress. The paradox is that the fitness demands of that style take away valuable practice time from other activities that might be devoted to developing those very same missing skills.

THE FUNDAMENTALS

12 DEVELOPING GREAT TOUCH

"Juggling makes every touch better."

Our very first steps were an adventure. That's why we were called "toddlers." But most of us were soon walking and then running with little thought or concentration. Practice created pathways between the brain and muscles that made those tasks essentially automatic (see chapter 7). Soccer players need to develop touch on the ball that is much the same, where controlling the ball becomes, in time, adventure free.

One of *the Game's* great challenges is that no one will ever get as much practice with a ball as they did with walking and running. But there are activities that can develop ball control that appears to be similarly effortless. Almost everything in this chapter gets perfected by players working on·their own. Learning to train independently—*when no one else is watching*—is a Life Skill with benefits that extend well beyond the soccer field.

12.1 START WITH THE TWO-SECOND END IN MIND

As players move to higher levels of play they will find themselves being scouted and evaluated, both by opponents and by teams seeking players to compete at higher levels still. One of the things that will be looked at is what the player does in the first two seconds with the ball.

Those who excel in terms of this **two-second standard** appear to be making decisions faster than one can consciously process all the incoming stimuli. But what's really happening is that with practice they've given themselves extra time—some describe it as extra bandwidth—in three ways.

For starters, their first touch "automatically" controls the ball; none of the two seconds needs to be wasted on a second touch for that purpose. Next, that touch and subsequent ones can be successfully taken with either foot; no additional concentration is required to use the "weaker" foot because there isn't one. Learning to juggle takes care of the first item; footwork exercises, juggling (see the following), and teaching to the weaker foot (see chapter 13.1) the second.

The third element is vision (see chapter 14.1), the ability to see and process what is happening on the field to make the best decision about what to do in those first moments with the ball. This, too, is something that happens before the two seconds begin, but it happens most effectively when controlling the ball requires minimal bandwidth.

Players with that triple competency—the ability to control the ball, to use either foot, and to see and process their surroundings—are rare in youth soccer. But it doesn't have to be that way.

12.2 FOOTWORK EXERCISES

Dribbling and footwork exercises have been described as "musical scales for soccer." (They also provide basic agility training that can be missing in P.E. classes.) Foot skills come in an endless variety; we know of a video with 245 of them. That's a bit over the top. Your players will be better served by learning a few sets of 10 to 12. They'll be able to remember the names in each set, and the exercises will cover the various ways that the feet control a ball on the ground.

1 Dribbling

These 11 dribbling exercises can be learned by the youngest players. While some include elements that will be found in the ball moves, their greater value is in helping players become comfortable with the ball, particularly the ball that is under the feet.

Players should be able to perform each dribbling exercise, gracefully and at speed, first over 10 yards non-stop, then 20. (Beyond that, an exercise becomes more about fitness than foot skill.)

> **CoachNotes**
> Some exercises use just one foot to touch the ball. It is with these that the earliest efforts to "eradicate the weaker foot" are found. This is done by having the players complete the exercise two or three times with the weaker foot for every repetition with the dominant. When persistently demanding this ratio over time, the cumulative impact on the ability to use the weaker foot effectively is significant.

Many players will rush to learn an exercise. Instead, it is better to **"do it right, then do it faster."** Challenging the comfort zone by going a little faster each time, or with a few more touches before a breakdown, will do the job. Once an exercise is repeatedly done correctly, there comes a time to do it "as fast as you can," then "faster than that." Here you want it to break down. This sort of deliberate practice is sometimes called **mistake-based training** (see chapter 8.5). Players should figure out what went wrong and then try again. Chances are, the next repetition will be better. And so it goes: two steps forward, one step back.

Except for Speed Dribbling, use these exercises at first in repetitions over 10 yards. But remind players that it's not who finishes fastest that's the winner, but the one who does the most touches. (20 touches over 10 yards is a good minimum.) And quickly get them to perform the foot skills with *"heads up."*

Make sure the players learn the names of these exercises. Check for understanding by asking *"What's this called?"* or give the name and say, *"Show me."*

Walk Ball. Walk the ball forward, rolling it across the body with the sole of each foot as that foot steps forward.

Boxing. Using the inside of the feet, box the ball back and forth while moving across the space. Now do the same thing going backwards.

Inside/Outside. (Sometimes called **Cut/Chop**.) Dribble forward, touching the ball alternately with the inside of the weaker foot then the outside, one touch with each step forward of that foot. The rhythm should be **"touch in, touch out, touch in, touch out."** The ball will follow a wiggling path. After two or three 10-yard repetitions with the weaker foot, do one rep using the stronger foot.

Snake Dribbling. (Sometimes called **Double Cut/Double Chop**.) Using the weaker foot, take two touches each, cutting ball inside then chopping it outside in an **"inside, inside, outside, outside"** rhythm. Take a step forward with the stronger foot for each touch with the weaker foot. (The weaker foot also steps down between touches.) The ball should follow a path that twists and turns like a snake in the grass, at least 4 to 5 feet side to side. Do three repetitions with the weaker foot, one with the stronger.

Forward Hops, Backward Hops. Hop forward on the stronger foot while rolling the ball forward with the weaker foot, **"ball under the toes."** Move the ball with each hop. Now do the same backwards. The forward hops are more easily done if the foot on the ball is out in front of the body with its heel down, lower than its toes. Go across while moving forward, then return backwards. Do it two or three times with the weaker foot, then once with the stronger.

Roll Around. Alternating feet, touch the ball forward under the ball of the foot on every step, **"right foot, left foot, right foot, left foot."** (Many players will have already done this standing in place.) Repeat while moving backwards.

Pull–Push. Pull the ball back under the toes of the right foot, then turn the toes down and push the ball forward. Repeat with the left foot, alternating right and left as the ball moves across the space. As speed increases, players will be double hopping on the foot without the ball. (**Variations** for more advanced players: a) Do this backwards. b) Pull–push only with one foot, hopping forward on the other.)

Sideways Hops. Hop sideways to the right on the right foot, touching the ball to the right with the inside of the left foot. Touch the ball with the left foot with each hop. Switching feet, now do the same in the other direction.

Side Roll and Stop. Standing sideways, roll the ball with the sole of the left foot *across the body* (to the right), stopping it with the right foot. Repeat, repeat, repeat at least 10 times. Then return to the starting point, using the right foot for the side roll.

Dribble Cut. Dribbling forward, cut the ball across the body with the inside of one foot, then push it on in the same direction with the outside of the second foot. Repeat, starting with the second foot. (Earlier, there was Snake Dribbling; this is Zig-Zag Dribbling.) This foot skill is an icon of the Coerver programs.

Speed Dribbling. It is amazing how infrequently youth players work on dribbling at full speed. Dribble 20 to 30 yards as fast as possible using the weak foot. Turn the foot slightly inward so that the ball is struck with the top of the outside toes. If running free on the field, the ball can be pushed farther away; closer control will be needed if the defender is near, even if this will be a little slower, so practice both. Do three runs using the weaker foot, then one with the stronger.

2   Fast Footwork

In the 70s B.C. (Before Coerver), the first import of the Dutch soccer methodology featured coach Franz van Balkom in a video series called *Soccer on the Attack*. Most of the fast footwork exercises from those lessons formed the basis for one or more ball moves. Unlike the Dribbling exercises, the player will stay in place (an area not more than two yards square), keeping the ball moving between the feet, often with a 90- or 180-degree turn.

The exercises follow a logical order, and it is best to keep them that order. This (and knowing the names) helps the players remember when they practice at home.

CoachNotes

A good teaching progression is to teach the first exercise and then the second. Now perform the first, then the second. Review the names constantly. Then teach the third. Now string them together: one, then two, then three. Now teach the fourth, and so on. (Once you get beyond the fifth skill, you will need to limit the repetitions of each foot skill so that footwork doesn't consume the entire training session.)

The description of each exercise is as precise as possible. Many are hard to describe. It's easier to follow along with a video. Remember that some athletes are better auditory than visual learners. They will need to hear the moves described as precisely as possible. Be very aware of key words such as "opposite" and "switch" and avoid "other" when talking about the feet.

These are rhythmic activities, and each footwork exercise has its own beat. In each the skill is done with one foot, then the other, then the first, and so on, often with a couple of touches in between. **What Could Possibly Go Wrong (WCPGW):** Players may "cheat" and do more with the easier foot. Insist that they don't.

These exercises generally are more difficult than the Dribbling exercises. Save them until players are 9 to 10 years old. **WCPGW:** Many players will rush to learn a skill. Again, slow them down. ***"Do it right, then do it faster."*** Over time, speed up until this becomes mistake-based training.

Side-to-Side. You will return to this between repetitions of the exercises that follow. Box the ball back and forth between the feet. Take quick touches and keep the head up. Turn right. Turn left. Stay relaxed, especially in the knees, hips, and shoulders, ***"not stiff like Frankenstein."*** Keep ***"heads up."*** Ask to see ***"Eyes."***

Step–Flick. From the Side-to-Side, grab the ball under the toes of the right foot, then flick it back to the left foot. After two more Side-to-Side touches, repeat left to right. Develop the following rhythm: **"step-on, touch, touch; step-on, touch, touch."** Again, heads up, body relaxed.

Side-to-Side Push Forward. From the Side-to-Side, with the inside of one foot, push the ball out at 30 to 45 degrees across the body. Grab the ball under the toes of the opposite foot and pull the ball back between the feet. Resume the Side-to-Side and, switching feet, repeat (i.e., using the second foot to do what the first one did before.)

Pulling the V. From the Side-to-Side, with one foot push the ball out at 30 to 45 degrees across the body (as before). This time, grab the ball under the toes of the opposite foot and pull the ball back beside the body while pivoting 90 degrees toward the ball. The ball has moved in the shape of a "V." Resume the Side-to Side and, switching feet, repeat so that you are now facing the same way as when you started.

Roll Behind Leg. From the Side-to-Side, once again push the ball out at 30 to 45 degrees across the body. Grab the ball under the toes of the opposite foot and pull the ball back beside the body until the ball is behind the hip, then use the inside of the pulling foot to pass the ball behind the opposite leg. (The pulling foot takes two touches, one to pull the ball back, the second to push it behind the standing leg.) Turn 90 degrees (toward the ball) and bring the ball back under control with the first foot, using a Step–Flick if possible. (If doing the Roll Behind Leg with the right foot, you turn 90 degrees to the left.) Resume the Side-to-Side and repeat, switching feet. **Teaching point:** Many players will incorrectly pivot 270 degrees to get back to the ball when they first try this. (When using your left foot to pull the ball, you will turn to the left by Pulling the V. You will turn right with a Roll Behind Leg.)

Side Roll. From the Side-to-Side, push the ball from the left foot to the right. Now use the sole of the right foot to draw the ball right to left across the body with a crossover step. Finish the crossover with the left foot now moving left to catch the ball with the inside of that foot. Resume the Side-to-Side and repeat, switching feet. The ball should be back where it started. **Teaching point:** The ball should move 6 to 8 feet sideways, possibly more, on a Side Roll. This may require an additional hop sideways on the first foot to stop the ball with the opposite.

Sole Roll. This is the one foot skill that is not connected to a ball move. Its usefulness is in lessening the likelihood that a player will crash and burn when inadvertently stepping on a ball.

From the Side-to-Side, step forward, rolling that foot toes-to-heel over the top of the ball—for an instant most of the player's weight is on top of the ball—and "popping" the ball backward with the heel, then quickly turning the foot and body 90 degrees inward as the foot lands. Now continue the turn 90 degrees more to complete the 180-degree turn, and bring the ball back under control with the opposite foot, using a Step–Flick if possible. Resume the Side-to-Side and repeat, switching feet, turning back though the same 180-degree arc. **Teaching point:** Many players will incorrectly pivot 180 degrees to the outside to get back to the ball when they first try this.

Figure 8. From the Side-to-Side, step over the ball right to left with the right foot (like the Stepover ball move). Land on the toes of the right foot (the legs are now crossed) and pivot sharply 180 degrees clockwise, *"making the grass squeak,"* and resume the Side-to-Side with a left-foot touch. Repeat, stepping over with the left foot. **Teaching Point:** In this move, the hips and shoulders turn 90 degrees counterclockwise, then 270 degrees back clockwise. WCPGW: Some players will incorrectly turn in a 180-degree counterclockwise half-circle.

Cruyff. Like the turn of the same name, from the Side-to-Side, turn a foot inward and knock the ball back between the legs. Land on that foot, foot turned inward, and complete the 180-degree turn. Resume the Side-to-Side, then repeat with the opposite foot.

On-Over. From the Side-to-Side, push the ball forward. With the opposite foot, step on and then beyond the ball, with the foot landing *turned inward* 90 degrees. Now continue to turn 90 degrees more in the same direction to complete the 180-degree turn. Use the first foot to gather in the ball and resume the Side-to-Side. Repeat, switching feet. (This is the basis for what is commonly known as the Maradona move.)

Pull–Push. Pull the ball back under the toes of the right foot, then turn the toes down and push the ball forward (**"tip of the toes, top of the toes"**). Repeat with the left foot, then the right, and so on. As speed increases, players will be double hopping on the foot without the ball.

3   Advanced Foot Skills

This wonderful collection of advanced foot skills, courtesy of Coerver Coaching, contains a mix of dribbling variations and others performed in place. For players 12 and older they provide a terrific mix of touch, agility, and quickness. These exercises are virtually impossible to describe in words. A rather feeble attempt follows, often using the names of ball moves that they include. Fortunately, purchase of this book gives you access to a video of the moves found on www.PlayersFirst.com.

Round the Leg. Pull-Cruyff, step-step, outside V, step-step. All touches with one foot.

Quickly Around. Pull-Cruyff, outside V. All touches on one foot, hopping on the other.

Four Pull Cruyff. Right, right, left, left, hopping on other foot.

Pull Cruyff Walk. Move backward, alternating pull-Cruyffs, right then left. You can also do this going forward.

Drag-Catch. Drag behind leg, pivot on opposite foot, catch with inside of first foot. All the touches are on one foot.

Under Toes. Ball forward then back with right foot while hopping or turning on the left.

Scissors-Roll-Catch. Scissors to the right, side roll to the left, catch under sole of the right foot > scissors L and so forth.

Quick Rolls. Side roll with the right foot, and then the right foot steps back. Left foot moves forward. The ball goes between with a catch at the left foot.

Side Roll, Stepover, Turn, Catch with stepover foot. Box and repeat with other foot. 4 E>W, then 4 W>E.

Outside V-Stepover. R-L-R outside Vee > Stepover L, R behind leg (hopping on stepover foot to catch under R) > L-R-L outside vee > Stepover R and so forth.

12.3 JUGGLING

"Juggling is just a trick," according to a coaching colleague. Who. Could. Not. Be. More. Wrong. The reality is that *"juggling makes every touch better."* The following five-level Juggling Progression (which can also be downloaded from www.PlayersFirst.com) will do for controlling the ball out of the air what the "musical scales for soccer" do for control of the ball on the ground. (Stop now and have a look at the following "Great Touch Juggling Progession.")

4   The Juggling Progression (★★★★★)

This started simply enough with a weekly test. Each player took four tries and then added together the best two results for a score. **Any Touch** counted, even the inadvertent ones off a chest, chin, or nose. When the *"4 tries, best 2"* score reached 100, players moved on to **Feet Only**, juggling rather than continuing with the Any Touch activity to scores in the hundreds or thousands. (You'll find that there's not much additional benefit in scores beyond 50, but 100 is a magic number.) The third original level was **Weak Foot Only,** where any other touch ends the turn. Then, after hearing that the base standard for juggling with the Women's National Team was a score of 13 in a precise pattern called **Progressive Juggling**, that became the fourth level (but with a target score of 15, which requires 120 touches in the pattern). Finally, from coach Anson Dorrance at the University of North Carolina, came what has become known as the "Diamond" level: **Body Parts Juggling**. (Interestingly, UNC's test now requires 12 body parts instead of 14; the Heels have dispensed with the heels.)

From the time the first players reached the second and third levels, their **first touch** showed improvement. It also became apparent that *all* the touches of the better jugglers—whether receiving, dribbling, passing, or shooting—were getting better than those of the lesser jugglers. What's more, the **hard skills** contributing to the first touch were allowing players much better opportunities with the touches that followed.

Ignition. Learning to juggle is soccer solitaire. It's a good activity for those arriving early to a training session, and most teams allow three to five minutes for practice before the weekly test. But as a rule, a team's training sessions are for other things. Players should learn juggling on their own in the backyard. Some will do that, but most players are more likely to put in the time when there's an incentive to do so.

What originally set players' progress on fire was the introduction of what the Positive Coaching Alliance calls a targeted symbolic reward. Each player getting a new personal best on the weekly test was awarded a lemon drop at the end of practice. "Drops" quickly became like gold medals. Then, in a camp setting, Skillzys tags (see www.skillzys.com) were awarded to each player upon finishing a level. The Diamond tags—for those finishing the Body Parts level—were numbered, with number one going to the camp's first finisher. Finally, during a weekly off-season indoor program, came the Bell. Players completing a level immediately went to a school bell placed in the middle of the practice field and rang it. These became moments when everything stopped and everyone cheered. Soon it seemed like the ringing was constant. More lemon drops were bought, more tags ordered.

As Things Progress. For younger players, **Keep Up**—where a bounce is allowed between touches—can be a good way to start. It does, however, require a firm, even surface. Dropping the ball then popping it back up into the hands, though, should be discouraged.

So should catching the ball when juggling. The efforts to get that one more touch are those which produce the most improvement.

CoachNotes

At the first (Any Touch) level, most of the juggling may be on the thighs. That's OK. This level is more about developing rhythm and balance than about controlling the ball. At Feet Only, most of the touches will be with the stronger foot. That's also OK, but it can be useful to start taking a Weak Foot Only score alongside the Feet Only to avoid having to reprogram a severely one-footed player.

Players need to maintain flexibility at the hip and knee, work to take any spin off the ball, and develop uniformity in the touches with the ball getting to waist or chest height between touches. Once players begin the Feet Only level, the ball starts on the ground for the test (although many coaches prefer allowing them to start from the hands until the "four tries, best two" score reaches 30). At Weak Foot Only, the "lift" is with the weaker foot. The "lift" is its own skill, and players will need to practice it separately. Most players find success by pulling the ball back and up on the toes, then flicking the ball up with the toes, lifting the whole foot or combining the two methods. Because this is difficult, a turn doesn't count against the the "4 tries" unless the player gets three touches or more.

It's common for players to get "stuck" at the higher end of Progressive and Body Parts juggling. Have them practice Progressive starting at 11 or 12 to get used to maintaining the pattern at higher numbers. With Body Parts and 14 in 14, practice 4 in 14—that is, getting both shoulders and both heels in 14 touches. Once this has been accomplished several times, then try 4 in 13, then 12, then 11. By 10, they'll have it. Be sure to point out how they can use these solutions as examples of how to get unstuck in other problem-solving situations.

THE GREAT TOUCH JUGGLING PROGRESSION

Juggling makes every touch better. It has an amazing impact on making your **1st touch** more productive, so the ball goes right where you want it to go with that touch. It also helps to make *all your other touches on the ball better*. Good jugglers always have confidence in their ability to control the ball. Learning to juggle is not easy (or everyone would be able to do it.) To get good, you have to work on this at home. This helps with your focus on soccer and helps you to develop the habit of training on your own, "when no one else is watching." That's something which all good players do.

If you're 9 years old or younger, you can start with "Keep Up". Here the ball is allowed to bounce once between touches. Then take two touches between bounces, then three, then four. After you can do this most of the time, switch to juggling. Once you switch to juggling, try to make every touch the same. And never catch the ball in your hands; getting that last extra touch helps to make you better. (When you catch the ball in your hands, your score for that try is ZERO!)

The juggling progression has five levels beyond "Keep Up." (Some younger teams divide Level 1 into three parts.) You move on to the next one when your score reaches 100. "The hard part is getting to about 15 touches at any level." You really won't get much better from making more than 25-30 in a row at any level. But it only takes a little more work to make that 25 into 50, which multiplied by 2 gets to a score of 100 – a magical number without a whole lot more effort.

Be patient. The next goal after you can do 5 touches is not 15. It's 6! Be persistent. 10-15 minutes of juggling 2-3 times every week works better than working for an hour once a week. No matter what, record best scores every week.

We've suggested goals that players should reach at different ages. Some teams and some players set goals to do it faster. But quite a few 9 year-olds have finished the progression, including Body Parts Juggling. Needless to say, their ball control is awesome! So **"Go For It."**

Beginners: Keep Up. (For players through under 8 years old.) Start with the ball in your hands. The test: take 4 tries, add the best two together. That's your score. *The ball is allowed to bounce only once between touches. Move on to level 1 – "Any Touch" - when your score – "4 tries, best 2" – gets to 50.*

Level 1- Bronze: Any Touch. Start with the ball in your hands. **The test: "4 tries, best 2"** That's your score. (Note: *only 4 tries, **no mulligans**, and if you touch the ball with your hands or catch it, the score for that turn is "0".*) Every touch counts, even the unintentional one off of the face or chest. *Goal: a score of 100 by end of first season of U11. Move on to level 2 – "Feet Only" - once your score gets to 100.*

Level 1B (optional): Any Touch. **The test: take 4 tries:** the best one of the four is your score. Try to get 100 touches in a row. *Goal: a score of 100 early in 2nd season of U11.* Even when you move on to the next level, do this test every month or so. After 150 touches, limit yourself to 3 tries, at 250 limit to 2 tries.

Level 1C (optional): "Mostly Feet". **The test: "4 tries, best 2".** Only touches on the feet count. *Goal: a score of 100 by end of your U11 year.* Some coaches have players move on to Level 2 once the score reaches 50.

From this point on, start with the ball on the ground. Any turn with a score of 3 or more counts.

Level 2 - Silver: Feet Only. **The test: "4 tries, best 2".** Only touches on the feet count, *and any other touch ends the turn. Goal: a score of 40 by the end of the U11 year, 100 by middle of the season at U12. Move to Level 3 - "Weak Foot Only" - after 100.*

Level 3 - Gold: Weak Foot Only. **The test: "4 tries, best 2". Starting with the weak foot** *from a ball on the ground, only touches on the weaker foot count, and any other touch ends the turn.* Start working on while you're still working on "Feet Only" – you don't want your "weak foot" to be just a shoe rack. *Goal: 50 by middle of the U12 year, 100 by end of that year. Move to Level 4 - "Progressive Juggling" - after your score gets to 100.*

Level 4: Platinum: Progressive Juggling. **The test: the best of 4 tries is your score.** Follow this pattern: "right(1), left, left(2), right, right, right(3), left, left, left, left(4), ..." All touches must be with the feet *and any variation in the pattern ends the turn. The Women's National Team standard was reported to be 13.* Coach or asst. counts once player reaches 12. *Goal: 15 (=120 touches) within a month of finishing "Weak Foot Only." Move to Level 5 - "Body Parts Juggling" - after 15. (Come back to this from time to time; try to get your score into the 20's or 30's.)*

Level 5 – Diamond: Body Parts. The fourteen parts are: four parts of each foot (instep, inside, outside, and heel), chest, head, each thigh, top of each shoulder. Players take as many turns as possible in **two minutes** plus whatever "extra time" is needed to complete last turn. Coach or Assistant Coach does the counting. Players collect as many body parts as possible in any order on a single turn. Each body part only counts once until all 14 are collected, even if the player selects to use some part multiple times. *When you get all 14 on a turn keep going, begin a 2nd collection on that same turn. (We've seen U13 boys and girls reach scores of 42, 3 times around!!!)* Record the best turn. (Another possibility: "14 in 14" – getting all 14 body part touches in exactly 14 touches.)

EVEN MORE: Head Juggling. This is also something to do every week, starting mid-U11 or at U12. Level 1 would be to get to 50 in "4 tries, best two". Level 2 would be to get to 50 in a row. Around the World: Foot to thigh to head to other thigh to other foot to first foot, etc. (add shoulders for the "Long Trip".) Rainbow: The number of times a player can pop the ball up over the head, turn and catch the ball on feet to continue (limit number of touches between rainbows). Sitting. or Standing to Sitting to Standing. Speed Juggling: touches in 60 seconds.

WCPGW: As the progression evolved over several decades, there were some failed experiments. Some tried to change the basic 4 tries, best 2 test (e.g., "add your scores from three tries"), but these methods put too much pressure on each repetition. Others went immediately to Feet Only, which was too much too soon and proved to be too frustrating for most players.

Jolly Ranchers, Mini Tootsie Rolls, and other candies have been tried as substitutes for the lemon drops. Lemon drops always worked better. That may be because kids see those other treats more often. Lemon drops are something that kids like but would rarely ask for when given other options. Here they become associated with something special you can only receive if your juggling is improving. (How strong is the association? Former players dropping off their kids for practice have always asked about lemon drops.) A few coaches also unhappily discovered that the cachet was lost when they used their supply of lemon drops to reward other things. (But it's OK to have a few butterscotch or peppermint drops on hand for the few who don't like lemon drops.)

Trust but Verify. Having players pair up to count for each other when testing is efficient, and it usually works. Assigning and rotating the pairs dampens temptations to fudge scores or allow an extra "mulligan" turn. Having a coach count once players get to a score of 12 on Progressive juggling and at the Body Parts level rewards those players with more attention from the coach and makes sure the standards are being rigorously maintained.

What to Expect. "S=E/T" (Success is a result of effort over time.) Advise patience and perseverance: 15 minutes two to three times every week will get it done. At each level, getting to where each rep is about 15 touches takes at least 75% of the effort. Players also need to know that *the next goal after you can do 5 touches is not 15, it's 6!* Once *4 tries, best 2* scores reach 50, they normally become 100 within a week or two.

CoachNotes

While 15 minutes two to three times works, astonishing progress will happen if players practice daily. Though not soccer specific, do an Internet search for *The Mental Trick That Unlocks Improvement* to read a great piece about daily practice.

Testing *every week* is essential. It shouldn't take more than five to seven minutes for two players to complete four turns. (Note that when testing, catching a ball earns a score of 0 for that turn.) If players are working on their own as they should, one-fourth to one-third of the team will be recording personal bests each week. When an individual's scores don't improve for three consecutive weeks, that's a sign that some kind of intervention by the coach is in order.

Collateral Benefits. For younger players, nothing will make them better more quickly than finishing the first three levels, through Weak Foot Only of the Juggling Progression. Tests of shooting power and serving for distance have shown that those at the Weak Foot Only level or above improve nearly twice as much as those at Feet Only or below.

Learning to juggle is definitely a grit builder. It's tough. It's all deep hard skill practice. (Reach–reflect–refine–repeat.) It's filled with failures. You spend loads of time at first chasing after that last touch gone bad, but each mistake is an opportunity to **"fail well,"** to learn, improve, and prepare for the next try. Players learn proper impatience doing the work to get through the levels, but with a realization that instant success is rarely attainable. At the higher levels, the precision required in Progressive juggling and the problem-solving aspects of Body Parts are important contributors to improving focus and concentration.

Keeping It Sharp (And More). Where the progression has been in use for a while, it is no longer unusual to have 10-year-old boys and girls earn their "Diamond" tag. At that point, additional juggling no longer produces great improvements in touch. Players will, though, need to do enough jugging to keep sharp, so they can regularly meet the completion standards for Progressive and Body Parts juggling.

That can get old in a hurry. Most players will want additional challenges. They can try to take their best Progressive scores into the 20s and 30s. Another favorite is **14 in 14**, collecting the 14 Body Parts in exactly 14 touches, then continuing into another cycle, aiming for 28 in 28, then 42 in 42. (Here, juggling has clearly moved into the *"just a trick"* realm.)

Some other challenges: **Speed Juggling**—100 or more touches in a minute using one foot or alternating feet. **Low–High**—where one touch goes no higher than the knee and the next no lower than the head. **Around the World**—foot to thigh to head to other thigh to other foot to first foot, and so on. (Add both shoulders for the "Long Trip.") **Rainbow**—the number of times a player can pop the ball up over the head, turn, and catch the ball on the opposite foot to continue (limit number of touches between rainbows). **Sitting** or **Standing to Sitting to Standing. In Pairs** (search YouTube.com for "Tobin Heath and Casey Nogueira Ball Tricks Battle," but use both feet for the "back and forth"). Search online for videos of Indi Cowie and the amazing Mr. Woo to see lots of tricks; even beginning jugglers will be inspired.

Making the Investment. Not every great juggler is a great player, but all great players can juggle. Learning to juggle demands of players and coaches both perseverance and that "proper impatience." It does amazing things for developing touch on a ball, is an essential ingredient in the ability to play faster, and brings the jugglers boatloads of confidence and poise under pressure. As a platform for growing not just skill but persistence and resilience, this Juggling Progression is top of the line. For both the player and the person, the payoff is well worth the time and effort invested.

CoachNotes

ZELMO is a team juggling game for a group of three to seven players with some juggling ability. It uses only one ball. The first player starts the ball from the hands or with a lift, depending on the skill level of the group, juggles, and then passes the ball along to another player. The ball can touch the ground once, either on the way to the next player or while in that player's possession. If the player can't keep the play going, the player gets a Z. A bad pass that the new player can't be expected to handle, judged so by the group, gets the passer the Z. The person "earning" the letter starts the next ball. Players are eliminated when they get Z-E-L-M-O.

You can set a variety of conditions on the juggler: The ball can bounce twice, but not in a row; there can be three touches in a row; you must touch the ball with both feet; only touch the ball with the "off" foot; you must juggle, pop the ball up over the head, turn, and catch the ball with the feet and juggle before passing, and so on. Let the winner set the condition for the next game.

This is a great restaurant game. Once the team has ordered, send them out to play Zelmo. (Having them in the parking lot can be less hazardous than having them remain inside.) The name is reputed to have come either from its founder or someone in the founding group who was either really good or really bad at the game. If you use the game, please honor the legend.

12.4 MEASURING "WEAK FOOT" COMPETENCY

The Foot Skills, Dribbling Exercises, and Juggling Progression build the hard skills needed to control the ball with either foot. Here's a rough-and-ready way to compare a player's technical ability to use the "weaker" foot with the same for the dominant one. It's been used as young as U10 and involves tests of Juggling, Shooting for Power, and Serving for Distance and Accuracy. Test results are then put into a formula with three parts:

1. **Juggling Milestones.** Player gets one award. Award points as follows: .5 for finishing Feet Only; 1.0 for a Weak Foot Only score of 50, 1.5 for finishing the level (100); 1.7 for a Progressive score of 10, 1.8 for finishing the level (15); 2.0 for finishing the Body Parts Level; and 2.3 for finishing 14 in 14. This is *Result 1*.

2. **Differentials.** Using a radar gun, record four Power Shot scores per foot for each player. Total the player's dominant foot scores and then the weak foot scores. Calculate the percentage that the latter is of the former. (The goal should be .9 or better, indicating the weaker foot is no more than 10% less powerful than the dominant.) This score is *Result 2*. Now repeat the process using the North Carolina Soccer Olympics Distance Serve test[1] to get *Result 3*.

3. **Compare With Others.** Determine the weak foot total on the Power Shot test that marks the 75th percentile level of the group. For each player, divide that number into the weak foot total to get *Result 4*.[2] Repeat using the Distance Serve data for *Result 5*.

Now add the five results. The total score will normally fall between 3.00 and 6.00. Above 5.5, the player has the ability to use both feet with similar efficiency. Whether the player is demonstrating this ability, however, will require game observation.

12.5 DYNAMIC TOUCH

Now let's turn to the "soft skills" using "hard skill competence" to best affect and make an impact on the game.

While this was being written, an Under-16 match involving two of the country's better teams provided a superb demonstration of what "great touch" looks like. One of the players repeatedly came from behind opponents to intercept passes made by their team. She did the same with the (way too many) poor balls played by her own team that the opponents looked certain to steal. It was a riveting performance. The most fascinating part was how, moving at full speed, her first touch moved the ball 6 to 8 feet, not only clear of the opponent, but also to a place where she could take the next touch in stride.

Those moments demonstrated the two key qualities of the **Dynamic First Touch**. The touches were productive—putting the ball in the best place for the next touch. And they were explosive, getting the ball clear of defensive pressure and in some instances putting immediate pressure on the opposing team.

There are many activities involving more than one player that provide opportunities to work on touch, either directly or as a challenge within a larger exercise. Here are some

---

[1] Lines of cones are placed across the field at 3-yard intervals to create an alley. The alley is 5 yards wide and starts 9 yards from the service line. There are two 2-yard wide side alleys on either side of the central alley. Players serve four balls with their right foot as afar as they can while the coach records where they land. Players then serve four balls with their left foot as far as they can.

[2] Using the 75th percentile is arbitrary. With a large sample group of widely varying abilities, you might use the 90th to base your number on what those in the top 10% can do.

common examples:

- Accordion Passing is where two players one-touch pass back and forth while varying the distance between them. This requires the passer to adjust the weight of the pass and the receiver to figure in that weight when making the return pass.

- Touch Then Pass. Here players are asked to receive the ball with a designated part of the foot, then pass back with a designated part of that foot or the other. Alternately, the ball can be served in the air (from the hands or feet, depending on the server's skill) to be received on a designated body part (e.g., top of foot, thigh, chest, head) and passed back.

- Smash Ball. Not for the little ones, here players rocket balls back and forth at each other over a 10- to 15-yard distance. The challenge is to absorb the weight of the pass, and then return another rocket. This can also be done between two lines of players, where the passer follows the pass and joins the back of the other line. Once players can control these inbound missiles, play in a triangle in order to force a first touch that goes toward the next point in the triangle.

- Challenges. It is a condition of our basic 3v1 and 3v2 keep-away exercises (see chapter 20) that "balls are not to be killed dead at the feet" unless that's the only choice (e.g., because of a badly served ball). While doing so does have uses in the Game, here we're working on the ability to play the "first touch away from defensive pressure." Forbidding one-touch play except in designated situations will increase the number of opportunities to play a quality first touch to oneself. Those same conditions can be applied to just about any activity or small-sided game.

- Pass the Steal. This is one of the six exceptions to the "Take Two Touches or More" Soccer Habit (see chapter 11), where a player wins the ball and passes to a teammate in the same touch. In a game, it can instantly put the opposing side in a world of difficulty. It's a simple idea, but not so simple a skill to execute.

12.6 THE BIG PAYOFF

Where touch is poor, much of a player's focus—up to all of it when receiving a ball—must be devoted to controlling the ball. Little is left to **"Think Ahead"** about what to do once the ball is under control. On the other hand, those with great touch—and anyone who has completed the Juggling Progression will qualify—possess neuromuscular pathways that do much of the work of ball control, as if instinctively or on autopilot. These players seem to be playing smarter. But what has really happened is that parts of the brain are now free to focus on all the other elements of the game, anticipating what's ahead and reacting and playing faster. *And that is a monstrous advantage on Game Day.*

13 THE SEVEN WORDS

"Our leading scorers are always those with the hardest shots."

–Anson Dorrance, University of North Carolina Women's Soccer coach

Did you know that two basketballs can fit through the hoop at the same time? In theory, 390 soccer balls can pass through a goal frame simultaneously. So why is it so much easier to sink a jump shot?

The biggest challenge involves time. You can complete 100 juggling touches in under a minute. With a partner, shooting 100 free throws will take longer, but still can be done far more quickly than taking 100 shots with a soccer ball. This places a premium on correct shooting technique. With far fewer repetitions to develop the neuromuscular pathways (see chapter 7) associated with powerful and accurate shooting, each repetition has an outsized importance. And each technically incorrect repetition is more damaging. What a coach must do is work to make each shot as "clean" as possible to maximize the neuromuscular benefit of each one.

Many players do shooting games with their teams. Few do repeated and systematic, supervised work every week on perfecting the hard skills of shooting technique. The result is that few even learn how to strike the ball properly, let alone develop the neuromuscular memory (more commonly called "muscle memory") that is needed so that the ball is struck correctly without thinking, every single time.

13.1 THE BEST IDEA EVER: "TEACH THE WEAKER FOOT"

The ability to strike the ball with the different surfaces of both feet is one of the most important things players can learn. Build this by teaching exclusively to the "weaker" foot.

That idea can be traced to a talented 10-year-old in a soccer camp who only played the ball with one foot. The ban that followed is known to this day as the "Dakota Rule." Noting his immediate progress, challenges were designed for a group of the camp's strongest players to encourage use of the "weaker" foot in more and more of their activities. At the same time, the players were required to use only the weaker foot when working on shooting technique and in the shooting games that followed.

In short order, radar gun measurements showed the gap narrowing between weak-foot and dominant-foot power. And surprisingly, *the dominant foot measurements were also improving*, even though the players were only getting a few repetitions with that one as "dessert" at the end of an activity. The camp soon was teaching only to the weaker foot at every age (the youngest players were 7-8); 9- and 10-year-olds regularly began sporting a pair of "cannons."

Understanding the neuromuscular basis of learning helps to explain this. Striking the ball correctly with the weaker foot initially requires far greater focus and concentration. It forces players to slow down. This leads to "getting it right" more often earlier on, wrapping the myelin, and developing neuromuscular pathways that are increasingly fast, powerful, and precise.

CoachNotes

Teaching to the weaker foot is very important. What the players learn will transfer to the dominant foot, a crossover that doesn't usually happen in the other direction. Do this without fail so that players don't even ask about which foot to use. But allow for "dessert," a few repetitions with the dominant foot as a reward for effort and progress with the weaker. And then prepare to be thrilled and amazed when the weak-foot juggling skills and the weak-foot shooting skills combine to make the weak foot vanish, allowing players to simply use whichever the situation requires.

SafetyNotes

The good news: With this program, players as young as 9 or 10 will be launching rockets. The bad news: At that age, those shots—even with the weaker foot—can break a wrist, especially when a player in goal is not trained as a keeper. When there's a player in goal during a shooting exercise, shots should come from no closer than 12 yards and even farther out for older players. If the activity requires that all the participants rotate into the goal, shot-stopping by catching the ball may need to be discouraged, if not prohibited.

Boys, in particular, love to randomly whack a ball, and pre-practice activity can quickly become a free fire zone. The fun comes to an end when that ball accidentally pegs an unsuspecting teammate or coach. (Some of the worst concussions we've seen.) It's a good idea to make it a part of your team culture that shooting a ball is something that happens only as a part of an activity that includes taking shots.

13.2 "IMITATSIYA:" THE IMAGINARY BALL

Imitatsiya is a great idea used at the Spartak Tennis Club in Russia (home at one point of five of the top 10 ranked women's players in the world). It is simply performing a ball move or ball skill with an imaginary ball. Have players do the move with a ball, then without, then with again. *Imitatsiya* use will promote increased muscle memory when learning things like ball moves, shooting and passing techniques, and other movements associated with soccer skill. It's a simple but very effective teaching tool.

13.3 VIDEO REVIEW: BLAST THE BALL

Blast the Ball videos are currently available from Soccer U on YouTube.com. They are a superb step-by-step guide to developing the ability to strike a ball with power and accuracy. The original *Blast The Ball* DVD was ahead of its time, offering many examples of things like chunking and *imitatsiya* before they were more widely used. It popularized the notion of the **soccer hop**—a different way to think of the last step before striking a ball—and provided inspiration for the **Seven Words** in the progression that follows. It included a number of technical exercises that remain useful for quick technical reviews before shooting games or finishing exercises. Condensed descriptions based around several of those exercises are included next. But it will still be valuable to see the long-form versions on SoccerU's YouTube site.

13.4 MECHANICS

Blast the Ball addresses seven types of shots: 1) the straight shot with the laces from straight on, struck with the sweet spot—the hard spot on the top of the foot; 2) the angle shot from about 15 to 30 degrees; and 3) the inside of the foot shot which is used in what is known as a push pass. More advanced are 4) the outside of foot shot, commonly used to bend the ball; 5) the straight volley; 6) the side of foot volley; and 7) the roundhouse volley.

5   The 12-Step Progression

The mechanics of each type of shot are similar and can be taught using essentially the same process and progression. First, the strike of the ball is broken down into three multiple-chunk parts. The first is the preparation for the shot, for which we will use three words to name the chunks: **Hop**, **Load**, and **Lock**. Next comes the strike, again three words: **See**, **BOB**, and **Swing**. Finally the follow-through, **Step**, with players finishing forward. These seven words will become a mantra and should be frequently repeated.

Part I: Prepare—Hop, Load, and Lock

MECHANICS ON A DEAD BALL

"HOP" into the shot, *accelerating* with the last step, not planting the foot, placing the "hop foot" precisely, **"ankle beside the ball"**

"LOAD" up with a big back swing (rotate back from the hip and stretch the quad) and **"set the V"** (flexed knee)

"LOCK" the ankle (making a **"fist with your toes"**)

"SEE" the ball – not the target - as you strike it

"BOB" - body over the ball

"SWING" - strike through the middle of the ball with the foot's **"hard spot"** – just above knuckle of big toe

"STEP"– leading with the knee bent and over the foot on the follow through, and **"finish forward"** landing with the body weight on the shooting foot.

These three chunks all happen together but are best taught in pieces. In this, as in all things, **"do it right, then do it fast"** needs to be observed.

1.   **Hop.** Have players one step (3-4 feet) from the ball, jogging in place. Then they take a hard hop step forward so that they land with the ankle beside the ball, the hop foot pointed toward where the shot is to go, and the shooting leg drawn back. The momentum of an aggressive hop step should cause the player to fall forward. If this doesn't happen, the step is what we call a **plant step**. The momentum of a hop step is forward, a plant step is downward. Guess which one produces a more powerful shot!

2.   **Load.** This is the backswing, with the leg taking on a V shape and stretching the quad. The bigger the backswing, the more power the shot will have. Now repeat step 1, still starting a step away, adding the **load** to the **hop** with an emphasis on the big back swing. (Have the players touch their toes in the quad stretch at the top of the load.) Again, the momentum needs to be forward.

3.   **Lock** the ankle. In most instances, this will involve **"making a fist with your toes."** Locking the ankle by making a fist should point the toes so that *the line from the knee to the toes* is almost straight. Now repeat step 2 with all elements in place.

Part II: Strike—See, BOB, Swing

These three chunks will also go together.

4.   **See.** *Repeat step 3*, making sure that the player sees the spot on the ball they want to hit. (They will keep their eye on that spot through the strike.)

5. BOB. *Repeat step 4*, making sure that the player is **"Body Over the Ball."** If the hop step and see are done correctly, BOB will automatically happen.

6. **Swing.** From step 5, have the player snap down into the ball, stopping just short of impact, with the most forward part of the knee even, or slightly in front of, the goal side of the ball.

CoachNotes

Many younger players will need to learn what it feels like when a foot properly strikes a ball. Kneel down, holding the ball on the ground in front of you with a Goalkeeper's W (to protect your thumbs). Have the player place the hop foot with the ankle beside the ball as in step 1. The shooting foot is touching the ball, the "sweet spot" of the foot (the bony bump midway between the ankle and toes) at the target point, toes pointed down, ankle locked by making that first. Have the player draw the shooting foot back *no more than two inches*, then swing gently forward, striking the ball so that the foot finishes touching the ball. If it's correctly done, have the foot drawn back 3 inches the next time, gradually increasing the distance until it's 12 to 18 inches. From about 8 inches out, you should be able to tell if the technique is correct by the solid "thunk" when the foot strikes the ball.

SafetyNotes

If doing this with older players, especially girls, limit the power of the strike since this can be a strain to the knees.

Putting Parts I and II Together

7. **Back and Forth.** Stand beside the ball, so the ankle beside the ball is about a foot from the ball. Load then swing back and forth, not striking the ball, with a little hop each direction, following through with knee to chest.

8. **1-2-3-Shot I.** Standing in place on the hop foot, take three *imitatsiya* "back and forth" swings, then take two steps forward and (finally!) strike a real ball.

Part III: Follow Through—Step

With so much forward momentum from the hop and swing, players should almost naturally finish forward, landing on the foot that struck the ball. But many won't.

9. **Step.** The knee should stay in front of the striking foot for as long as possible with the bodyweight shifting totally to the foot that struck the ball. (Weight on the back

foot usually indicates the last step was a plant instead of a hop.) Most will land "toe first" on the foot that struck the ball. The ball will tend to go in the same direction as the step. Now, still using *imitatsiya*, you'll put all three parts together, first with a *full stop* hesitation between each, to isolate the "step." Gradually blend the three parts into a whole. a) Start standing beside the ball. b) Next, repeat step 7, striking through an imaginary ball. c) Now, repeat step 9 with the step after the strike.

10. **In Pairs, Back and Forth. (★★★★★)** Starting no more than 10 feet apart, play the ball gently back and forth with perfect technique so that the ball **dies at the feet of your partner,** a) first from a standing, post-hop position beside the ball and then b) from the "feet moving" starting position in step 1. c) Gradually increase the distance between partners, but shrink it back if technique goes bad.

11. **1-2-3-Shot II.** Moving forward from 20 to 30 yards away, hop-load-BOB-swing-step three times on three imaginary balls, then strike the real one. WCPGW: It's not unusual for technique to be fine for the first three and then dissolve on the real shot.

Part IV: Shooting on the Run

Four tips: a) Go directly to goal; no detours to the side. b) Don't chop steps (you lose speed). c) **Get the hop step right!** Step slightly past the moving ball into the Hop. (The ball will catch up by the swing.) d) Accelerate through the ball with the shot.

12. **Stride, Dribble, and Shoot (1-2-3 Shot III).** Set cones 12, 18, 25, and 30 yards out from a goal. At the 30-yard mark, place the hop foot beside the ball. Gently strike the ball forward with perfect technique (as in the Back and Forth exercise). Take three long strides, then stride and strike gently with good shooting technique through the ball (**"Step"**) at about the 25. Repeat at the 18. Finally, with the fourth touch, strike the ball forward into the goal without breaking stride. Start at a walk. Gradually increase speed from a walk, to a jog, to a run, but with the 1-2-3 always as gentle shots, the last at full power. In time, set a five-second time limit from start to the final shot. Note: Pay particular attention to placement of the hop step as well as the follow-through step after each strike.

WCPGW: Throughout the process, things fall apart the moment you try to focus on more than one word at once. In step 2, when the player steps forward and loads with the leg, the hop step often becomes a plant or ends up in the wrong place. With a moving ball, the hop step will often be well behind the ball; reaching for it, the player abandons BOB, leans back, and puts the ball over the goal.

Shots wide come from incorrect placement of the hop step or missing the target spot on the ball with the swing because the eyes are up, not seeing the ball. Players will often look up at the goal as they shoot, and the shot's rise will follow the head's raise. The correct order of things is **"See the target, see the ball, shoot."** Players also need to learn that what they look at last before the shot is where the mind will tell the ball to go. So if it's a look at the keeper...

Typical causes of shots that lack power are a) a "plant" instead of the "hop," b) insufficient "load," c) failure to lock the ankle, d) failure to strike through the ball and "finish forward" with the "step," or e) various combinations of those five.

CoachNotes

When assembling chunks into a whole, players will initially struggle to get more than three or four of the seven words right. For the coach, learning to see all seven simultaneously—you actually see six but the hear the lock's "thunk"—is no easier. Both player and coach performance improve with repetition. Until you can see all the parts of a player's shot as a single event, it's OK to focus on specific chunks. In order, "hop," "step," and "see" and that "thunk" are the parts that will need the most correction. Start there.

Additional Thoughts

Always work slow to fast. Back up a step or two if you need to. It takes patience and perseverance. Work on technique every week.

This learning process will be enhanced by devoting much greater time and emphasis at first to technical activities than shooting or finishing exercises. Constantly repeat the Seven Words. Knowing the mantra will allow even very young players to **"Fix It"** by themselves when a shot goes wrong. Once the technique has been taught, insist on it *all the time*, even if you're not working on passing or shooting. And remember to remind players that every incorrectly struck pass or shot wraps myelin in the wrong places, scrambling the muscle memory.

Take 5 to 10 minutes to review one or two steps of the 12-Step Progression as an introduction to any other shooting or finishing exercise. It has also proven beneficial to repeat the full 12-Step sequence each season. (It will take about 30 minutes as a review. When teaching this the first time, get through step 7 or 8 the first day and finish things the next.) Older players can be reluctant to practice the steps individually. So pair them up—strongest to weakest works best—facing each other and have them alternate repetitions, with each required to "sign off" on the other's technique. Leg swings (step 8) can be done side by side with a hand on the partner's shoulder.

13.5 NOTES ON OTHER TYPES OF SHOTS

Straight Shot. Here the ball will be struck with the **laces**. Once the basic technique is mastered, this becomes the best type of shot to use in teaching how to shoot on the run.

Angle Shot. The placement of the hop step will need attention; the shot will go toward where the toe points.

CoachNotes

Opinions differ on whether to teach the straight shot or angle shot first. The geometry of the straight shot is more two-dimensional, which makes it simpler. The longer arc of the angle shot's leg swing produces more power. There's also less potential for the stubbed toe when coming from an angle, so some players will prefer this approach to the ball.

Inside of the Foot Shot. This is identical to the side-of-the-foot **push pass**. It is the one shot that does not lock the ankle by making a fist with the toes. Instead, lock the ankle by forcing the heel down and toes up. Strike the ball below the knob of the ankle bone. Train this with Triangle Passing: There are three players. Each receives with a touch, then pivots into the hop for the pass with the second touch. Set up the exercise so at least two-thirds of the passes are with the weaker foot. (There are endless variations to this simplest of exercises. The template: a) which part of which foot is used to receive the ball; b) what happens between the first touch and the pass; and c) the pass.)

Straight Volley. To keep the ball low on this shot, you will need much more BOB, and the knee of the shooting foot will almost touch the chest (or chin) at the end of the swing. To train this shot, first prepare by having a player toss a gentle ball ("two hands underhand, no spin") to a sitting partner, which the partner strikes back into the server's hands. Then use a) **the Toss**: toss the ball into the air so that it will bounce in front of you 10 to 18 inches off the ground, then volley it into the net just as it hits the ground the second time and b) **the Drop**: lean forward, holding ball at knee-cap height. Drop the ball and, just as it hits the ground, volley it into the net. (These are actually what are called "half-volleys" and will be a coordination problem for some at first. Some players will find it easier to strike the ball just before the bounce.) Stringing a rope 2 feet off the ground between the goal posts will challenge players to get over the ball and keep shots low.

Roundhouse Volley. Players do step 8 while lying on their sides. Then with a ball placed on a batting tee.

13.6 OTHER TOOLS AND EXERCISES

Two great ways to make it more challenging:

- Futsal Balls. No-bounce balls are harder to strike properly, require proper technique, and will increase passing crispness.

- The Pirate Eye Patch. Wearing one (you can buy them for about $1 apiece) over the dominant eye seems to sharpen neuromuscular memory. It certainly slows players down and demands greater concentration. Most find it a difficult challenge, a few are unfazed, but all think it's fun.

6   Finish Forward Contest

Place a ball between two discs. The player sets the hop foot on the line and strikes the ball, finishing forward with an exaggerated step. Mark each player's farthest forward landing point. **Variation:** Allow a run-up to the strike.

A rule of thumb is that the step should land two-thirds of one's height forward of where the ball was struck. The most powerful shooters (find videos of Michele Akers and Zinadine Zidane) would regularly finish farther forward of that spot than they were tall.

7   A Ball and a Wall

Nothing beats using some sort of rebounder to build "strong pathways" by pumping up the number of repetitions. This really sharpens the placement of the hop and makes the step habitual. Garage doors are common targets, but quickly (and expensively) break down. Most school buildings have stretches of brick wall without windows. Even recreation centers have racquetball courts where all kinds of ball work games can be created. a) From 4 to 6 feet away, use perfect technique to gently strike a stationary ball toward the wall; if you get a rebound, strike that one, too. b) In a two-touch rhythm, strike with the weaker foot, touch the rebound with that foot to the other, strike with the stronger foot, and so on. c) **Shot juggling**: Same pattern, but one touch, weaker to stronger to weaker, and so on, then twice with the weaker, once with the stronger. d) Any pattern, but with a 360-degree turn after each strike to develop the ability to find the ball quickly e) Now use different surfaces of the feet.

10-15 minutes of this once or twice a week will quickly make a huge difference in the power and accuracy of passes and shots.

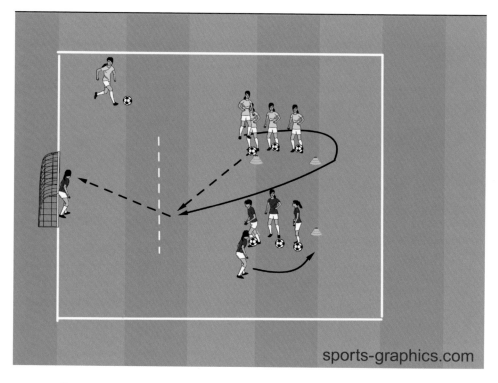

sports-graphics.com

Teams Yellow and Blue line up side by side 20 to 25 yards out from the goal. Each player in the lines has a ball except the players first in line. Team Blue has a player in the goal.

Yellow 1 loops away from the goal around the end of that line and sprints toward the goal, receiving a ball passed forward from Yellow 2, then shooting a driven ball with the first touch. The shooter then takes over as the goalkeeper unless the shot is not on goal, in which case the shooter must retrieve the missed shot first, leaving an open goal. *The first Blue player on line begins the looping run as soon as the pass is made.*

For Safety: All shots are taken from at least 12 yards away, and only the team's goalkeepers are allowed to catch the ball.

All shots are taken with the weaker foot; you can play a "strong foot" game at the end for "dessert." Teams keep score aloud, with **"Minus One"** for an open goal missed. (Think up a different penalty for a shot over the goal.) The game ends when a team reaches X points or makes Y shots in a row.

Variations: a) Use the other types of shots. b) Configure the activity so that service comes from in front of (or from the side of) the shooter.

9   Nonstop Shooting

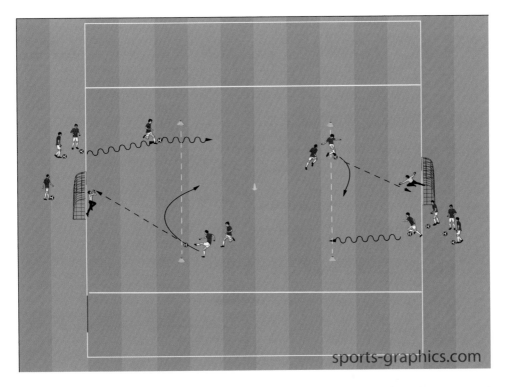

sports-graphics.com

This high-paced activity provides lots of repetitions under pressure. Using a longer central area can add a fatigue and fitness factor.

Each player has a ball and lines up beside their goal. The first at each end dribbles into the central zone and shoots (driven ball, weaker foot) before reaching a restraining line set 8 to 12 yards from the goal. At the shot the next player in line at that end takes off, dribbling into the central zone to get a shot as the prior shooter chases to prevent it. (The shooter chases whether or not the shot goes in.) This exercise goes clockwise to maximize weak-footed shooting. Natural lefties must dribble diagonally across the central area while their chasers must detour around a central cone.

Variation: You can play this as a contest between two teams. Scorers call out their goals (e.g., "blue"), double ("blue, blue") for a shot into the goal's far inside triangle, and "minus one" for an open goal missed. Teams say their scores aloud.

This activity is normally done without goalkeepers unless there are two for each end who can alternate between shots or every three to four shots. To simulate a keeper's presence, hang a pair of ropes from the crossbar to create a middle third of the goal; shots there don't count.

Where two large goals are not available, pairs of Pugg Goals can be used at each end to simulate shooting for the corners of the goal. A shot into the farther one earns the "blue, blue."

Variation: Require the shot to be into the far third of the goal.

10 Scott's Game

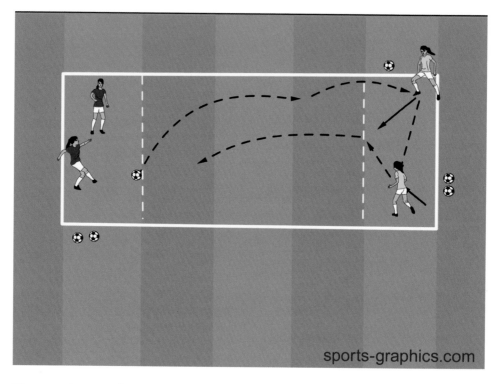

sports-graphics.com

The space is 12 yards wide, 30 to 40 yards long, including 8-by-12 boxes at either end. Have extra balls ready for **positive recovery**.

Two Yellow players are in one end box versus two Blue in the other. A Blue player serves a ball that must touch the ground at least once in the center zone and then enter Yellow's zone. The Yellow players have two touches to control the ball and return service to the Blues. The last team to successfully serve into the opposite box gets a point. "Losers" serve to restart the game.

Play to five. Have two or three games going. Winners stay on to play the next available team of two.

13.7 HEADING

Heading has become a controversial subject in soccer. Fear of head injuries and concussions has led youth soccer authorities to mandate *"eliminating heading for children 10 and under and limiting the amount of heading in practice for children between the ages of 11 and 13."*

Our experience is that concussions in soccer are most commonly the result of contact between the head and ground, goalpost, another head, or an opponent's arm. Concussions from a ball to the head are very rare and are usually from a ball that unexpectedly strikes the side of a head. That said, the days of serving "satellite balls" to see who had the courage (or foolishness) to head them are well behind us, and it can certainly do no harm to limit intentional head-to-ball contact while the brain is still growing. We'd even recommend taking the goalkeeper punt out of soccer altogether. *The Game* would be better if balls controlled by the keeper's hands had to be distributed with those hands. Players would have no choice but to learn how to play out of the back.

> **CoachNotes**
> In a moment of questionable sensitivity when a player's scalp has been opened up by another's while competing for a header, one coach's first words of comfort to the injured player were "bad technique." But it was true. When heading, **good technique is safe technique.**

Good technique starts with eyes open, mouth closed (the equivalent of the Seven Words' *"eyes"* and *"lock"*) and learning to strike the ball at the place on the head where "the hairline meets the forehead." Getting the **arms up**, hands to shoulders in a football player's blocking position, makes head-to-head contact much more rare and all but impossible if both players are arms-up. (The bleeding player cited had jumped like a *"popsicle stick,"* hands to the side.)

When the time comes to teach heading, the impact of multiple repetitions can be limited by using volleyballs. These are much lighter and therefore less intimidating for the neophyte. The most common progression used to develop proper heading technique involves serving balls **"two hands, underhand"** from a few feet away to players who will head the ball back to the server from a succession of body positions: a) lying down on the stomach, which isolates the head and neck movement but is sometimes too difficult for a total beginner, b) sitting, where the emphasis is on snapping forward both the neck and from the waist at the same time as the **arms up** are "rowing the boat," c) as before, only as part of completing a sit-up, d) kneeling, e) kneeling, diving forward, f) diving from a sprinter's start, g) standing, driving the ball low as you would with a shot, and h) standing, heading for height and distance as if clearing a ball.

Once players are comfortable with the basics, players can try to head juggle or head back and forth. Triangle heading comes next. Here **A** serves to **B** who heads to **C** who catches then serves to **A**, and so on. A key technical point here is that the header's upper body turns to face the target player before heading the ball.

13.8 HEADING GAMES

For the next two activities, split the team in half and either set up two of one game or one of each (change after 5-7 minutes). If using volleyballs, each activity will need three to four, but since balls are served from the hands, the headers are relatively low impact if using regular soccer balls.

11   The Heading Game

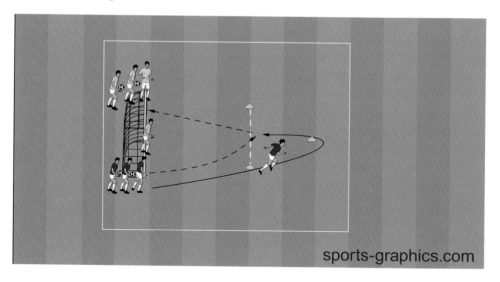

sports-graphics.com

Teams Blue and Yellow line up on either side of the goal, with the first player from team Yellow in the goal. Blue 1 races out and around a cone set 15 yards from the goal then back to goal as Blue 2 serves a ball (**"two hands underhand"**) to be headed in from at least 5 yards away. Yellow 2 starts his run as soon as Blue 2 serves the ball. Blue 1 becomes the next goalie, but must first retrieve any ball that was not shot on goal.

Keeping score: 1 for a goal, 2 if the goal is from a diving header, 3 for the keeper's team if the shot is saved with a header. Keep scores out loud.

12   Four Flags

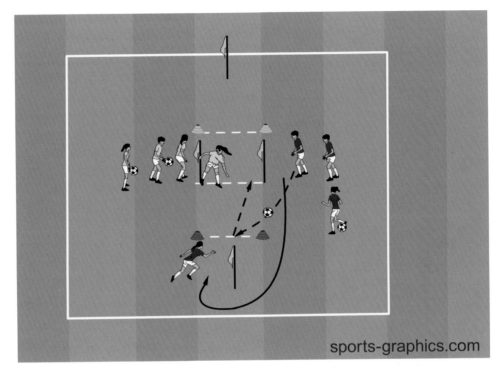

sports-graphics.com

Use a pair of corner flags to make a goal 6 to 8 feet wide. Set two other flags, one each, 12 feet out from the center of the "goal." Teams Blue and Yellow line up on their respective sides of the goal with Yellow 1 in the goal.

Blue 1 sprints out around the flag, is served a ball (**"two hands underhand"**) from Blue 2, shoots on goal (header) from at least 6 feet away, and then becomes the goalkeeper as Yellow 2 sprints out and around the other flag.

Keeping score: 1 for a goal, 2 if the goal is from a diving header, 3 for the keeper's team if the shot is saved with a header. Keep scores out loud.

CoachNotes
Games involving diving headers and wet, muddy fields are a hit with kids. Games involving kids, diving headers and wet, muddy fields are less popular when the carpool driver doing the pick-up arrives in a straight-from-the-dealer's-showroom Buick Regal. ("How was I to know?") The solution—it involved use of the car's spacious trunk—might be frowned upon these days.

13 Throw, Head, Catch

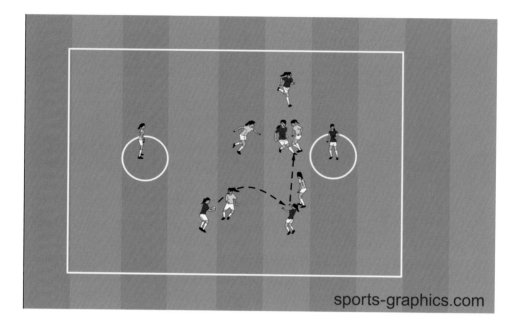

sports-graphics.com

Using the penalty area, use discs to mark out a pair of 6-foot diameter circles of cones 20 to 25 yards apart. Each team has a "target player" in a circle.

Teammates must play ball in a throw-head-catch manner, eventually heading the ball to the target player. Players may not run with ball and have 3 to 5 seconds to throw after catching. The throw cannot be obstructed, and the ball may not be touched with hands before it is headed. The defending team, though, can try to intercept and head the served ball and may catch any ball after it is headed. When the ball hits the ground, possession is lost by the team that last touched the ball.

This activity is often used as the first game that involves players competing to head a ball. **"Arms up"** will need to be reinforced continually. As a warm-up, the coach can serve balls to pairs of players standing side by side, with each player competing to win the header.

This becomes a wonderful tactical game once players can play it at speed.

Variations: a) The player heading the ball may not head it back to the server's hands. b) Give a bonus point if the ball headed is then successfully headed on by a teammate. c) Several bonus points if two players complete a header give-and-go (i.e., 1 serves to 2 who heads back to 1 who heads to 2 who catches the ball). **Where's Waldo** (see chapter 14, activity 18) is a fine addition to this game.

14 DEVELOPING VISION

"See, then think."

–Xavi

14.1 AZERBAIJAN DIARY

It is the final Group B game of the 2012 U17 Women's World Cup at Bayil Stadium in Baku, Azerbaijan. The United States and North Korea enter the match with a win and a tie apiece. The Koreans, though, hold the goal differential tiebreaker from the earlier group games. Only one team will advance.

Lightning strikes quickly, with the US scoring in the first two minutes and the Koreans equalizing barely a minute later. Korea has the better of the play after that, and the US is fortunate to get out of the half at 1-1.

In the second half the game evens out, but a flaw in the US's game is becoming increasingly evident as players are repeatedly dispossessed by Korean players coming in from behind. It isn't just forwards receiving balls with their backs to goal. Midfielders and defenders—whether in possession or about to be, whether back to goal or facing it, even sideways on—are surprised again and again by Koreans behind them. As the Koreans figure this out, they ramp up their response.

The most important soccer habit is to **"look before receiving."** Almost without exception, these US players lack that habit. The result is over 30 possessions lost, certainly enough to have had an impact on the game's result—a 1-1 tie. North Korea goes on; they will lose on penalties to France in the finals. The US goes home.

"I always know what I'm going to do with the ball before I get it." The words are those of Xavi Hernandez, the long-time Barcelona midfielder who regularly *completed* more than 100 passes a game. He does not mean this literally, but he does know beforehand what all his options are and the risk and reward of each.

A player like Xavi is always scanning the field to know where the other players are, both teammates and opponents. **Vision** is that combination of what you see and the ability to process that information. **"See, then think."** It's a critical skill, the key to anticipating the game, the catalytic compound in playing faster. Even when they were not being stripped of the ball, the thinking of the US players was delayed by failure to see enough of the play in advance.

Perhaps the US coaches could have worked on this more, but how much they could have accomplished is uncertain. Vision must be developed over time, trained and practiced so that you not only see more with each turn of the head but process what you've seen more quickly. The younger that players learn to **look**, the better. 17-year-olds can no doubt improve their vision, but it will never become as good as if it were trained from early in their soccer careers.

Developing vision starts with training the hard skills of looking before receiving and constantly scanning the field. In a 4v4 game of 7-year-olds, the eight players mostly see one thing—the ball. The first step on the road to Xavi-dom is to get them to see anything else. To do that they'll have to become *"bobbleheads"*. With girls' teams, *"ponytails"* is a good prompt because they're always flying when players' heads are on a swivel.

There are lots of ways to make this happen. A basic one starts with a pair of players passing a ball back and forth, requiring that the receiver to **look** over one shoulder (then both) as the ball is on the way. Next, have three players A, B, and C in a line, the end ones—A and C—each with a ball. A passes to B who must look as the ball is inbound to see if C has one or two hands in the air. After the pass is returned, C passes to B who must look for A's hands. How many does B get right in a minute? That simple start sets the foundation for players to develop ever better vision, to actually see something. A look by a young player may not take in more than one or two other players. With practice, each look sees a little more. With more practice, the player begins to recognize patterns of player positioning (still mostly a hard skill), then develops the (soft skill) abilities associated with processing that recognition into options for action.[1]

Over time the brain processes more and more with each look. Xavi's look takes in all the players in his field of vision (which will also by practice be wider) and what they're doing. The highly myelinized part of his brain that deals with decision-making instantly combines this information with other recent looks as well as with a vast storehouse of looks in thousands of situations. In an instant, he recognizes his options and the degree of risk and potential reward associated with each. His response (e.g., the pass) is a mix of the highly developed soft skills of his decision-making process with the highly developed hard skills of his passing technique, buffered by hard or soft skills that control such things as surface of the foot used and weight of the pass.

---

[1] Daniel Coyle's book *The Talent Code* has a fascinating section (p. 76-78) on how chess masters see the board. It's not much of a leap to see the implications for soccer.

14.2 PONYTAILS AND BOBBLEHEADS

There are a variety of products and programs on the market for developing vision. But the following simple activities are extraordinarily efficient without all the bells, whistles, and flashing lights.

14   The Rule (★★★★★)

The most effective method of developing the habit is to use a very simple rule in any training activity: *"You must look before receiving."* For the Rule to be effective, it needs to be an all the time challenge—in play during any small-sided game—that becomes part of a team's culture. With the Rule, there is always a consequence for not looking. If a player on Team A calls out a player on Team B (e.g., "Didn't look!") for failing to look before receiving, the offending Team B player gets penalized. At first, the offending player must turn the ball over to the opposition. But soon, being called out also means you must leave the game.

CoachNotes

Having the players make the call keeps their focus on looking whether their team has possession. And if a player fails to call out an opponent who doesn't look, the coach calls out the inattentive one while the original guilty party gets off free. This diabolical twist to maintaining the Rule really sharpens players' attentions. Not only must they focus on their own head movement, they have no choice but to keep close watch on and call out their friends on the opposing team.

Once out, the player can get back in by calling out an offender from Team A or in a general amnesty after either team scores. (You can allow an exception when there's no time to look because the inbound ball is a worm-burner coming too quickly or from too close. But even that exception is nullified if an opponent steals from behind. A player always needs to be aware of the nearest opponents.) It takes a while to reach the point where you can use the Rule without constantly stopping play. Find opportunities to build the hard skills of the habit, where players must always be moving their heads. Many of the warm-up activities (see chapter 17) have a place for this.

15 Secret Scoring

This activity will be a memorable introduction to teaching players to see more than the ball and is particularly useful with teams at U10 and older who will be working on head movement for the first time.

Before the training session, divide the team in half. Make three rosters that list players, one team listed on each side of the page. Enlist as confederates three parents from those on that day's carpool duty.

Have the teams play a five-minute game across half of the field. No keepers; everyone is a field player. Tell the players to keep score. When the game ends, send the players on a water break. While the game is under way, the parents will watch players for five seconds at a time, following the roster list, putting a Y next to the name of any player who looks at anything other than the ball, a N next to one that doesn't. In 5 minutes, each of the parents should be able to get through all the players on both teams at least three times. During the water break, tally the scores.

When the players return ask, "Who won?" and then "What was the score?" Now give the "secret score" and explain how that happened. Briefly discuss the importance of constantly looking around and the idea that if you go more than five seconds without scanning the field you might as well be wearing blinders.

Now play a second game with the parents again keeping score. It will be better.

CoachNotes

This tends to be a one-time activity, but it can be a useful measure of progress to keep score in this manner during some of the team's games. Enlist as scorekeepers a couple of parents who might need to be doing something else than criticizing the referee or shouting instructions from the sidelines.

---

16 Name Game

In learning to be constantly scanning the field, the first priority is the look before receiving. This progression, which emphasizes several **Great Soccer Habits** (see chapter 11), is a fine place to start.

Spread players around a circle 15 to 20 yards in diameter. The coach calls the name of a player and passes the ball to that player. That player...

1. Must, *before receiving the ball*, call out name of the teammate to whom he or she will pass. It can be any of the other players except the passer and the ones to either side. *Using two touches*, pass the ball **on the ground** to that player.

2. Must now **Look** (scanning left and right) and call out name before receiving, **take two, *pass on the ground***.

3. Must **Go to the Ball, Look,** call the name, **take two.**

4. Must **Go to the Ball, Look,** call the name, **take two** with a **dynamic first touch** (moving the ball 6-8 feet with the first touch), pass, then follow the pass to take the place of the target player.

Variation: Add a second ball, then a third.

Keeping score: At each stage, you can make this into a game by sitting down those who mess up. *Make the players call out the violation.* If using more than one ball and two passes are made to the same person, the passer who called the name last is out.

17 Walk Ball

In this activity, the players may only walk. It can be added to any game that is 2v2 or more and is a good one for early implementation of the Rule.

18 Where's Waldo? (★★★★★)

This activity requires the players to see, not just to look. It can be used as an add-on to any game that is 2v2 or more. At any point the coach can call out **"Waldo."** The players immediately freeze in place with their eyes closed.

In a 2v2 setting, players immediately point at their teammates. Then the coach asks them to point at each of the two opponents. A perfect score is 3. At 3v3, each player immediately points at his or her two teammates. Players who get that correct are asked to call the names and point in turn at the three opponents. A perfect score is 5. Tracking the perfect scores is a good way to evaluate players' progress in being able to see the game.

Scoring variations: Make it tougher. 2v2: 1 point for your partner, remaining 2 if you get both opponents; 3v3: 1 point for each partner, 2 for 2 opponents, 4 for all three.

At 4v4 or more, once the coach selects a player from each team to remain eyes-closed, the other players can open theirs. The coach then asks the "blind" players to point to specific teammates (often to the great amusement of the others). The player who gets the most correct earns a bonus point in whatever game is being played.

Other variations: The "blind" player is asked to point to specific teammates *and opponents*. The coach can also question the player (e.g., "If you had the ball, who would be the best passing option? Why?"). This can be particularly useful when you **"Waldo"** the player with the ball. Use this activity regularly (and unexpectedly) as a "pop quiz."

14.3 AND MORE

One touch play goes against the **"Take Two Or More"** habit, but is a good activity for developing vision and the ability to Think Ahead.

No Pinnies, especially when everyone's in a common uniform, adds significant difficulty to sorting out what you see.

Playing Back to Goal requires that the attacker know where the defender is and the level of pressure that's coming. **Back-to-Goal Continuous** (see chapter 19, activity 54) is good for training vision, better still when played 2v2 or 3v3.

Wall passes (see chapter 19.2) require that two players see the same opportunity. Give a bonus point for a successful wall pass, with an additional point if the wall pass leads directly to a goal.

At the older levels Pass the Steal—where a player wins a ball and passes to a teammate with the same first touch—is a tool for developing speed of play in transition. A much more difficult feat—always a **Game Over** moment—is when the next touch returns the ball as a wall pass.

The Double Wall Pass has two versions. **A** to **B** to **A** to **B** (beating two defenders in three touches), and **A** to **B** to **A** to **C** to **A** (beating two in four). Either is difficult, maybe a **Game Over** moment.

Silent Running is where players in a scrimmage are not allowed to speak. It is particularly useful in developing vision when connected to the Where's Waldo activity.

14.4 DECISIONS, DECISIONS, DECISIONS

"In an instant, the player must choose to pass, dribble, or shoot; choose whether to combine play with teammates or take the individual option; choose whether to play for possession or to risk losing the ball with a more daring or aggressive play toward the goal."

That's a lot, and it's largely dependent on the player's vision.

Many of the exercises in the following chapters are structured to mimic different elements of the full-sided game. Among them are multiple variations and challenges to further isolate specific situations.

Each modification in an activity's structure will alter the variables involved in problem-solving and making decisions. Players will need to reassess a) the new information they'll require to adjust their responses, b) the impact of the changes on the actions of teammates and opponents, and c) the uncertainty factor, especially WCPGW.

By posing at each change a few questions to individuals or groups, a coach can help players "to open up to new perspectives or information to guide their perception and action."[2] Repeated use of this process will allow the players to use those experiences to generate the right questions on their own, and identify keys both to the essence of the new problem and to its solution.

---

[2] footblogball.wordpress.com/2016/03/30/the-role-of-representative-learning-design-in-creating-a-learning-space.

15 THE INDIVIDUAL OPTION

"I don't teach ball moves because the girls wouldn't know how to use them."

–Coach of an Under-13 team

"I can beat you myself..."

–Mantra of the two-way player (part I)

15.1 INTRODUCTION

Shortly after the first Women's World Cup in 1991, the coaches of the U.S. Women's National Team presented a clinic where they stated that the team did **some sort of 1v1 activity at *every* training session.**

This was the team of the Three-Edged Sword—Michelle Akers, Carin Jennings, and April Heinrichs. They carved up the opposition with their individual skills on the road to winning that first Championship. Also on the team were future Hall of Famers Julie Foudy, Mia Hamm, and Kristine Lilly, who would shred defenses with their one-on-one skills for years to come.

Would that same regimen of 1v1 training work as well if applied to younger players? The answer, based on thousands of training sessions in the years since that clinic, is an emphatic resounding **YES**. Training the one-on-one situation is, for several reasons, an essential part of developing a complete soccer player. Those duels, where you must beat players or stop players in 1v1 situations, are the most frequently encountered tactical situations in any game. Their outcomes have an outsized impact on the result of the match.

Next, players need to become **two-way players**. When faced with a defender, they must be able to say: *"I can beat you myself,"* the **individual option**, or *"I can beat you using my teammates."* Far too many players develop only the second option because their coaches fail to train the first. Finally, developing strong 1v1 skills is wonderfully empowering, giving the player control over game situations that another who can only pass the ball will never enjoy. For those reasons, training the one-on-one situation is a foundational component of the Players 1st program, something to be done every time players are on the field, even as a part of pre-game warm-up.

"They know not the joys of being able to field a full team of bad*** ball handlers."

15.2 ABOUT BALL MOVES

A primary goal of the Players 1st program is to develop individuals who are magicians with the ball. At the core of this "Ball Magic" is a set of moves for players to use in their individual duels. These moves fall into three categories:

- Turns. Moves that turn the ball 180 degrees; alternatives for players who would simply want to pull the ball back with the sole of the foot.

- Beaters. Moves to get by a defender, either in the open field or to get off a shot. Most of these moves involve getting the ball past the opponent at about a 30-degree angle to the ball's original path.

- Stop-and-Go. Ways to shake off an opponent running alongside. The ball does not change direction in these moves.

The collection of moves that follows is by no means complete; there are many others in all three categories. These were chosen because they are, for the most part, simple, easy to teach and learn, and effective. Some can be grouped together as variations on a single theme, where the first element of a move can be turned into a Beater, a Turn, or a Stop-and-Go. Players must be able to do each move with either foot. They may cheat and do more with the easier foot. Insist that they don't. In fact, requiring a 3:1 ratio of use with the foot that's more difficult will produce the same kind of benefits as weak-foot juggling (see chapter 12.3) and shooting (see chapter 13.1).

Players should learn to perform all the moves correctly and should initially be required to use them all in practice activities. Gradually a player will develop a collection of personal favorites that he or she will use more often. At this point it's time for a player to **own** one or two moves that can be used successfully no matter how good the opponent.

Teaching Ball Moves

There are several common elements in any ball move. First, the attacker must s**et up** the defender. If hoping to beat the defender, the attacker should **dribble at the defender's shoulder**, not center mass. This will get the defender moving laterally. At the same time, the attacker must **attack with a sense of urgency** since **time favors the defender**. Finally, players must **explode** away at the end of the move, taking at least two **getaway touches** to put the defender in the rearview mirror.

Getaway Touches: *Beat 'em and leave 'em.* A move done not so well may still succeed if the dribbler explodes away with the ball. A move done precisely but without the getaway touches will give a defender another chance. Build the habit by demanding that the player take a *second* getaway touch at the completion of a move.

Levels of Pressure. Players progress from learning the hard skills of ball moves (*doing* the move correctly) to the soft skills associated with *using* the moves effectively. Teaching the moves needs to recognize that continuum.

Initially a move is performed without any limit on time or space and free from defensive pressure. The emphasis is on the technical elements, notably the footwork, body position, and getaway (always two touches, always an explosion). *Imitatsiya* (see chapter 13.2) (including the getaway touches) is a valuable teaching tool at this stage. Check for understanding by asking players to describe or **"Show me"** the move. Gradually challenge the comfort zone by adding pressure by a) increasing speed from walk to jog to run or b) piggyback four to six repetitions in succession. Note that many players will rush to learn or perform the skill. If it goes wrong, slow them down. **"Do it right, then do it faster."**

Introduce defensive pressure gradually, first with a passive defender. At this point the **Three Step Rule** gets introduced. That's about how far away an attacker should be from the defender when the move is initiated. The next level of pressure has "mirror attackers," two players dribbling directly at each other, performing the move, exploding by. At this point the Three Step Rule will make sense. Again, work from slow to fast.

Adding a live defender is the moment where work on ball moves transitions into learning the soft skills of 1v1 play. This is done in competitive 1v1 activities (see chapter 16.4). These games add pressure in the form of restrictions on time or space. The coach controls those variables to keep the decision-making factors at the level of a "just right" challenge.

Levels of Learning. With each move players will go through four levels of learning.[1]

1. **Performance.** The player performs the move correctly under no defensive pressure: an approach at proper speed, correct footwork/fake/feint, the ball goes where it should and is taken away in an explosion. Players should reach this level during the season in which the move is taught.

2. **Conditional.** The player is using the move with some success in a controlled one-on-one situation, demonstrating not only the move but the ability to set up the defender for the move.

3. **Functional.** The player uses the move with some success in scrimmages and games but is still thinking about the move when preparing to do it.

4. **Instinctive.** The move just seems to happen, without thought, in a game or scrimmage situation. The player has made the move "her own." When teammates cheer the move, the player may even ask, "What did I do?"

---

[1] These levels of learning will also apply as players develop their dynamic first touch (see chapter 12) and their ability to strike a ball (see chapter 13).

It takes, *at a minimum*, hundreds of repetitions to attain instinctive use of a ball move.

15.3 THE MOVES

The description of each move is as precise as possible. Many are hard to describe. If unfamiliar with a move, find them on video—the earlier Coerver videos are a good source—or get an older player to demonstrate them.

CoachNotes

In an earlier time, most ball moves were named after the players who first used the moves to greatest effect. This had the added benefit of teaching younger athletes at least something about *the Game's* iconic players. That practice ended when a few decided they needed royalty payments for the use of their names. The solution has been to use names that are descriptive of the move. In this chapter, we will use descriptive names (although the use of "Cruyff" and "Matthews" in association with those moves is considered generic), but will also provide historical context. Players should learn the names of the moves in one form or another as they are learning the moves themselves.

Be aware that some athletes are better auditory learners than visual learners. They will need to hear the moves described as precisely as possible. Note key words like "first," "opposite," and "switch" and try to avoid "other" when talking about feet. Make clear that using the "outside of the foot" really means a foot that is turned slightly inward and partly turned over so that the ball is struck with the top of the outside toes.

19 Turns

These moves turn the ball 180 degrees and are used mostly to turn away from defensive pressure or to turn the ball upfield when facing your own goal.

Figure 8. (associated with ZICO) Dribbling forward, step over the ball left to right with the left foot (like the Step-Over beater). Land on the toes of the left foot and pivot 180 degrees counterclockwise, sending the ball in the opposite direction with the inside of the right foot, exploding away with that touch.

Outside Cut. (Franz BECKENBAUER) Dribbling forward, cut the ball backwards with the outside of the foot. Explode away with the ball. While this turn lacks the deceptiveness of the others, it is useful if done quickly in a tight situation.

Cruyff. (Johan CRUYFF) Dribbling forward, take a longer step forward and stop on one foot. Turn the opposite foot *inward* and knock the ball back between the legs. Set that foot down and continue the turn, exploding away with the ball. The next touch taking the ball away can be done with the outside of the first foot.

On-Over. (Pierre LITTBARSKI) Dribbling forward, step on the ball, then over 2 feet *in front of the ball*, turning the foot inward. (Note: Now the ball is shielded from the defender.) Plant that foot, then explode away in the opposite direction, pushing the ball away with the outside of the opposite foot.

CoachNotes

Use the clock as a description. An attacker with the ball is facing 12 o'clock. A Turn will reverse the ball to 6 o'clock. If using a Beater, the first getaway touch at 30 degrees should put the ball by the defender to 11 o'clock or 1 o'clock. Using a Stop-and-Go move doesn't change the direction of the ball. It's still going toward 12.

---

20 Beaters

These are the moves used to get by a defender. All will change the direction of the ball about 30 degrees (11 o'clock, 1 o'clock, no more) so that the dribbler and the ball end up behind the defender. Once an attacker has beaten a defender, the player should NEVER cut the ball back to give that defender another chance. Meanwhile, keep a regular focus on the angle of the getaway touches. The first getaway touch as the defender is beaten is at 30 degrees. The second should touch the ball back inward to put the defender behind the dribbler.

Side Step. (Karl Heinz RUMMENIGGE) Dribbling forward, take a sharp step to one side while dipping the shoulder in that direction (what they call a "jab step" in basketball), then push the ball away to the other side at a 30-degree angle with the outside of the opposite foot. Explode away with the ball.

Scissors. (Marco VAN BASTEN) Dribbling forward, fake a pass with the outside of the dribbling foot, circling that foot over the ball *inside to outside* (a **scissors** step). Land on that foot, then push the ball away to the other side at a 30-degree angle with the outside of the opposite foot. Explode away with the ball. (A scissors with the right foot will explode away to the left.) Get the foot up over the ball, not just around it. A defender's eyes and momentum will often follow the knee cap.

The Double. (Combines the Side Step and the Scissors.) Step right, scissors left, explode away. This is not a double scissors. The Side Step part need not be convincing; the idea is for the defender to bite on the Scissors. Explode away with the ball.

Double Scissors. This move is two Scissors moves put together. Scissors right, scissors left, explode away.

Step-Over. (Roberto RIVELINO) Dribbling forward, fake a push pass with the inside of the dribbling foot, circling that foot over the ball *outside to inside* (a **step-over**). Land on that foot so that this leg is crossed over the front of the other. If the step over has been done correctly, momentum will have the player falling away from the ball. Take a small step with the opposite foot, just enough to regain balance, then push the ball away at a 30-degree angle with the outside of the first foot. At the same time explode away with the ball off the foot used to regain balance. (A step-over with the right foot will explode away to the right.)

Teaching points: a) The rhythm is *"Cha, Cha, Cha,"* like the dance. b) Get the foot up over the ball, not just around it. *"The fake is in the knee cap."* c) Use *imitatsiya* to make sure that players know a Scissors from a Step-Over.

Matthews. (Stanley MATTHEWS) Dribbling forward, lightly touch or drag the ball in (across the body) with the inside of one foot while hopping in the same direction on the opposite foot, then quickly touch the ball the other direction with the outside of the same foot. (The rhythm: *"touch in, touch out."*) Explode away with the ball off the hop foot.

Matthews Reverse. Dribbling forward, touch or drag the ball in (across the body) with one foot, as in the Matthews move. But this time allow the ball to go farther and take it away with the outside of the opposite foot in the fashion of the Dribble Cut (see chapter 12.2). Explode away with the ball. This move can also be done with a couple of quick Sideways Hops with one foot before the ball is taken away with the opposite.

Matthews With Scissors. Dribbling forward, touch or drag the ball in (across the body) with one foot, as in the Matthews move. Now scissors over the ball with that foot and take it away with the outside of the opposite foot. Explode away with the ball. This move can also be done with a couple of quick Sideways Hops with one foot before the scissors.

Foundation. Dribbling forward toward a defender (cones will do at first), pass the ball by the defender with the outside of the left foot, exploding by to the right of the defender to catch up with the ball. Emphasize that the explosion must come *as the ball is played by* and that the ball must be played close to the defender's foot.

The Lunge. (Marc OVERMARS) Dribbling forward, lunge forward so that the foot lands well in front of the ball, like a fencer going for the kill. The foot must land directly in front of the ball. Before the ball rolls up the heel, use the inside of the opposite foot to drag the ball behind the leg and forward at a 30-degree angle. Momentum will have you falling away to the side the ball is on. Recover as you explode away.

V Move. (Ferenc PUSKAS) Dribbling forward, use the toes to pull the ball back under the body with the dribbling foot, pivoting on the opposite foot in the direction of the first foot to shield the ball from the defender. Now explode, pushing the ball away with the inside of the first foot. Note: This move sends the ball forward in a 10 o'clock or 2 o'clock direction.

On-Over Move. (Dennis BERGKAMP, GARRINCHA) Dribbling forward, step on the ball, then over *at least 1 foot in front of the ball*, turning the foot inward. (Note: The ball is now shielded from the defender.) Plant the toes of this foot and continue to spin 360 degrees inside while dragging the ball forward with the bottom of the opposite foot. A more common but slightly different version of this move, associated with Diego MARADONA, does the 360-degree spin without having the foot touch down in front of the ball. The second touch drags the ball forward before the first foot touches down.

On-Over Nutmeg. Dribbling forward, step on the ball, then in front, as with the On-Over Stop-and-Go moves. (See the following: The foot stepping on the ball must be back out of the way.) As the first foot is landing, push the ball forward through the legs of the defender with the inside of the opposite foot. *Explode past the defender* to collect the ball.

Cut-Catch. (Zinadine ZIDANE) This move is often used by a dribbler on the wing when a defender is angling in from the side. A "defender" is needed to teach the move. Dribble forward down the left wing as a defender comes from the right to intercept. As the defender arrives from 4 or 5 o'clock, cut the ball with the left foot inside and under the body. Open up the right foot and push the ball away behind the defender's back (between 2 and 3 o'clock), with the second getaway touch exploding toward the goal. The ball makes a Z. Quickness is required, with the right-foot touch coming as the left foot is touching down.

Fake Kick. Dribbling forward, hop and load (see chapter 13.4), drawing the leg back as if winding up to shoot the ball at the defender. Start the "swing" with the foot driving down toward the ball. Just before contact, stop the foot and push the ball away past the (hopefully flinching) defender with the outside of the same foot. Explode away with the ball.

Hot Fudge Sundae. (So named, legend has it, because the coach must award the same to a player who uses the move successfully to beat a defender in *a game*.) Dribbling forward, step up onto the ball with the ball under the toes of the dribbling foot. Pass ball behind the opposite leg in a J motion as the opposite foot steps forward. Explode away with the ball. The first getaway touch is usually with the outside of the foot past the defender.

21 Stop-and-Go

Stop-and-go moves are used most frequently by players dribbling along the flank as a way to get away from a defender running alongside. But they are just as effective in other dribbling scenarios. Too rarely trained in youth soccer, their use has the potential to become a team's secret weapon. In each the ball or dribbler stops, followed by an explosion forward. The ball does not change direction at all. Because these moves are so often used at speed, they should be trained at full speed as quickly as possible.

Fake Figure 8. Dribbling forward, step over the ball right to left with the right foot (like the Step-Over ball move). Land on the toes of the right foot, like starting a Figure 8, but hesitate, allowing the ball to roll forward. Take a small step forward with the left foot, then push the ball forward with the laces of the right. The ball does not change direction. This move is very much like the Step-Over, with the ball going *forward* rather than away at a 30-degree angle.

Pull Push. Dribbling forward, grab the ball under the toes of the foot and pull it back slightly. Then push the ball forward with the top of the toes (toes pointed downward) of the same foot. Explode away with the ball.

The Wave. (Giovane ELBER) Dribbling forward, wave a foot forward over the ball then back as you hop up on the opposite foot. Now push the ball forward with the top of the toes (toes pointed downward) of the first foot. The High Wave goes over the ball as written. The Low Wave waves the foot next to the ball. Explode away with the ball.

On-Over Drag. Dribbling forward, step on the ball, then over, turning the foot inward. (Note: The foot stepping on the ball must be back out of the way.) Using the inside of the opposite foot, drag the ball in the same direction as it was going and explode away.

On-Over Side Roll. Dribbling forward, step on the ball, then over, turning the foot and body inward. (Note: The foot stepping on the ball must be back out of the way.) Using the opposite foot, Side Roll the ball in the same direction as it was going and explode away.

The Shimmy. (Peter BEARDSLEY) Dribbling forward, fake a kick to the left with the right foot, turning the hip toward the defender. Allow the right foot to hit the ground in front and to the left of the ball. Then take the ball away with the outside of the right foot. (The upper body turns 30 degrees, then back forward.)

Bonus Moves

These fall outside the three categories.

The Twistoff. This adds a second 90-degree cut to the Outside Cut, creating a 270-degree turn. (If you use the left foot, you end up going 90 degrees to the right.)

Pull–Cruyff. Dribbling forward, take a longer step forward and stop on one foot. Pull the ball back with the bottom of the opposite foot, then use the inside of that foot to pass the ball behind the standing leg. (If you use the left foot you will turn 90 degrees to the right.)

Foundation II. (Shannon MacMILLAN) This is a foundation move used in a man-on situation with your back to the defender. As a ball is passed in, touch the ball by the defender using the outside of one foot, then spin off in the opposite direction around the other side of the defender.

The Man-On Turn. Posting up with back to (and in contact with) the defender as the ball is played in, rake it across the body and past the defender (to 4 or 5 o'clock if using the left foot) with the sole of the foot. Continue to spin by the defender, following the ball.

Which Moves When?

You probably do not want to teach all 30 moves in the first season, so try these.

The Basic Dozen. (Any age) Turns: all four. Beaters: Side Step, Scissors, The Double, Step-Over, Foundation. Stop-and-Go: Pull–Push, Wave, Shimmy.

The Next Set. (U8.) Double Scissors, Matthews, Lunge, V Move, Twistoff, Pull–Cruyff.

Fun and Fancy. (U9-10) Fake Kick, Matthews Variations, Cut-Catch, Hot Fudge Sundae.

On-Over Variations. (U10.) Use this group to teach players how to use one variation of a move several times to set up a defender for one of the other variations.

All the rest. (Whenever) This is also the time to work on combining moves.

15.4 MAINTENANCE

"If you're not getting better, you're getting worse." This is not just some coaching bromide, and you don't just get worse compared to others if you're not trying to improve. The research shows you really get worse and lose competencies if you just try to maintain your skills and are not actually trying to get better. *"Automated abilities gradually deteriorate in the absence of deliberate efforts to improve."*[2]

Coaches often focus on helping players to improve on their weaknesses. But players should continue to develop their strengths, the things that make them special and set them apart, that define what coaches call a soccer personality.

---

[2] Ericsson, A. 2017. *Peak.* Eamon Dolan/Mariner Books, p. 13.

Here are some other ways you can keep old things fresh.

22 Ronaldo Ball

Prior to a Champions League game in Marseille, Christiano Ronaldo was warming up before a very hostile crowd. With each ball that came his way he would do "a little something" before playing it on. The crowd saw this as "hot-dogging," but he continued to do it throughout the game. Sometimes it was a ball move, sometimes a minor change of pace or direction, sometimes—in a sprint of five or six paces—one step was shorter than the rest. It was part of his game.

During the game, the effect of those subtle actions—hard to see when watching the televised replay—was to unbalance his nearest opponent ever so slightly. At that level of play, it was an important advantage. Having players do this as a challenge at practice gets them thinking about how and when to use their foot skills and ball moves. Start with, *"You must do a move before you can pass."* Then switch to, *"You must use a move* (against a defender) *before you can pass."* (But a shot is always allowed.) Note that *"a little something"* can also be done just before a ball arrives at the feet. Players who make Ronaldo Ball part of their game create the same advantage at their level of play as Ronaldo does at his.

23 Move of the Week

To encourage use of the moves in games, select one or more moves to be the Moves of the Week. Emphasize the moves during the week's training sessions. On game day, reward those who successfully use the move with a mini-bar of some sort of candy.

If players are just learning the moves, try to wait at least two weeks until the move becomes a Move of the Week. In addition to individual moves, some weekly selections have been any Turn, any Stop-and-Go, and any On-Over move. An end-of-season favorite is **Choose Your Own Moves** where each player chooses three moves (one of each type) to try in the game. Note: To keep some players from going overboard on this you might have to limit the number of prizes a player can earn in a week. (Not that that should actually be considered a "problem.") In addition, players can be asked to keep a checklist of moves tried and used successfully at practice and in games.

24 Outrageous Soccer

This challenge, which can be added to almost any activity, is used to encourage clever, creative, and especially outrageous play with the ball. It's for play that demonstrates *"spontaneity and daring"* with the first touch when dribbling, passing, or shooting. Players have total freedom with the ball. Score is kept by the coach's reaction as follows:

1 for an **"Oh,"** 2 for **"OH!,"** and 3 (or more) for an **"OH MY!"** In just a few minutes with this challenge, you should see players shaking off the chains of safe, conventional, and comfortable play.

15.5 Individual Defending

When to teach individual defending is an interesting question. On the one hand, you want players to have success in their early attempts as attackers in 1v1 settings. On the other, you will want their take-on skills challenged as they begin to improve. What follows is adapted from the coach's handbook of the North Carolina Girls Soccer Camp. It's a great set of a dozen ideas made easy to remember by the wonderful use of vivid language to highlight important concepts.

Body Position. You never want to be standing straight up, you should be **(1) in a knees-bent, focused (2) crouch (3) with one leg in front of the other**. You never want to stand square with your legs apart because you can be beaten to your left, your right, or through your legs. With the one foot forward you can **funnel the attacker to one side**. This also allows you to turn and chase quickly. You want to get your **(4) butt down**, lowering your center of gravity.

Movement. When the player makes a move, you want to **(5) move with the attacking player**. The critical thing when learning to defend is that **(6) your feet are in constant motion**. Every time the ball is touched or the attacker makes any move, you as a defender are moving and adjusting with them. The **worst defenders are like those with feet set in concrete**, more rooted into the ground than active. The **feet of the best defenders are like they're barefoot on blacktop on a 95-degree day**, in almost a **machine gun-like staccato** as they are adjusting to every offensive move. This keeps you active and allows you to move quickly and adjust to any attacking move.

Winning the Ball. (7) Select the correct time to step in—when opponent pushes ball too far out, or when support exists, or your goalkeeper says to **"step in." Never dive in unless you are _sure_ you can win it**. As soon as a player makes a mistake **(8) pounce on the ball _hard_**. Tackle for the ball like it is _behind_ the opponent's feet. Understand that **tackling isn't just a stab**. The initial contact is only **Stage One** of the tackle. **Stage Two** (which weak tacklers never figure out) is **(9) a fight for possession after the initial collision**.

Additional Defensive Emphasis for 1v1 Games. (10) Close the attacking player down _while the ball is moving_ by getting out of there quickly to _absorb the attack_, then slowing or delaying the attacker to your speed. **(11)** When you close the attacker down, get _eyes only on the ball_. Then **(12) try to funnel the attacker** either to the poorest shooting angle or onto her weakest foot (or if possible both) but in general close down opponents **away from the center of the goal**.

An Introductory Activity: Pressure Your Partner. In a 5-by-10-yard alley, a) Players pass the ball back and forth. When one stops the ball, the partner closes down to proper distance and in position to direct the dribbler one way or another. b) Passing back and forth, when one player lets ball run between the legs and turns after it the partner closes down and does not allow the turn. Introduce having the pressuring defender call *"Ball"* when closing down the attacker (see chapter 20, activity 57).

16 COMPETITIVE 1V1 ACTIVITIES

"The team that wins the majority of a game's one-on-one duels wins the majority of those games."

–Dettmar Cramer, director of the first USSF Coaching School

16.1 INTRODUCTION

There are scores of 1v1 activities. The ones that follow are loosely arranged from the easiest for the players to the most difficult. Some feature straight-up head-to-head duels while others are structured as games for teams of 3 or 4. Some are general-purpose activities; others focus on specific elements of the 1v1 situation. Collectively they will develop competency in those encounters, add to the fitness level of your players, and enliven your training sessions.

16.2 CONDITIONS AND CHALLENGES

There are many conditions and challenges a coach can apply, singly or in combination, to vary the pressure level of an activity. Some of the most common:

Space. The size of the area used is the first condition. Size matters a lot. As a general rule, *"If it's not working, the space is too small"* for the current skills of the players. But with too large a space the game becomes too easy or turns into more of a fitness exercise than intended. Note that an 11-by-11-yard box is 21% larger than a 10-by-10; 12-by-12 almost 50% larger.

Time. Women's National Team players playing **Top Gun** battle at full intensity in two-player duels for three minutes! Younger players will have passed out by then.[1] Most 1v1 activities carry a strong, game-like fitness component. So start with 30- to 45-second games and work up, figuring that a 90-second duel at U14 is a long one. Shorter games are used for intensity, longer (or shorter times between matches) for fitness.

---

[1] The body is marvelously self-protective; you'll pass out before you die.

CoachNotes

"Time favors the defense," and that is never more true than in a one-on-one situation. Attackers must play with a **sense of urgency**. (When that's not happening and the attacker is merely dancing with the ball instead of taking on the defender, one coach starts to call out, "one, two, three, four..." eventually saying, "That's how many defenders will be on you if you give them that much time.")

Illegal Moves. Using the inside of the foot in an attempt to power by an opponent and turning by drawing back the ball with the bottom of the foot are to be strongly discouraged because these tactics will be much less effective when players get older. Likewise, the coach can make certain moves off limits to the team or individuals if they become too dependent on them. The use of an illegal move can be made a **give-it-up** offense, where the ball must be given over to the opponent.

Designated Moves. When a **Move of the Week** is designated, for example, that move can earn an extra point if it leads to a score.

Mental Focus. Where cones are used as gates or goals, points are scored only for **clean goals** (i.e., where balls pass through the goals on the ground without touching the goal posts). Requiring that little bit of extra precision helps players to **think around the goal**.

16.3 KEEPING SCORE

Keeping score is important in developing the competitive mindset of players, particularly among those whose personal style is to be more collaborative than combative. These athletes can find it difficult to play hard against their friends during training sessions. They need to learn that *"It's OK to compete,"* and to understand that, *"You can't train one way and expect to compete in another."* At the very least, all players are expected to know the score of their game at all times. When they don't know their or their team's score, the score is 0.

Have players call out the score when they score a goal. This emphasizes that the activity is a competition and helps the quiet ones to develop their on-field **soccer voices**. It will also limit disputes when a game ends.

How often a coach *records* scores is a separate issue. At the highest levels of *the Game*, scores for every activity are often recorded (and results posted) since playing to win is at the very top of the team's priorities. With younger players coaches need to be more selective. Playing to win is not always compatible with playing to improve.

A **"Go-For-It"** mentality—trying new things, being bold, and taking risks—is the express lane to improvement and needs to be encouraged, no matter the inevitable failures and losses as a result along the way.

16.4 THE ACTIVITIES

Note: Not every variation is indicated for each activity. Mix and match conditions and challenges to serve your purpose on a particular day.

25   Cone Soccer/One-on-One Ladder

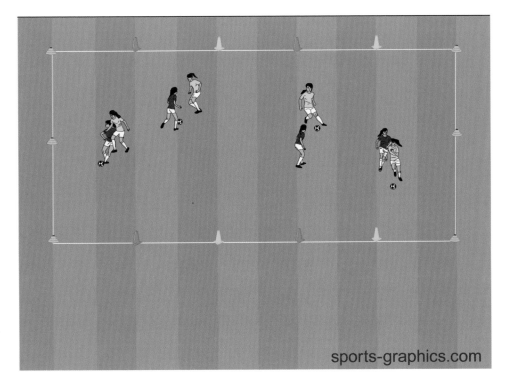

sports-graphics.com

Set two rows of cones 10-12 yards apart. The spacing between cones is 5 yards, with as many cones as there are players. (With younger players use pairs of cones to make the "goals" bigger and the game easier.)

In pairs, players will defend their cone while attacking the cone of their opponent on the other side of the 10- to 12-yard space. Start with a face-off at the midpoint between their target cones, each player with a foot on the ball. All pairs play at the same time. Games last 45 to 60 seconds. Score by hitting the opponent's cone with the ball. Balls are out-of-bounds if they go beyond the cones; there is no out-of-bounds sideways.

The winner is the player who scores the most goals, who scores last if the score is tied (comebacks are harder), or—if it's 0-0—who has possession at game's end. (Some add a 15-second **Golden Goal** period if there is no score at the time limit.)

At game's end, winners go to one side, losers to the other. All then rotate one position clockwise. It becomes like a tennis ladder. As players move up and down the ladder, some may play each other several times over the course of six to eight games. After the last game, players rotate, and then the coach records each player's place on the ladder. This is the starting point the next time the activity is used.

26 Many Goals Game

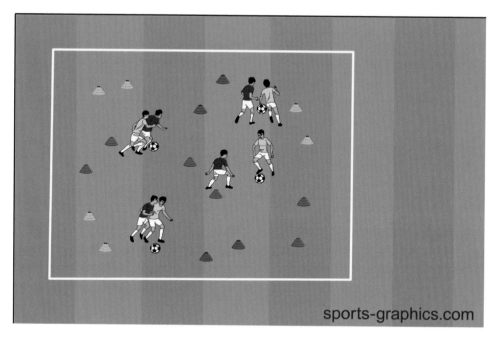

sports-graphics.com

This is a good game for players just starting to work on their dribbling skills. For older players, it is often used more as a fitness exercise than a contest of dribbling skills.

In a 25-by-25 area, place pairs of cones randomly to create at least as many goals as there are pairs of players. Goals are 4 to 5 feet wide. Make goals with differently colored pairs of cones if you have them. Start with players paired 10 feet or so from any goal, each with a foot on the ball. All pairs play at the same time. Play six to eight 45- to 60-second games, depending on age.

Players score by *dribbling* through any goal in any direction, (i.e., touching the ball on both sides of the goal without the opponent touching it or the ball touching the goal). Keep score out loud. Players may score multiple goals on a possession, but may not score through the same goal twice in a row.

Variations for older players: A player can only score through any goal once. Another variation: win by dribbling through two or three goals of the same color.

Scoring Variation: Because it is very hard to win a ball in this game once the other player has possession, give two points for each goal scored after a takeaway change of possession.

Comment: "Heads up!" The game requires vision to avoid the other pairs and to find the next goal to attack.

27 Shark Tank

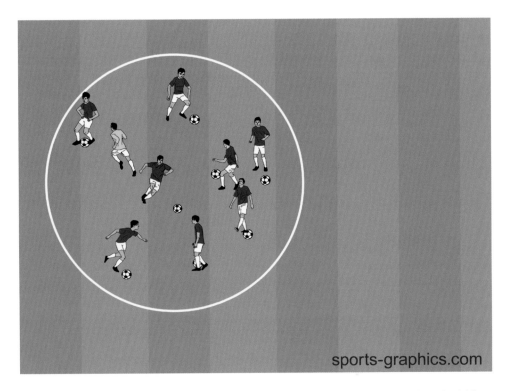

sports-graphics.com

Everybody plays Sharks and Minnows. Both of the following versions are played within a circle about 8 yards across.

Sharknado. Every player is a shark, has a ball, and must keep it in the circle while trying to knock out those of the other players. (If your ball goes out "by accident," too bad!) This can be played single knockout or where players can retrieve their ball and come back in (perhaps after performing some ball skill). In either instance, the winner is the one player left in the circle. The winner can be given an extra turn in the traditional Sharks and Minnows game.

Sharks and Minnows (see figure). Each player, one at a time, races the clock while attempting to dispossess the other players. But we've added a special challenge: once the shark goes after a target, the shark must stay after that minnow until the player's ball is knocked out of the circle. Give the shark 40 to 60 seconds to knock out as many minnows as possible. Sharks and Minnows is usually thought of as a game for little kids, but older kids still love it. It's one of those activities you can use to revitalize a training session that's not going well. And that "special challenge" makes the game more than a pleasant diversion.

28 See You Later (★★★★★)

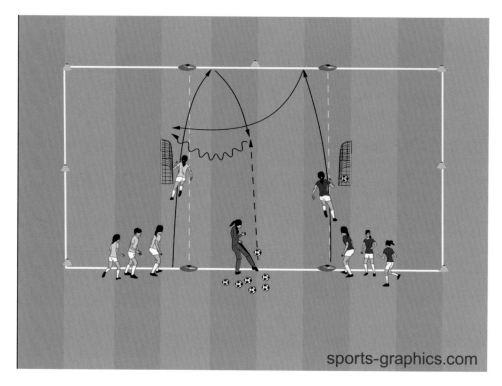

This game is often used to work on turns. It is played in a 10-by-20 grid, with two Pugg Goals (at ends, in middle as shown, or on a sideline). The coach stands at the midpoint on one side with all the soccer balls. Players are divided into two teams, one on each side of the coach. The coach plays the first ball into the grid as the first players from Yellow and Blue race across to the touch the other sideline, then back to win the ball and score. Players keep score out loud.

If the ball goes out of bounds, it's **"see you later"** for both players, and the coach plays in a ball for the next two. A player who scores stays on, touching the far sideline again before resuming play against the next opponent. The player who put the ball out of play— or was scored on—must fetch the ball and return it to the coach.

Another standard rule is that a shot that misses a wide-open goal costs the team a point. (In the same way that an open goal missed on Saturday is like giving the opposing team a goal.) We call this the Minus 1 rule.

Mantra: Coach: **"If I have an open goal..."** Players: **"I will score."** Coach: **"Fix it!"** Players: **"See the goal, see the ball, step** *(follow through the shot)***."**

In this and all "team" 1v1 games, it is important that the players start their turns without prompting from the coach. This demands their constant attention while waiting for their next turn. In this game, a player will sometimes jump the gun, coming on when it's *not* their turn (e.g., after a teammate scores). When that happens the penalty for the offender is a trip to the end of the line.

Variations: a) Players score to designated goals; b) players can score at either end; c) goals are placed back to back in the middle of the grid. In any scenario, the game is very well suited to work on turns.

Scoring Variations: a) A player gets 1 point for the first goal scored in an "appearance," 2 for the second, and so on. b) A player must do a turn before scoring a goal, must do two different turns (which can include the turn used for the first goal) before scoring the next, three different turns before the third, and four for the fourth. A player getting a "1" and a "2" in one appearance goes for "3" on the next. The game ends when the first player gets a "4."

Comments: This is a game they will play forever. Very high paced, it can be a great way to end a practice. It works just as well in 2v2 and 3v3 scenarios. If you have 12, 14, 16 players and no assistant, you can serve out a second or even a third ball to keep players from standing too long in line. It's chaotic, but games are like that. And it helps players to learn to keep **"Heads Up."**

29 1v1 Continuous (★★★★★)

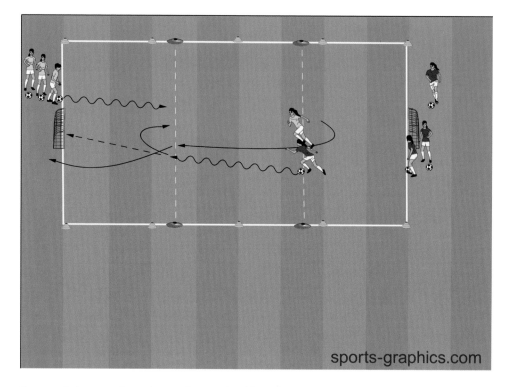

sports-graphics.com

Teams of three to four players line up beside 6-foot-wide Pugg Goals at either end of a 10-by-20-yard box. The first players from each team come out, one with a ball. All other players wait, standing with a ball.

In this game, a player stays on the field until the ball goes across the end line he or she is defending (whether a goal is scored or not, no matter who plays the ball over the line). As the ball crosses the end line the next player waiting at that end *immediately* dribbles out to take on the remaining player—if not getting a full breakaway. (No prompting from the coach; encourage a player who scores to steal the ball from the feet of an inattentive player and score again.) A player must be in the attacking half (or third) to shoot. Put cones at these points and refer to this as the **Pink Cone Rule**, no matter the color of those cones. Players keep the score out loud. If any player doesn't know the score, his or her team's score goes back to zero. This is another game that players will do forever.

Scoring Variations: a) Bonus points for goals that come as the result of the designated **Move of the Week.** b) Bonus points for a player's second goal (worth two points), third (three points), and so on, on a single turn. c) Point deducted for missing a wide-open goal (**Minus 1**). The coach or an assistant can also keep track of who scores and who is scored on.

Rule Variations: a) Both players go off if the ball goes out of bounds on the sides three times; b) any player using an **illegal move** must give ball to the opponent. Another variation uses the **chaos** challenge.[2] In this scenario, two games play through each other, intersecting in a 10-by-10 square. **"Heads up!"** Goals cannot be scored from that central zone.

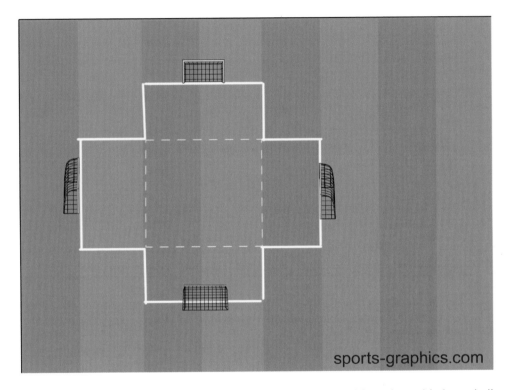

sports-graphics.com

The 10-by-40 Alley variation uses that much longer space, with each goal being a ball placed on top of a disc. When a ball goes out of bounds or beyond the goal, the coach plays another ball in and then a third. (A new pair comes on, though, if the third ball goes out of play without a score.) This grit-building variation is very much a fitness activity, not suited to younger players.

---

[2] Hat tip: Roby Stahl.

30 *Along the Line*

sports-graphics.com

This game and the following one are particularly useful when working on Turns and Stop-and-Go moves. Place pairs of cones 6 to 8 yards apart as goals, making the goals 3 to 4 feet wide. There will be two players per line, so make as many parallel lines, five yards apart, as you'll need for all the players. (This is a cone-intensive activity!)

Two players face each other between the goals, one either side of the line. One has a ball. The player with the ball will try to get the ball to either goal, "squashing the ball" there (not shooting it through) before the "defender" can get a foot into the same space on her side of the line. (**Coaching points for the attacker:** a) stay **sideways on** to the line to maximize the effectiveness of Turns and Stop-and-Go moves and leave the defender behind; b) keep the defender moving all the time.) If successful, the "attacker" must take the ball back to the midpoint before scoring again. Play on if unsuccessful.

The defender cannot cross the line or try to win the ball. (**Coaching points for defender:** face the line and move as much as you can, using shuffle steps; you'll be more easily beaten if the attacker can make you cross one leg in front of the other.)

All pairs play at the same time. After 40 to 60 seconds, players change roles. The winner is the player who "scores" the most (i.e., only the "attacker" can score). Play six to eight games in a tournament, ladder, or round-robin format.

Comment: The focus of the game is entirely on quickness and deception using turns and stop-and-go moves. It also does wonders for defensive quickness and footwork. This is a demanding game on both sides of the line.

31 Four-Goals Game (★★★★★)

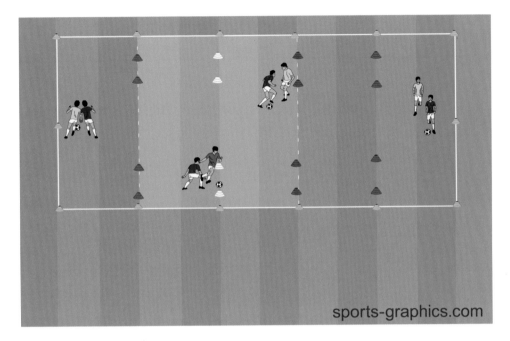

This game uses the same setup as Along the Line, but with an additional 3 to 5 feet of playable space added to each end of the line. In this game, either player can score by dribbling through either goal in either direction (i.e., four goals). The attacking player *must dribble through*, touching the ball on *both sides* of the goal, not just pass it through for a point.

The space for each pair includes those yards outside the goals between the adjacent lines to either side. So the Red versus Purple duel shown in the figure is being played in a 10-by-12-yard space, parts of which are also being shared with players in adjacent games. **"Heads up!"**

Players start in a face-off between the goals on their line, each with a foot on the ball. A player who scores keeps possession ("winners" in basketball parlance) and tries to score again. Going back through the same goal is OK, but the attacker must take the ball back to the midpoint before scoring again. Each game will be 40 to 60 seconds long.

This game has it all: quickness, poise with the ball, deception, the ability to use all three types of moves. When you do a full round robin with your team—over two days, of course—and keep score (3 for a win, 1 for a tie), you regularly end up with a ranking that accurately shows who's your top player, who's your least, with the others properly arranged in between. For that reason, the Four-Goals Game makes a great 1v1 activity for a tryout.

32   Box Game

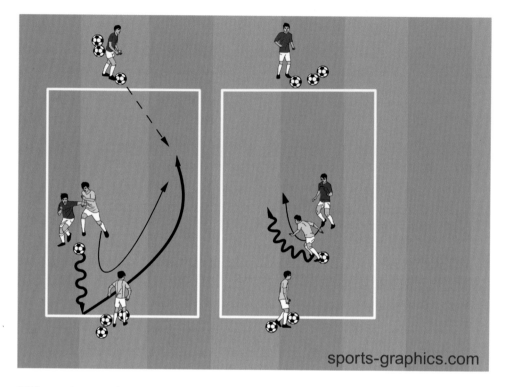

sports-graphics.com

Different 1v1 exercises are particularly good for specific elements of the 1v1 situation. In the Box Game, the focus is on individual defending (see chapter 15).

In a 10-by-15 box, players play 1v1, scoring when one player dribbles across the end line of the box. Each player also has a server on his or her defensive end line. (12 players = 3 games) The rules: When a player scores, he checks back **at an angle** to get another ball from the partner, usually receiving the ball with back to goal. When a ball is played out of bounds, the player who last touched it out will be the defender as a new ball is played in to the opponent by his teammate. A defender can attempt to intercept any ball that's being played in. Play for 45 to 75 seconds before the inside and outside players switch roles. The pair giving up fewer goals wins.

33 Top Gun

sports-graphics.com

Several one-on-one activities have this name. This one is adapted from a Women's National Team training session. It is the most intense and demanding 1v1 game of the twelve in this chapter: unlimited space, two players, one ball, one cone as the goal, score by hitting the cone.

What makes the game challenging are the conditions placed on the attacker and defender. The attacker must *always* be going for goal, not shielding, dribbling for possession, or dancing with the ball. The defender must *always* be trying to win the ball, not guarding the goal or merely trying to contain the attacker. When a ball is played past their "goal," both players must sprint after it.

This is a **"Go-For-It"** game, only played "all out," and the coach awards a goal to the opponent when a player fails to meet to those conditions. Coaches must be totally heartless about maintaining this level of intensity (e.g., awarding a goal to the opponent even when a shooter stops to celebrate scoring the goal).

The rules: In an unlimited space, place cones with "top hats" (discs) at least 10 yards apart, one "goal" for each pair of players. (Younger players: Use two or three cones together make a bigger target.) Games are 40 to 60 seconds long, but could be up to 20 seconds longer if the team needs extra work on intensity or fitness.

Players start with a face-off, each with a foot on the ball, 5 yards from their target goal. Then 1) *Both players must play the ball at all times*, trying to hit the cone with the ball. 2) Winners (i.e., the player who scores) keep possession until the opponent can win the ball. Award 3 points for a win, 1 for a tie. Because this game is all about competitive intensity, scores should always be recorded by the coach. Use this activity weekly if your team is always getting beaten to the ball.

34 Combat

sports-graphics.com

There are times when your team will come up against players (or teams) who play outside the rules. This activity can prepare your players to deal with it, particularly when you know that it's coming. **It is NOT designed to teach players to play outside the rules.**

Combat has been associated with former Women's National Team captain and coach April Heinrichs. You can see video of this activity on her *Training to Win* DVDs. The activity progresses through four variations:

1. **Push Combat.** In a 5-by-5-yard square, two players face off, each with a foot on the ball. At the signal, each player tries to win the ball. When one does, she must try to maintain possession by shielding the ball. (**Teaching points: "Shield sideways on,"** not with your back, getting low for leverage and keeping possession of the ball with the foot farther from your opponent.) The other player may use her hands or body to push her off the ball. If this player wins possession of the ball or pushes her opponent out of the grid (with or without the ball), the ball is now hers, and she must immediately protect it against the opponent's challenge. If a player knocks the ball out of bounds, she must retreat to the other side of the box until the ball is

brought back in. The player with possession at the end of 40 to 60 seconds wins. Switch opponents between games. Play three to five games.

2.   **Pull Combat** is next. Here players are allowed to pull their opponent off the ball or out of the square. Hair pulling is frowned upon, but other than that...

3.   **Anything Goes** isn't really, but the player without the ball is allowed to push *and* pull.

4.   **By the Rules.** Always finish with this. Here players are not allowed to push or pull. Most will discover that they're now much better at holding on to the ball under pressure.

In all instances, the player with the ball can be encouraged to **"use your hands"** against her attacker. But legally, not grabbing or pushing. Holding off the opponent with a hand or forearm low against the waist or hip will rarely be called as a foul in Saturday's game. An arm straight out from the body *will* be called.

CoachNotes
You will know this activity is being done with the proper intensity when the laughing stops.

Most players will love this game and want to do it often. A few will absolutely hate it. It is to be used sparingly, rarely more than once a season, and is best used when you know you'll be up against a very physical opponent or one that has been taught to play outside the rules (which we've seen, sadly, as young as U11.)

It is important to emphasize to the players—both at the beginning and the end of this activity—why you're doing this. It's not to teach them to play outside the rules but how to deal with those who only think they can win by cheating.

35 Battle and Shoot

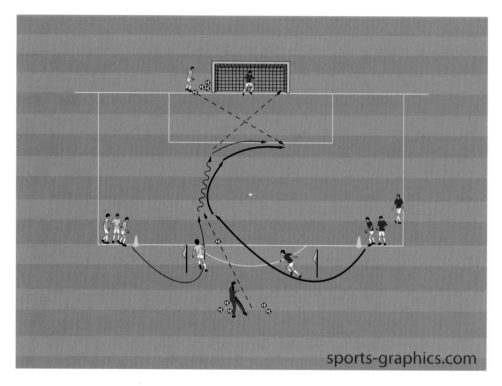

sports-graphics.com

Form two lines of players. On the coach's signal, the first player from each line sprints around the nearest flag or cone. The coach serves a ball. Players battle to win the ball and score. The player who did not shoot becomes the next goalkeeper.

Variation: As shown in the figure, after the first shot, a second ball is served out from the end line by the player who took the last shot from the previous pair. Players must retrieve balls after their turns and return them to the serving points.

36 The Squares of Truth

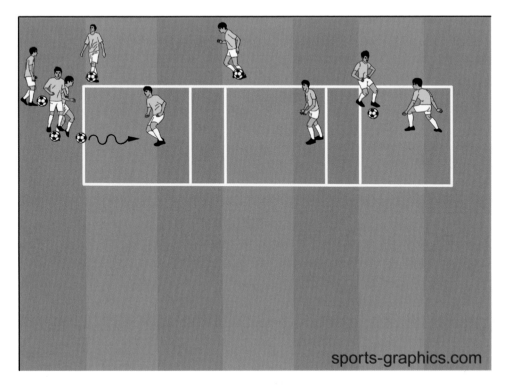

In this **"Go-For-It"** game, three 5-by-5 boxes are arranged in a line, with a 2-by-5 neutral zone between them. There is a defender at the back end of each box. The first attacker takes on the defender in the first box. If he beats that defender, he immediately takes on the next, and then, after beating the second, takes on the third. The first player to beat all three in a single turn wins the game.

If the first defender makes three stops (including balls played out of bounds) that defender joins the attacking line, the other two defenders move up a box, and that third losing attacker becomes the defender in the third box. If any defender steals the ball, the attacker takes over that box.

37   1v2 (★★★★★)

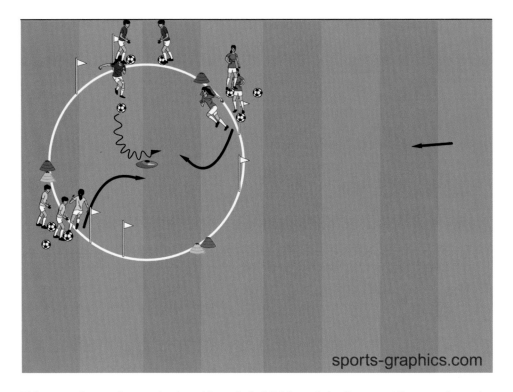

This very advanced game is played in a circle 15-18 yards in diameter. Three goals on the perimeter divide the circle into thirds, with a disc in the middle that serves as a *Pink Cone*. It will work with teams of three, but fours are better. Each player needs a ball to start and the game benefits if there are extra soccer balls available.

Attack Two Goals. Teams line up beside their goals. A player comes out from each team, one dribbling a ball. Players can score in either goal not their own. A player scoring checks back **at an angle** (see chapter 19, activity 53) beyond the pink cone to get another ball (and an **instruction**) from a teammate and then takes on two new opponents. Otherwise, if a ball goes out, it's **"See You Later"** for all three players, and the next ball is dribbled in from the line closest to the goal where the ball went out. Treat any goal scored with a **Pink Cone Rule** violation as if the ball has been played out of bounds: Everybody off.

Attack One Goal. This variation is more difficult (see figure on next page). Now each team starts from across the circle from the one goal where they can score. Again, a player who scores must check back beyond the pink cone to get a new ball and then to face two new opponents. Treat any **Pink Cone Rule** violation as *"See You Later"* for all three players; no goal, but allow the offending team to bring on the next ball.

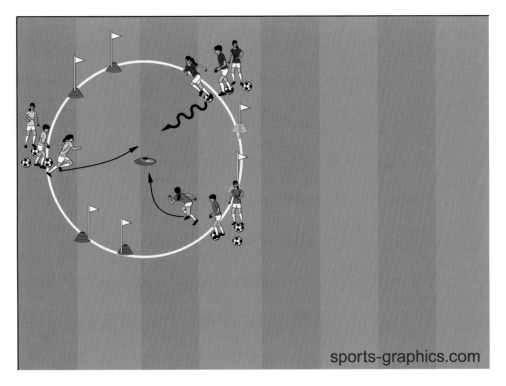

sports-graphics.com

Scoring: This game is so fast paced that keeping score is all but impossible. One way is to award the game to the team of any player who scores on each of the other pairs of players on a single turn. Another is to award the game when a player scores after a **Killer Dribble**, one that splits the defenders before the shot. A third is to award a loss if a team commits two **Minus 1 Rule** violations.

Comment: It's common for a team to run out of soccer balls. The three teams will have to work together to keep the game going. When all the balls have been scattered, though, it's *"Everyone get a ball."* The first team doing this gets to start with the ball once everyone is back.

16.5 FINAL THOUGHT

The cumulative impact over time of regular one-on-one play does not turn every player into a take-on artist—although it does for some. But it uniformly produces players who possess uncommon poise and confidence under pressure with the ball at their feet.

17 WARM-UPS AND SKILL BUILDERS

Fundamentals are always fundamental.

If dribbling and footwork exercises are the musical scales for soccer, skill-builder warm-ups are the instruments on which the notes are first performed.

17.1 THE WARM-UP SETS THE TONE

Training at its best takes place under a fundamental philosophy that *if you chase perfection doggedly enough you'll catch a healthy dose of excellence in the process.* This requires a learning environment that sets standards above the norm, constantly challenges the players' **comfort zones**, but also accepts, even welcomes, the mistakes that happen as the athletes learn to train at the edge of their game so they will play at the edge of their game.

Basketball's Stephen Curry is changing the way many athletes approach their pre-practice and pre-game warm-ups. His amazing routine (you can find it on YouTube) isn't just something he does to get ready for what follows. Rather it is a demanding arrangement of technical exercises—**deliberate practice** all—that pushes him to a) get uncomfortable, b) get intense, c) make mistakes, and ultimately d) get better.[1] (You can make a fine mantra to use at the beginning of practice from those four items.)

17.2 FIVE SIMPLE WARM-UPS

What follows are five basic warm-up exercises to be used for the first 15 to 20 minutes of a training session. Each shows just a few of the many variations a coach can use, and with sufficient intensity will easily get every player 1,000 touches or more on the ball. Once established, these activities should be used to make sure that all these hard skills of footwork and ball moves are reinforced and sharpened at *least every* two to three weeks.

There's also a good 20-minute pre-game routine that will further reinforce essential skills. Warm-up activities should always be used to provide lots of work with players' weaker feet, maintaining a 2:1 or 3:1 weak-to-strong ratio when possible. Players should also learn to perform their skills with **"heads up."** Coaches should always see **"eyes."**

---

[1] thetalentcode.com/2016/10/06/stop-warming-up-start-learning-up/.

38 Alleys

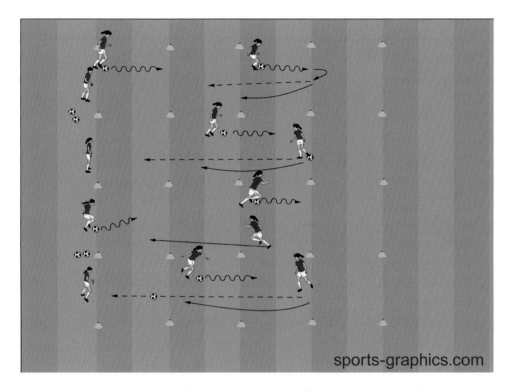

sports-graphics.com

Divide the team into groups of three. Each group will work in an alley 5-by-10 yards. To start, the first of the three dribbles across the space using a designated Dribbling foot skill (see chapter 12.2). Upon reaching the far end the player turns, passes to the next in line, and then follows the pass while calling out how many times the skill was performed. Where the foot skill uses just one foot to touch the ball, players take two to three turns using the weaker foot for each with the stronger.

Note that this is not a race across the space. The object is to have the most touches with a minimum of 10 to 12 repetitions of the foot skill per turn. Emphasize, in this order, 1) proper technique, 2) body control, 3) speed (more reps done faster). **"Do it right, then do it fast."** *Note that any warm-up with dribbling components can also use some of the* Advanced Foot Skills. (see chapter 12.2.)

39 Four Corners/Stars

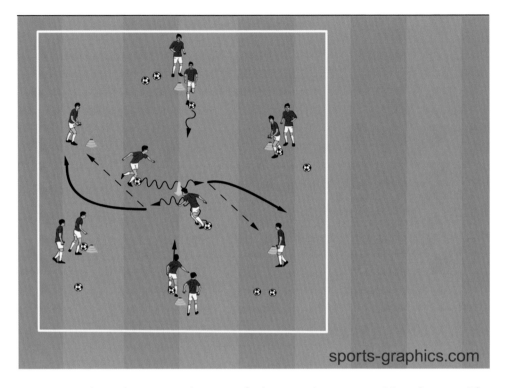

sports-graphics.com

Have two or three players at each corner of a box or point on a star 20 yards across. The first players from two groups opposite each other perform the Dribbling foot skill to the center of the space with good technique, pass to the next player at the opposite side, and follow the pass. The exercise moves clockwise; the next pair starts when the previous pair is halfway to the middle.

Now use the same exercise to work on ball moves. Players on opposite lines dribble directly at each other, perform the move the proper distance from the partner (**Three-Step Rule**), and pass to the next player at the opposite line. Specify the foot to be used (e.g., *"Scissors left, getaway right"*) to prevent collisions in the middle, and demand the two explosive getaway touches. Gradually have players increase the speed of their approach to the move.

40 Ladder

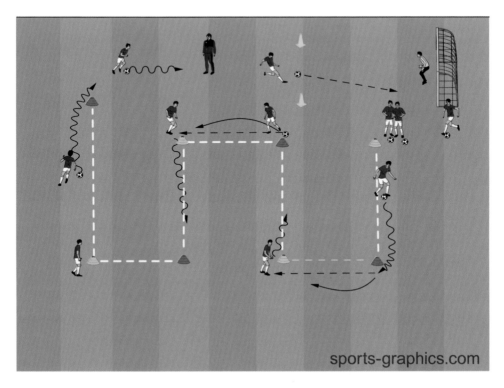

sports-graphics.com

Players perform a Dribbling foot skill from gold to red, pass "up the ladder" to the player at the next gold, and follow the pass. From the last red cone, the player speed dribbles back to the start, beating the coach with a move, and taking a long shot with the weaker foot, then following up by shooting any rebound.

Variations: a) Dribble across performing a designated ball move. b) Dribble across with a move, turn, dribble back including the same move, turn, cross again with that same move, and then pass. c) Use a Pull-Cruyff or Twistoff at the red corners before making the pass.

41 Partners and Pairs

Players are in pairs within a circle 20 to 25 yards in diameter. Each pair, A and B, have a ball.

1. **As** will perform as many repetitions of a Fast Footwork foot skill (see chapter 15.3) as possible in 15 seconds. Then **Bs** will try to beat the partner's score. Switch partners after each round. Again, note that any warm-up using Fast Footwork components can also use some of the Advanced Foot Skills.

2. **As** will circle as many **Bs** as possible with a ball in 30 seconds. Then **Bs** will try to beat the partner's score. **Variations:** a) circle with inside of foot, b) outside of foot, c) right foot only, d) left foot only, e) speed dribble to a **B**, pass between legs, speed dribble to the next **B**, f) as before, only **B** is opening, closing legs (use a Foundation Move or other designated Beater if closed). Switch partners after each round. Players in pairs on the circle's perimeter. The first player dribbles toward the center of the circle using a designated foot skill. At the center, the player turns, using a designated turn (see chapter 15.4). As the player approaches the center, the partner checks away then back **at an angle** as the first player turns, looks up, and passes with the weaker foot (Note: Insist on the **Step** at end of pass). The second player a) **goes to the ball**, b) with a **look**, c) receives, and d) begins using the foot skill toward the center while the first player returns to the starting point.

Good combinations to use: a) box and Cruyff (weak foot), b) cut-chop and figure 8, c) double cut/double chop and figure 8, d) roll-around and on-over turn, e) dribble cut and outside cut (weak foot).

42 The Scottish Circle

sports-graphics.com

Emphasize use of the weaker foot when possible. Divide the team into three groups and then scatter the players around the circle. Each player in the first group has a ball.

1. First group's players do 6 reps of a designated Fast Footwork foot skill and then do a Dribbling exercise to the middle, turn, explode back, and leave the ball to one of the outside players.

2. Fast Footwork, then Dribbling to the middle, ball move, explode away (two getaway touches), pass to a waiting player, and follow.

3. Now put the first group in the middle, as shown in the figure, the second and third—every player with a ball—around the perimeter. The central players go to and call for a ball from a perimeter player, make a return pass, and then sprint off *through the middle area* to get the next ball. Central players will work for 30 to 45 seconds. Groups switch on the fly. **Make it competitive:** See which team or individual returns the most passes.

Return pass **variations**: a) inside of foot push–pass; b) receive to outside, then pass with inside of same foot; c) take across the body with inside (or sole) of foot, then pass with the inside of opposite foot. Next, with the outside players serving balls **two hands underhand**: d) volley with inside of foot; e) return with a header; f) cushion the header and then pass back with the foot; g) chest then pass; h) head, chest, pass; i) juggle three touches, pass back; j) let the ball run through legs, turn, pass back.

17.3 BEFORE THE GAME

43 Pre-Game Warm-Up

Having a consistent pre-game routine—45 minutes in all is sufficient—helps players zone in on the game to follow. This 20-minute set of three exercises reinforces the most important components of the training regimen. It needs only a 20-yard square space, which can be useful if there's another game still on the field. Once the routine is established, the team's captains can manage the activity while the coach warms up the goalkeeper.

Use discs to set up a 20-by-20 square. Use cones to set up 5-foot wide "goals" along two of the four sides. Have four sets of four pinnies, one color per goal.

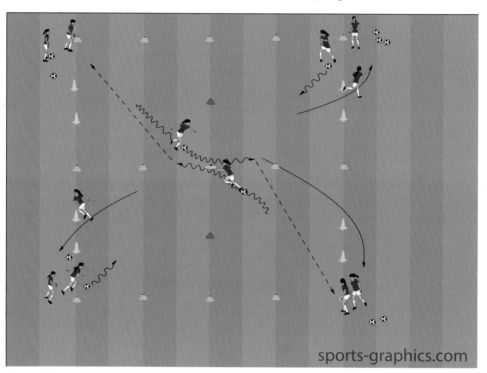

sports-graphics.com

1. **Fast Footwork and Ball Moves: Four Corners.** (See activity 39.) Players start in the four corners, stretch between reps. a) Facing pairs use a foot skill to the middle, then a turn, and pass back to next player from their corner. b) Facing pairs dribble to the middle, perform a designated ball move—including Moves of the Week—pass to the next player at the opposite corner, and follow the pass with dynamic stretching (5 minutes).

2. **3v1 and 3v2 in a Box.** (See chapter 20.1.) Use two, three, or four boxes depending on the number of players. a) Regular. b) Five-Touch Rule. (7 minutes)

3. **1v1 Continuous.** (See chapter 16, activity 29.) (Pick up the red discs.) Two four-minute games. Keep score. Second Game: Winners versus winners and losers versus losers. Loser of "losers game" collects cones, discs, and pinnies. (8 minutes) (Use Back-to-Goal Continuous (see chapter 19, activity 53) if the team has begun to train the Back-to-Pressure scenarios.)

By now the team should be able to take the field. Use the remaining time to complete the pre-game routine with finishing runs (see chapter 21, activity 66) or a keep-away game. You will also need a warm-up routine for your goalkeeper. Use at least half of it to reinforce technique. **Do not ruin the keeper's preparation by having the team pepper the goalkeeper with dozens of close-in shots (even if you see most of the other teams doing it).**

BUILDING BLOCKS OF

TEAM PLAY

18 ORGANIZING FOR TEAM PLAY

What's on this page covers what are called the Principles of Play for soccer. While you might pass some of these ideas on to players as they reach the U12 to 14 age, we include this mostly as a lesson in soccer vocabulary. Note that each **attacking task** has a comparable **defensive task**.

18.1 SPACE—OPEN FIELD, NO BALL, NO DEFENDER, NO ATTACKER

Dangerous Space—Behind the goalkeeper (in the goal), behind the defense (especially a "flat" defense), between the midfielders and defenders.

Use a **Pass to Space** as the final pass in Creating the Easy Goal (see chapter 21). Another example of a Pass to Space is a Pass to the Corner Flag for a wing forward to run on to the ball.

- On Offense, we want to try to Exploit Space (take advantage of it), particularly Dangerous Space.

- On Defense, we want to Deny Space, particularly Dangerous Space and Space Near the Ball.

18.2 OFFENSIVE TASKS—TO EXPLOIT SPACE

Penetration—The person with the ball gets it into space by dribbling or passing. Passes can go through, over, or around the defense (although we rarely use "over" yet, since we want to keep the ball *"On the Ground."*)

Support—The players near the one with the ball who can get the ball in one easy pass. If possible, there should be Support to either side. There should always be *Support Behind the Ball.*

Width—Attacking players two or more passes away who are looking to **Exploit Space**. These players are often used as targets when a penetrating pass is used to go around or over the defense.

Mobility—Players making runs to Unbalance the Defense. These runs can be used to try to **Get Behind the Defense** by a Run Into Space, or to **Create Space** with a Run Off the

Ball which pulls a defender away and creates space for a teammate. Checking back to a ball is a run into space that also creates space.

Creativity—The ability to mix dribbling and passing and to use a variety of Combinations to get the ball up the field.

- How a team does these things defines its Attacking Shape.

- Always keep in mind the What If Moment: What happens if we lose the ball?

18.3 DEFENSIVE TASKS—TO DENY SPACE

Pressure on the ball to stop penetration.

Cover—To back up a player who is putting Pressure on the Ball while also being able to Pressure the Supporting Attacker if a pass is made.

Compactness—Getting a lot of players around the ball to provide Pressure and Cover, also to Deny Dangerous Space. We want to Double Team in All Directions.

Balance—Tracking runs by attackers into Dangerous Space, especially in the penalty area, but not getting pulled out of position by Runs Off the Ball being used to Create Space.

Predictability —Forcing the attacking team to move the ball in directions the defenders choose - using the *Angle of Pressure*, the *Positioning of Covering Players*, and choices about *Which Runs to Track* and which to let go.

- How a team does these things defines its Defensive Shape.

- Always keep in mind the What If Moment: What happens if we win the ball?

19 TWOS

"...or with the help of a teammate."

—Mantra of the Two-Way Player (Part II)

In a 2v1 situation the attackers have six ways to beat the defender. Five utilize both attackers: **Blind Side Runs**, **Overlaps**, **Takeovers**, **Wall Passes** (the give-and-go), and **Posting Up** on the defender. Then there is the **Individual Option**, which is something not only to be allowed but encouraged in a **"Go-For-It"** culture.

When? There's no rush to get this done. If Saturday's game is in a 4v4 or 5v5 format, it's too early to focus on this since they're still mostly playing 1v7 or 1v9. U8s have learned to use wall passes in games, but the learning would have come quicker if the coach had waited until U9.

19.1 THE TACTICS

44 2v1 to the Line I

Posting up is an element of playing back to goal (see chapter 21). In this exercise, we will look at the other four ways to beat a defender with the help of a teammate. In each scenario, the important elements include a) visual cues, b) the technique of the exchange, c) timing, and d) communication.

Set a 10-by-20 box for each group of three players with two attackers wide at one end. The defender is 6 to 8 yards from that end. For each scenario, the pair will attack five to eight times, then change the defender. The attackers start by passing the ball back and forth as the defender adjusts but does not try to win the ball. The object of the exercise is for one of the attackers to stop the ball on the opposite end line. *(Restart the next repetition from whichever end line is closer.)*

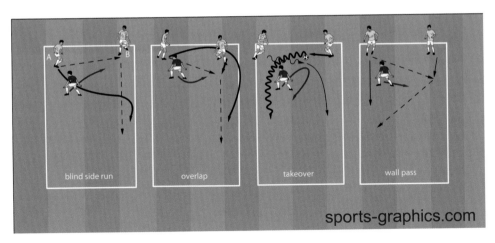

Blind Side Run. After a pass (diagonally slightly back to draw the defender in), the passer (**A**) runs diagonally behind the defender for a return pass. That pass goes *straight down the line*; it's a pass to space for the teammate to run on to. The blind side run goes close enough behind the defender to be within arm's reach. If possible, player **B** takes two touches, the first toward the defender, the next the pass down the line, preferably with the outside foot.

Visual cue: B is slightly behind **A. Communication:** It's visual, not verbal since **B** can clearly see A's run. A is calling for the ball with the movement.

Overlap. After a pass (slightly forward), the passer (**A**) overlaps **B** who makes a return pass to space straight down the line. Again, **B** should try to take a touch toward the defender to freeze the defender in place and be encouraged to use the outside foot for the pass.

Visual cue: B is slightly ahead of **A. Communication:** A calls out *"hold"* when running behind **B** so that **B** will hold the ball, then *"going by"* as the overlap happens.

Takeover. A dribbles square toward **B**, using the foot farthest from the defender. To avoid collision, **B** runs by **A** so that **A** will be between the defender and **B** during the exchange. As **B** gets to **A**, **A** steps off the ball and toward the defender, leaving the ball for, not passing it to, **B**. Player **A** also has the option of keeping the ball. In either case, both players explode away from the exchange and turn up the field.

Visual cue: A dribbles toward B. The **communication** is visual: whether or not A steps off the ball and into the defender.

Wall Pass. B is at an angle 30 to 45 degrees ahead of A and almost square with the defender. A passes to B and then runs straight down the line for the return pass. The return pass should be one touch with B planting the foot away from the incoming pass (and pointed to where the pass is to go), then using the inside of the near foot to push pass the ball back to A. Footwork at the wall is important. Players will want to use their stronger foot, and for some it feels more natural to pass with the away foot. But there's a huge difference in balance when passing with the nearer foot and that has a significant impact on the accuracy of the return pass.

Visual cue: B is ahead, square with the defender. **Communication:** *"and go"* as A passes the ball and sprints forward.

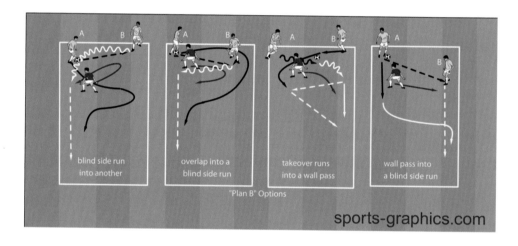

Plan B. Sometimes B will not be able to play the ball back to A. On a Blind Side Run, Overlap, or Wall Pass, B should dribble square as A makes a Blind Side Run behind the defender. The best Plan B for an unsuccessful Takeover is for the other attacker to check back, to set up a Wall Pass.

45 To the Line II

Once all four options have been trained, make the activity into a competition within the groups of three. The attacking pairs get X attempts to beat the defender using each of the four 2v1 options.

Variations: a) Attackers get six attempts using any of the four 2v1 options *or* the individual option, but may not use any of the five methods more than twice. b) In 15-by-20 space, using teams of two, the attacking team goes against each defender three times with 10 to 15 seconds to beat the defender to the line.

Keeping score: a) Attackers earn two points for each ball stopped on the line, one for success using a Plan B option. A defender earns two by winning the ball. No points to anyone for a ball kicked out of play. b) Assign points based on difficulty of tactic used: blind side run = 1, overlap = 2, takeover = 3, wall pass = 4.

19.2 THE WALL PASS

Perhaps because a give-and-go happens more suddenly, its impact on a defense tends to be disproportionately larger than that of other 2v1 tactics. For that reason, wall passing is not just a tactic, but rather an essential skill. But it is one insufficiently taught to or used by youth players.

CoachNotes

Of the four 2v1 tactics, the wall pass is the most difficult to learn. It takes two passes to complete, which is why it's also called a give-and-go or a 1-2 pass. The blind side run, overlap, and takeover each need just one.

It's common to teach the four 2v1 tactics in the easy-to-hard order presented here. But a case can be made for starting with the wall pass, even with younger players who are just learning to solve the 2v1 situation. Here's why: The wall pass requires vision and the ability to read the game, both to set up the defender to be beaten and to have the wall in the proper position. By teaching the wall pass first, players will develop their vision and movement skills at the same time. It takes a little longer, but this approach has been used successfully with players as young as U8.

---

46 Wall Passing 1, 2, 3

There are several good exercises for developing the technical, hard skill elements of the wall pass.

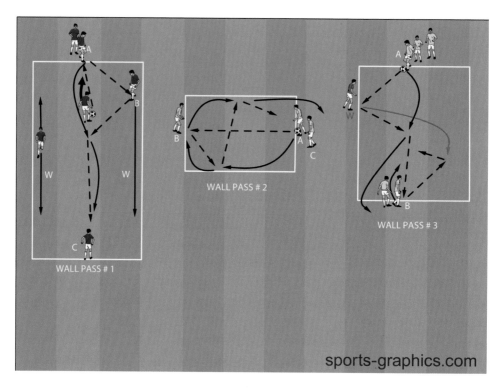

Wall Pass 1. (★★★★★) To start **B** passes to **A** then steps forward and stops in front of **A**. **A** makes a wall pass around **B** using either wall player, sprinting blind side by **B** (so that **B** cannot see both **A** and the ball). On receiving the return pass, **A** passes long to **C** then sprints forward and stops in front of **C**. **C** makes a wall pass around **A**, sprints blind side, passes long to **B**, and so on. The "walls" constantly move back and forth to be in good *"OPEN"* supporting positions. Start with two-touch play—except at the wall which should be one-touch whenever possible. (But **don't turn one bad ball into two** just to attempt a one-touch pass.) **Variation:** Use the outside of foot for the "give" pass to add a bit of deception.

> **CoachNotes**
> Be aware of a tendency for all passes at the wall to be with a player's dominant foot. Correct, balanced footwork at the wall has a significant impact on the accuracy of the second pass. The "wall" player should plant the away foot with that foot pointed in the direction the pass will go, then push with the nearer foot. Reaching to use the away foot provides a less balanced platform for the pass.

Keeping score. Once players can get this activity into an all-one-touch rhythm, make it a contest between two groups. The winner is whichever team completes the longest string of one-touch passes in 3 minutes (plus "extra time" for a string started before the time limit.) Demand precision: start a new string any time a) there is *"wrong foot"* footwork at the wall, b) when a player runs ball side after the "give" pass, c) when that player fails to stop in front of the next passer, or d) a poorly played pass.

Wall Pass 2. A passes to **B**. **B** plays a wall pass off **A**, then passes to **C**. **C** plays a wall pass off **B**, then passes to **A**, and so on. Since this is done in a relatively small space it's a good activity to have players use the outside of the foot for first the pass of the give-and-go combination.

Variations: a) Two-touch (except at the wall), b) one-touch only, or c) vary the distance.

Wall Pass 3. In teams of four or five, **A** completes wall pass with **W**, passes to **B**. Now **W** moves for a wall pass from **B**. (*Note: **W** stays as the wall throughout.*) The game ends when all **A** and **B** players are back to their starting points.

Variation (shown in figure): **A** completes wall pass with **W**, who passes to **B** as **W** overlaps **A**. With two teams, the game ends when all a team's **A** and **B** players are back to their starting points.

Focus on body position and footwork of the players at the wall: sideways on, planting the away foot, passing with near foot.

47 2v2 With Outside Help

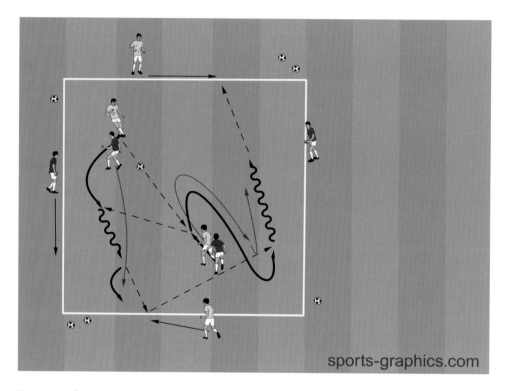

sports-graphics.com

Two two-player teams occupy a box or square. The four players on the outside of the rectangle are neutral players. Passes between neutral players are not allowed.

Variations: a) Add a neutral player in the middle, b) 3v3 or 4v4 in the middle, or c) limit the touches of inside/outside/neutral players. *In this activity, the outside players are normally limited to one touch.*

Keeping score: A team scores by completing five consecutive passes. **Scoring variation:** The scoring sequence must conclude with a one-touch pass to an outside neutral player followed by a one-touch pass back in to a different attacker.

Variations: This activity can be played to goal with or without keepers. More: a) with one teammate from each team on each touch line (these outside players can move anywhere along the line, but opposing outside players may not defend), b) with both outside teammates on the opponents' end line, teammates must combine off of one of those players (with a wall pass or the return pass to the third man) before a shot, or c) used to train the wall pass, awarding one point for a wall pass using outside help, three points when it's done by two inside players without the outside help.

48 2v2 versus 2v2

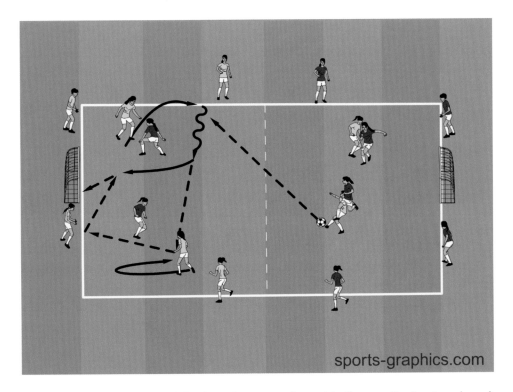

sports-graphics.com

Use two 18-by-18 squares, joined at the center line with Coerver Goals at each end. 2v2 in each box, with one pair designated as the attackers. Each team has two to four supporting players outside its attacking end. Supporting players are limited to one touch. Change the middle players every 3 to 4 minutes.

When a defender wins the ball, she passes to a teammate in the other end. (**Six-Second Rule variation**: A point for any ball won back before the pass to the other end.) a) Limit the number of *passes* in the attacking end. b) Limit the number of *touches* 1) in the attacking end, 2) by the shooter, or 3) both. This activity can be played with or without goalkeepers.

Variation: Allow the long shot from the defensive end—worth two points.

Scoring options: a) Bonus point for a score with the weaker foot, b) bonus point(s) for use of blind side run, overlap, takeover, wall pass, or c) bonus point for each successfully executed back-to-goal play (see chapter 19.4), passer calls the situation, receiver reacts appropriately.

Variation: Add a neutral player who switches ends a) as an attacker or b) as an extra defender.

49 Wall Pass Keep-Away (★★★★★)

Use a 30-by-30-yard space or larger. Play 6v6 or 5v5 with two neutral players. Emphasize setting the defender up (**"pick on a defender"**), getting the walls (support players) to either side of the ball, and clearing the space behind the defender for the return pass. Players will also be learning to figure out when the play is **on** or when it's **not on** and when a longer pass to reset things might be a better option. It helps at first if the neutral players already know how to create and use wall passes. Use older players or perhaps another coach, if available, in this role.

Keeping score. A team scores by completing a wall pass around an opposing player. The pass at the wall must be one touch.

Once players are achieving some success in this activity, there are a number of ways to modify the game or the scoring: a) having two balls in play (shown in figure), b) calling out (*"didn't look"*) an opposing player who did not **look before receiving** (the Rule; see chapter 14.2) means that player must leave the game until either team scores, c) apply the same penalty when an opponent just *gives* a ball away (*"giveaway"*), d) award bonus points for when a lost ball is regained in under Six Seconds, e) bonus points for a pass made with the same touch that steals the ball (pass the steal). And always, it is **Game Over** when pass the steal becomes the first pass of a successful give-and-go.

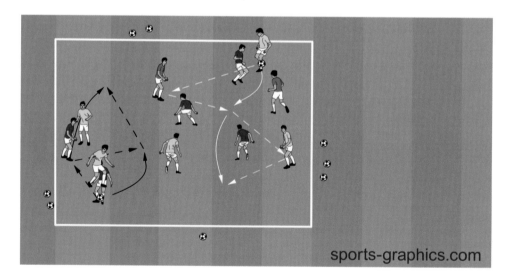

sports-graphics.com

The Double Wall Pass. This should be a **Game Over** moment in any practice activity. It comes in two versions, both shown previously: a) **A** to **B** to **A** to **B**, where a pair of teammates complete two wall passes in three touches, and b) **A** to **B** to **A** to **C** to **A** where a player combines with two teammates in four passes.

19.3 GAMES FOR TWOS

50 Down and Back

This is an adaptation of a common basketball drill. Use a 15-by-25 space with a Pugg Goal at either end and cones set to indicate that the Pink Cone Rule is in effect.

Keeping score: Players earn a point for involvement in any attack that ends in a goal. The pace of this activity makes scorekeeping difficult, so have players call their teams' scores out loud after each point earned.

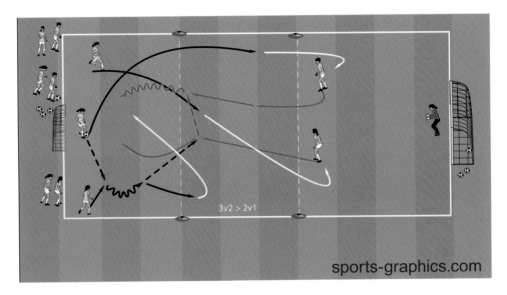

2v1 to 1v1. Two players attack one defender using a) blind side runs, b) overlaps, c) wall passes, d) takeovers, or e) players' choice. If one of the attackers scores (or misses or gives up possession), that player becomes the defender in a 1v1 back the other way. The partner becomes the defender who will face the next 2v1. The 1v1 segment ends when the ball goes out of play or is won by the new defender.

3v2 to 2v1. (Shown in figure.) This is a larger version of the previous exercise. Use a 20-by-30 space (longer if using a goalkeeper), with a mini Coerver or futsal goal and a keeper at one end and a Pugg Goal at the other.

Three players attack toward the large goal against two defenders. If one of the attackers scores (or misses, or gives up possession), that player becomes the defender in a 2v1 back the other way, while the teammates stay to become the defenders in the next 3v2. Emphasize attacks where the players don't just stay in their lanes, but instead use blind side runs, overlaps, and wall passes.

51 Speed Gates (★★★★★)

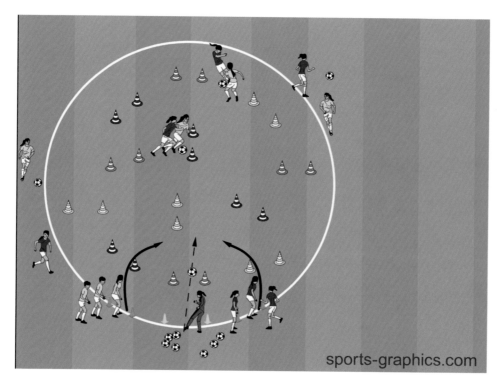

sports-graphics.com

This progression (which players love) becomes a wonderful exercise in problem solving on the fly. You can easily spend up to 30 minutes with this activity. Keep score of each part separately, or use the different scoring values in a single game of many parts. There are far more challenges available in this activity than the examples that will be given. In a circle at least 20 yards across, set pairs of cones as 4 feet wide gates. Use cones of different colors to make four gates each of three different colors.

Two teams line up to either side of the coach, with all the soccer balls at the coach's feet. The coach plays a ball in as players enter the playing area through the closest gates to either side.

1v1. (1 point to the team for winning a duel) A player scores by dribbling through a gate, touching the ball on each side of the goal line without the ball touching either a cone (a clean goal) or the defender. a) Dribble through three gates of the same color, with the opponent playing to a different color and b) dribble through three gates, one of each color. Play for the pair ends if the ball leaves the circle. The winner, or a player who puts the ball out of bounds, returns the ball to the coach. Have two or three pairs dueling at the same time. This requires players to keep their **"heads up"** in addition to reducing time spent standing in line.

2v2. A pair wins (worth 2 points) a) by dribbling through three gates of the same color, with the opponents playing to a different color, b) when each player on the team dribbles through one gate of a color and then completes a pass through a third gate of that color, or c) when teammates each dribble through a gate of a differing color, then complete a pass through a gate of the third color. Again, two matches can be going on at the same time. *In variations where both teams must score in gates of more than one color, a gate where there has been a score becomes off limits to the other team.*

3v3. To win (3 points), a) two players of a team dribble different gates of the same color and complete a pass through a third of that color to the third teammate, b) two players dribble different gates of two colors, complete a pass to the third teammate through a gate of the third color, or c) players can construct a challenge.

4v4. To win (4 points), a) the team completes passes through two (or three) gates of the same (or different) color(s), b) three players dribble through gates of one color, complete a pass to the fourth player through the fourth gate, or c) two players each dribble through a gate of one color and their teammates complete a pass through a gate of the third color.

At the 3v3 and 4v4 levels, the problem-solving and decision-making challenges are massive. If you smell something like an electrical fire, it's from brains overheating. This is an activity that produces the scrunched-up-face look that comes with total concentration.

52 Four-Goal Progression (★★★★★)

This summary activity has a succession of 1v1, 2v1, 2v2, 3v1, 3v2, and 3v3 situations for players to solve. It is another variation of the 1v1 Continuous game, only now there are two Pugg Goals set wide on each end line. The Pink Cone Rule is in effect. The exercise is to be played at a furious *"Go-For-It"* pace. It is also used to encourage bold or outrageous attacking by individuals or teams.

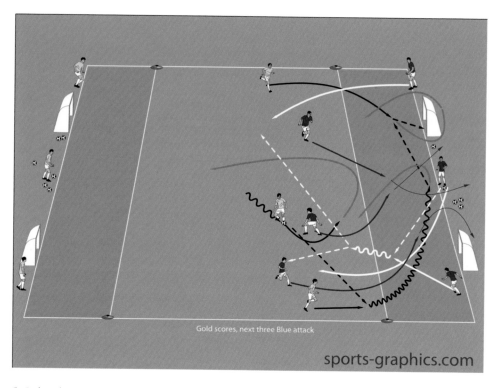

Gold scores, next three Blue attack

sports-graphics.com

1v1. (20-by-25 playing area) Players end up with tons of breakaways. When a player gets one, make him or her do some **Ronaldo Ball** (see chapter 15.5) to toy with the chasing defender. Two or three pairs can be playing at a time. When a ball crosses the end line, the next attacker comes on to take on the closest opponent.

Gamesmanship: When a ball crosses an end line, the next attackers must attack immediately. If they don't—maybe they're not paying attention—defenders are allowed and encouraged to steal the ball off that next attacker's foot and score. *Award double points for this.*

2v2. (20-by-30 playing area) The player who puts the ball over the end line must run around one of the goals at that end before becoming a defender (and around *both* goals if he has not scored). This creates 2v1 situations as the ball goes in the other direction. The next pair of attackers starts from outside the goals to create width. They attack with a *"sense of urgency"* to exploit the 2v1 situation before the chasing defender gets back. Both attackers must touch the ball before the pair can score. (A defender winning the ball, however, should immediately counterattack and can score without the teammate touching the ball.) Attackers can earn bonus points for completing a wall pass or changing "lanes" by means of coach-specified overlapping, blind side, or takeover runs. *Goals scored where players have not changed attacking lanes earn no points.*

3v3. (Shown in figure; 25-by-30 playing area) Attackers start from three lines, one in the middle, one outside each goal. The ball starts in the middle with a pass and the passer's movement to change lanes. Diagonal movement of players and the ball is encouraged; do not allow attackers to stay in their lanes.

Now when the ball goes over the end line: a) If it's a score, the scorer must run around that goal before defending, leaving teammates facing a 3v2 situation; b) if it's not a goal, the two partners must each run around a goal, leaving the shooter facing a (well-deserved) 3v1.

Keeping score: This game is often played using Outrageous Soccer scoring. This rewards clever, creative, and especially outrageous play with the ball, play that demonstrates **spontaneity and daring.**

Scoring: 1 point for something that makes the coach go **"Oh,"** 2 for **"OH!,"** and 3 (or more) for an **"OH MY!"** A score of zero is also possible, but points can be awarded for clever play that does not result in a goal. **Game over:** any move that breaks an ankle (puts a defender on the ground with a ball move). After just a few minutes of this activity players will be shaking off the chains of safe, conventional play.

19.4 PLAYING BACK-TO-GOAL

Players often find themselves in back-to-goal (or back-to-pressure) situations as a ball comes their way. How to handle that situation will depend upon the proximity of the defender and how aggressive the defensive pressure is. In any scenario, the importance of a **look** cannot be overstated. What follows is a very simplified progression for training players to deal with pressure from behind. While the focus will be on turning a ball toward the goal when there's pressure from behind, the basic ideas and skills apply in any situation where pressure is coming from behind.

CoachNotes

This progression is based on the one taught at the North Carolina Girls Soccer team camp. Girls teams with strong skills at the end of their U14 year (and U13s with exceptional skills) will enjoy the camp's training environments, particularly those where the challenge is to use those skills against teams a year or two older.

---

53 Back-to-Goal Tactics

In this activity players will learn to deal with three levels of defensive pressure from behind: a) light, where there will be time to *"turn"* with the ball, b) closing, where there's still time to receive the ball and turn it to *"face"* up against the opponent, and c) raging, where the opponent will be *"man-on"*, rarely more than an arms-length away and closing hard. Players who stand and wait for a ball to arrive often discover that the pass never gets there, having been intercepted by a defender. Even a *"look"* may not save you here. So the first habit that should be in play is to *"go to the ball,"* checking back not directly but *"at an angle."* This does three things. It starts the process of turning the body in the direction you'll want to take the ball. It makes the look easier. And it creates space to use when receiving the ball.

CoachNotes

Space is defined as an open field where there's no ball, no attacker, and no defender. An attacking team will want to create space for a pass or dribble with movement designed to draw opposing players away from some piece of the field. Other examples include the finishing runs of the Easy Goal patter (see chapter 21.2), clearing the space behind a defender for a wall pass and getting out of the way of a dribbler headed to the goal. A common movement pattern will have a player check into space to show for a ball, not get a pass, and then clear the space for a teammate to show.

Meanwhile, the passer should read the situation and give an instruction to the receiver—*"turn"*, *"face"*, or *"man-on"*. But that instruction never removes the receiver's responsibility for having a *"look"*, preferably two—one early on when checking back and the other just before receiving.

In a *"turn"* scenario, there's little or no defensive pressure. A proper pass will be to the receiver's farther, upfield foot as the player gets sideways on to control the ball and turn it upfield. If the pass is perfectly weighted, it may be possible to let the ball go by and simply turn and follow. In a *"face"* situation, there's still time to receive the ball and turn it while getting faced up to the opponent. Again, a proper pass will be to the receiver's upfield foot and be collected across the body. Quick use of a ball move can then beat a closing defender. In a *"man-on"* situation, defensive pressure from behind is close and immediate. Here the pass will be to the front foot so that the receiver's body can stay between the defender and the ball. Three ways to defeat this pressure are 1) by raking the ball across the body with the receiving foot and exploding away (the **man-on turn**; see chapter 15.4), 2) the MacMillan Move, using the outside of the receiving foot to touch the ball behind the defender, then spinning off by the defender's other side (a back-to-pressure version of the Foundation Move), and 3) the **double pass**, a wall pass variation where the receiver returns the pass then spins off behind the defender for a second ball.

Training, In Twos. Pairs of players, one with a ball, start at opposite ends of a 12-by-20 rectangle. They'll play against an imaginary defender. One player checks back *"at an angle"* (all the way to the side of the box) to get open for a pass from the partner. The receiver looks once at the beginning of the checking run, again just before receiving. The passer gives an instruction based on the "phantom defender's" pressure and passes to the receiver's correct foot. The receiver plays the ball with the appropriate technique, taking it back to the end where she started. Now roles reverse. Train each scenario separately: a) light pressure (*"turn"*), b) closing pressure (*"face"*), c) raging pressure (**man-on**), and then d) mix it up, where the receiver must react to the passer's instruction.

Training, In Threes. Now there are two players at one end: an attacker and a defender. The attacker checks back *"at an angle"* as before, with the defender applying the level of pressure appropriate for the technique being trained. Once the attacker receives the ball, turns it, and is taking it back to the end, he checks into the defender and then back *"at an angle,"* becoming the attacker as the former passer now takes the defending role. Train each scenario separately, as before. When training scenario b) the receiver needs to get faced up with the first touch then quickly use a ball move to "beat" the (passive) defender. When training d) the defender decides the pressure; the passer must read the game and give the correct instruction.

54 Back-to-Goal Continuous (★★★★★)

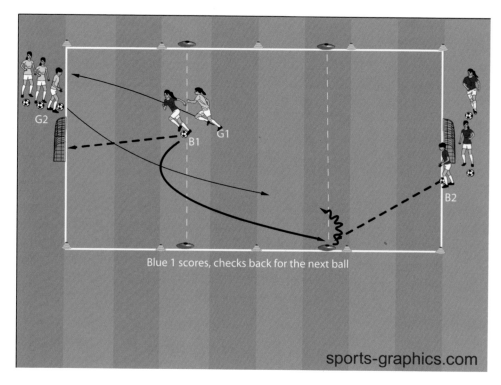

Blue 1 scores, checks back for the next ball

sports-graphics.com

This variation of the 1v1 Continuous activity (see chapter 16, activity 29) removes the unopposed break-aways from that game, creating more opportunities for face-to-face individual attacking and defending. It is also a superb exercise used to train attackers in the back-to-pressure situation.

To start, Blue 1 sprints out past the halfway line, then checks back at an angle to receive a pass from Blue 2 as Gold 1 applies defensive pressure. Blue 2 must read the defensive pressure and give the correct instruction; Blue 1 must *"look."* **Blue 1 scores** and checks back *"at an angle"* for another ball from Blue 2 as a new defender (G2) comes on. (If Blue 1 had played the ball across the goal like without scoring (*"minus one"* if it was a wide-open goal), Gold 2 would race out to the halfway line then check back as Blue 2 comes on to defend and Blue 1 chases down the ball.) If Gold 1 wins the ball in the original duel and scores, she will check back for another ball from Gold 2 as Blue 2 comes on as the defender.

Attacking players check back to the ball *"at an angle,"* both to create space to use with the first touch and to be able to receive the ball *"sideways on."* The player should also *"look before receiving,"* maybe more than once, to recognize the level of pressure that's coming.

The passer should always *"give an instruction"* to the receiver based on the level of inbound defensive pressure—although the instruction is no substitute for the *"look"* by the receiving player. When there's no pressure, the player can *"turn"* onto the ball as it goes by. When pressure's coming, the player receives the ball while turning to *"face"* up to the defender. Finally, when there's full *"man-on"* pressure, beat the defender with the man-on-turn, a MacMillan move, or by using the passer to execute a double pass.

Those not in the play or next in line will need to be retrieving soccer balls. If every player brings a ball to the training session, teams of four or more will be needed so that there are enough soccer balls for the activity. This activity also works 2v2, with both players checking back to get the next ball. **The Rule** (see chapter 14.2) must be enforced. Any player who does not look can be called out by any player on the opposite team. Penalty: The ball is dead, defender checks back for another ball.

55 Turning Series Game

This high-paced activity is similar to Outside Help (see chapter 19, activity 47), but now the outside helpers are assigned to a team. Blue goes north to south; Gold goes east to west.

Playing 2v2, 3v3, or 4v4 in the middle, players pass to an outside teammate at either end. That player passes to any other central teammate, giving the correct instruction for the receiver to turn the ball toward the other end. The outside player exchanges with the one who made the pass outside. The outside player is allowed two touches. For an even faster pace, make it one. Award points for a ball successfully turned based on degree of difficulty of the turn: 1: **Turn**, 2: **Face**, 3: **Man-On**. A MacMillan Move is a **Game Over** moment.

Variation: Opposing middle players are paired up in a must mark condition, where each can only mark the other.

20 POSSESSION IN 3S TO 6S

"Everything that goes on in a match, except shooting, you can do in a rondo."

–Johann Cruyff

A **rondo** is a small-sided keep-away game played in a limited space where the attacking players outnumber the defenders. Rondos are used to develop the ability to possess the ball under pressure. At higher levels of play, most rondos are structured to replicate game situations that happen in specific parts of the field. Our focus will be more general: foundational exercises for developing possession skills. Over time, the pressure will be gradually increased by modifying the size of the grid, by changing the number of touches required of the player with the ball, by adding defenders, and by changing the ways a defender can win the ball.

20.1 3V1 AND 3V2 IN A BOX (★★★★★)

These two exercises introduce the main ingredients of possession play. They should be used regularly both to sharpen the fundamental skills of possession and to set the table for more advanced possession games.

Two Basic Rules

1. Players must **take two touches or more,** no one-touch play (although there will be some exceptions when we add defenders).

2. The ball must be played **out from under the feet** (not "killed" at the feet) with the first touch—a **first touch away from defensive pressure**. Again, there's an exception, when a ball is so poorly served that stopping it with the first touch is the only option.

Violations of either rule result in a turnover, but *only if the defender(s) recognize it and make the call*. This forces the defenders to think and be aware, not just chase the ball. In these basic activities, the player called out also becomes the "monkey in the middle," a defender instead of an attacker.

Activity Management

1. The player in the middle has a scrimmage vest in hand.

2. The first pass is always free (i.e., the defender must allow the ball to be *passed*, but doesn't have to allow the ball to be *received*).

3. Maintain the pace of the activity by having the player winning the ball drop the vest and immediately make the next "first pass."

4. The new player in the middle must pick up the vest before defending.

5. Follow this rotation if you have an extra player: The player who loses the ball goes out (and readies an extra ball to play in should it be needed); the outside player picks up the vest and becomes the defender.

56 3v1 in a Box

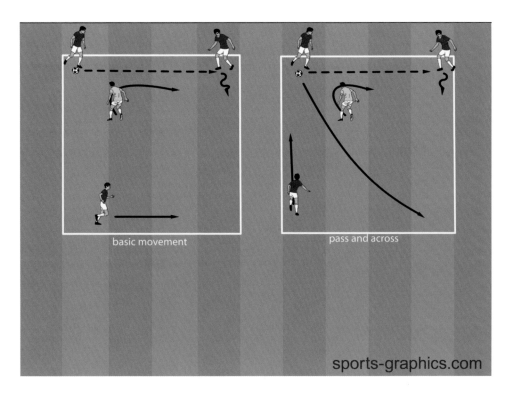

basic movement

pass and across

sports-graphics.com

In a 10-by-10 grid, three players combine passing and dribbling to keep the ball away from the fourth player.

Support. The attacking players start in three corners of the box, the players without the ball creating a triangle by supporting in the corners nearer to the player with the ball (not in the corner opposite). The supporting players stay as wide as possible so that they are **not just** open **for a pass, but** *open*. With each pass the triangle resets so that the player with the ball always has support to either side.

Responsibility. Players will sometimes make a **blind pass** to where a teammate *should* be, but is not. If that ball goes out of play, the *passer* goes to the middle. *The player with the ball is responsible for what's done with it*, no matter what a teammate does.

Four Levels of Defensive Pressure.

1. **Light pressure:** The defender is essentially passive, putting only token pressure on the ball. This level is used to introduce the basic movement pattern of the attackers. Players rotate through the defensive spot.

2. **Medium pressure:** Defender(s) can do everything but touch the ball. They can win possession three ways: by forcing a pass out of bounds or calling *"one-touch"* and *"killed it"* violations.

3. **Full pressure:** The defender can now win the ball a fourth way, by **squashing it** under the foot (stepping on the ball.)

4. **Ultimate pressure:** Sometimes in 3v1 play, the attacking players get so good at keeping possession that just touching the ball wins it.

The Five-Touch Rule. Players must touch the ball at least five times before passing. This adds a 1v1 element.

Five-Touch teaching points: A dynamic first touch **away from defensive pressure** is essential. **Keep the ball moving** and avoid getting "triple teamed" in a corner by the live defender and the two boundaries. Even with this movement, in five touches the defender will be there: **"use your 1v1 moves"** to get free to make the pass. When the player with the ball dribbles toward a teammate, the teammate should make a takeover run (filling the space vacated by the dribbler), instead of trying to back out of the way. *Takeovers are allowed on any touch.*

The Progression So Far.

1. 3v1—light pressure.

2. 3v1—medium pressure.

3. 3v1—full pressure, **"squash it to win it."**

4. 3v1—five-touch, medium pressure (defender can also "win" the ball by calling out an attacker taking fewer than five touches.)

5. 3v1—Five-touch, **"squash it to win it."**

6. 3v1 – ultimate pressure, **"touch it to win it."**

7. 3v1—five-touch, **"touch it to win it."**

Reading the Game. This activity can build the bad habit of **coca-cola passing** where the passer "stops to have a cold one" after playing the ball. To correct this problem the next step in the progression is what's called **pass and across**. Now the player who passes the ball moves to the corner opposite. This requires the third attacking player to move to the corner vacated by the passer. Develop this using the same progression of 7 steps listed previously but also including:

8. 3v1—pass and across, medium pressure.

9. 3v1—pass and across, **"squash it to win it."**

Teaching point: Make sure the passer gets **sideways on** from the middle of the run across the box, never losing sight of the ball because the next adjustment may be needed before that run reaches the far corner.

Pass and Choose. Once players have some mastery of pass and across, allow the passer to choose whether to pass and support or to pass and go across. The third attacking player must now read the passer's form of support and react accordingly. This is always played as:

10. 3v1—pass and choose, **"squash it to win it."**

WCPGW: Some players will make a pass, take a step like they're going across, then switch to support. Others will pass, then hesitate like they're supporting, then go. This confounds the third attacker's ability to read the game. Whatever the passer does, it must be immediate and decisive.

57 3v2 in a Box

This activity uses the same general ideas and progression as the 3v1 exercise (e.g., five-touch, pass and across, pass and choose, read the passer's movement.)

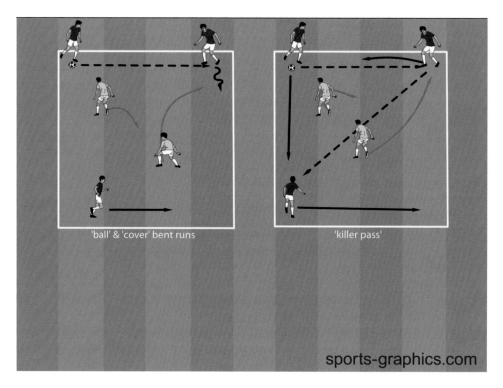

'ball' & 'cover' bent runs   'killer pass'

sports-graphics.com

Killer Balls. Players still *"take two"* (touches or more) although a pass that splits the defenders, the **killer pass**, can be on any touch, and a takeover can happen at any time. Especially in the five-touch scenario, players should be encouraged to *"Go-For-It"* by splitting the defenders with a **killer dribble**.

Defending With Two. Defenders work as a team. That's why the defender who has been in the middle longer "drops the vest" even if the partner actually wins the ball. Initially both defenders will often chase the ball. This leaves the supporting players wide open (as shown in the figure) and makes killer passes and dribbles much easier. Instead, one defender needs to pressure the ball while the partner provides cover. When the pass is made, the second defender now pressures the ball, bending the approach just enough to pinch off the gap between the defensive pair. Meanwhile the first defender steps back and toward the ball, switching into the covering role. Until the rotation becomes natural, it can be useful to have the defenders call *"ball"* and *"cover"* as they switch roles.

In the End. The long-term goal (it will take two to four years depending on the age and touch of the players) is to be successful playing *"3v2," "five-touch," "pass and choose,"* and *"touch it to win it"* in a 10-by-10 box. This is more difficult than it sounds, but players who can do this will be able to possess the ball under extraordinary pressure. They may still *give* a ball away, but they'll have so much poise and confidence with the ball that they'll rarely have it *taken* away. Imagine what it's like when all a team's players have this skill.

20.2 VARIATIONS WITH THREE ATTACKERS

The remaining eight possession activities generally go from easiest to most challenging, although most offer a lot of versatility in terms of degree of difficulty. All are designed as competitions so you can keep score. Grid size will be important to the effectiveness of these exercises: change as needed. Note that many of the variations given for one exercise work in others as well.

58 Adjacent Boxes

This pair of activities introduces possession in more dynamic environments that require enhanced problem-solving skills.

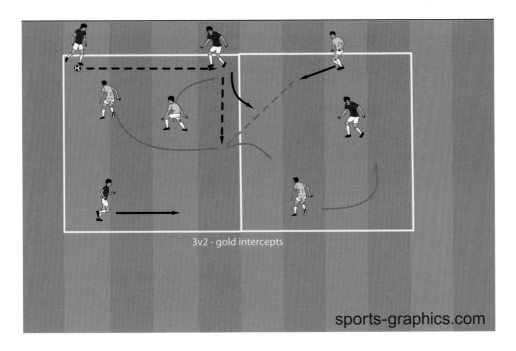

3v2 - gold intercepts

sports-graphics.com

3v1 In Adjacent Boxes. Two teams of three—3v1 in 1 box, the one player's teammates in the other—occupy adjacent 10-by-10 squares. (At first, the squares may need to be larger.) The one player must win the ball, pass it to the teammates in the other box, and follow the pass. The player who lost the ball becomes the defender in the adjacent box.

Variation: Allow a defensive second player in after a certain number of completed passes.

Keeping score: The attacking team earns a point for every certain number of passes completed without a defender touching the ball. Defenders earn a point if the player winning the ball completes a pass to a teammate with the touch that gains possession, what we call **Pass the Steal**.

3v2 In Adjacent Boxes. (Shown above.) Two teams of four: 3v2 in one box, the two players' teammates 2v1 in the other. When the two defenders in the first box win the ball, they must pass to one of their teammates in the other box. Whoever makes that pass follows it into the adjacent box, as does the player who lost the ball. Defenders in the adjacent box will need to maintain width and be ready to check to the ball.

Variation: Use the Five-Touch Challenge.

Keeping score: Same as 3v1.

Variations: Attackers earn bonus points for a killer pass or killer dribble, also if they can win the ball back before the defenders pass to the adjacent box.

59 3v3v3 Neutral Zone

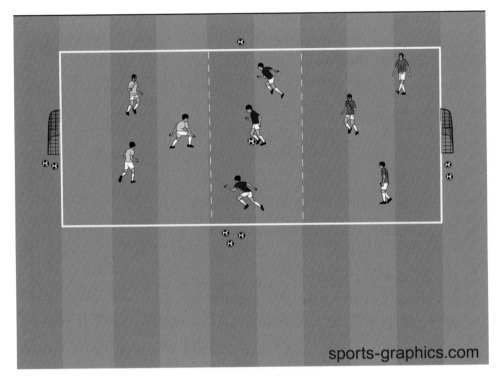

This is a 3v3v3 continuous game. Team Blue attacks team Gold, trying to score. Team Blue tries to win the ball and get it into the neutral (center) zone, then attacks team Red. If a team scores, they get the ball and attack the team waiting at the other end.

Variation: The attacking team can defend back into the neutral zone when they lose possession. That would have Blue chasing Gold in the scenario shown.

60 Four-Box Game

sports-graphics.com

Divide a 20-by-20 square into quarters. There are two teams of four, one player from each in each box. A third team (Red), divided into two pairs, will be neutral players. Using one pair of neutral players, play 3v1 in one box. When the one player wins the ball, it is passed to a teammate in another box, who is then joined by the second pair of neutral players. The game is played in three four- to five-minute segments, with each team taking a turn as the pairs of neutral players.

Keeping score: A point is awarded for four passes completed within a box, but all three attackers must touch the ball. When a point is scored, the ball is immediately played to a teammate in another box. **Game Over** happens when a team scores in succession (i.e., without losing possession) in all four boxes.

This is a great game for so many different aspects of the game: **vision**, switching point of attack, third-man running, combination play, short and long passing, body position for receiving, support, defending.

CoachNotes
In youth soccer, much of the communication among players on the field consists of players repeatedly calling the name of the player with the ball in an attempt to get a pass from that player. The most common result for the caller is to attract the attention of a defender. If possible, players should **call for the ball with their movement.** Avoid name calling. If not where the player with the ball can see a supporting teammate, communication should be in the form of an instruction sandwich. "Back, Sam, Back" will be much more effecting than, "Sam. Sam! SAM!"

61 6 (2 In) versus 3

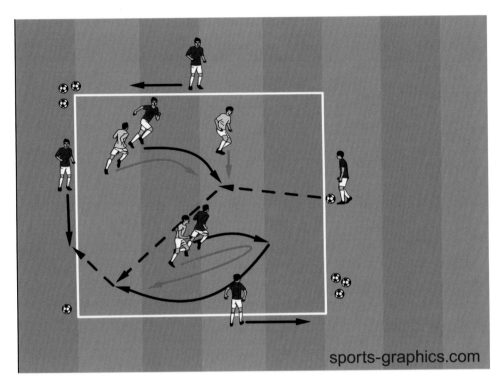

sports-graphics.com

Four players outside the boundaries of a 15-by-15 square have two teammates inside the square against a team of three. The six-player team seeks to play the ball from one outside player to another through *both* of the inside players. The defenders try to win the ball and keep it away from the two inside opponents. If the two players regain the ball, they then reset by passing to one of the outside players. Play a four- to five-minute game, then switch players into different roles and play a new game.

Keeping score: The team of six scores by playing the ball through the central pair with each of those two touching the ball. The team of three scores by completing four passes in succession, with a bonus point for each killer pass and three for a killer dribble.

62 3 in the Middle

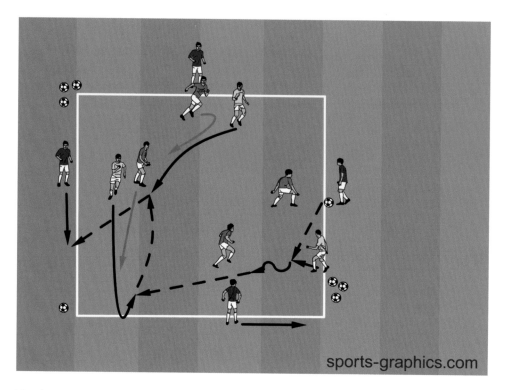

Youth teams commonly play their strongest players centrally. This rondo is used to take advantage of that concentration of ability and build an attack that goes through the middle.

In a 20-by-20 square, three central players (Gold) play "numbers down" against four defenders (Red). A second team of four players (Blue) is spaced outside each side of the square. The object of the exercise is to move the ball from one outside player to another through the central players *without the defenders touching the ball*. The central players must complete a pass among themselves before passing to an outside player.

Keeping score: The central and outside teams earn three points for a sequence that moves the ball through the central players from one side to the opposite side (as shown in the figure), one point for a sequence that moves the ball from one side to an adjacent side. Defenders can earn a point in two ways: 1) for every three passes completed after a ball is won or 2) for completing a pass from the first touch as the ball is won (pass the steal). The central attackers can also earn a point by 1) winning back a lost ball within 6 seconds or 2) passing-the-steal to another central player.

Scoring Variations: a) a bonus point for any team in the middle completing a wall pass, b) a bonus point when all three central attackers (or all four defenders) touch the ball without it being touched by the opposing group in the middle.

Play for four to five minutes, then have the defenders and the outside team change places. Note that 20 minutes of this demanding activity will usually be more than enough for the three central players.

Variations: As competence develops, use additional challenges (singly or in combination) to ramp up the demands on the central three: a) make the space smaller, b) require two* or three passes among the central players, c) require that the pass to an outside player be a one-touch ball, d) limit the outside players to one touch, or e) require outside players to pass back to a different central player.
(*Make two passes the minimum requirement as quickly as possible.)

When the central players are regularly succeeding at this activity, change the playing space to a pentagon and add a player to both the defending and outside teams. The central players are now 3v5. Attacking points can only be earned by sequences that go across to the farther sides of the pentagon (not to the adjacent sides.)

20.3 4S AND MORE

63 Three Teams Game 1 (★★★★★)

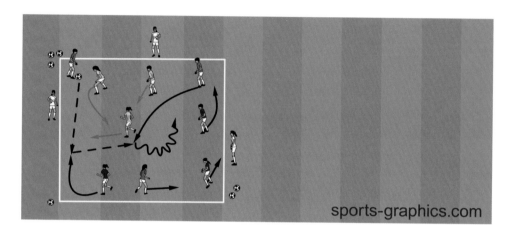

sports-graphics.com

Three teams, each in a different color scrimmage vest, play 3+3 v 3 (up to 6+6 v 6), using a square 20-by-20 or larger. One team defends as the other two play keep-away. When one of the attacking teams has lost possession three times, including balls played out of bounds, that team becomes the defending team. (The "times lost" score of the team remaining as attackers resets to zero.)

Variation: Defenders who win a ball and complete three passes switch roles with the team that gave up the ball

Useful **variation**: Provide rest—and ball retrieval—by having a fourth team (as shown in the figure) which will also keep track of possessions lost by attackers. This team rotates in as defenders when the current defenders become attackers. The three that would have otherwise become the defensive group goes off.

While this activity is good for developing the ability to find the killer pass, it's even better suited to help supporting attackers find and exploit seams in a defense. Have the attackers position themselves on the perimeter of the space. A player farther away from the ball checks into the central area for a pass. If the ball is played in, the receiver plays it back out to a different attacker. If it's not played in, the player vacates the space and a different teammate looks to find a seam. Players love this game.

Keeping score: Score one for the attackers if they complete five consecutive passes. Score one for the attackers if they can regain a lost possession in six seconds or less.

Variation: To encourage the **"Go-For-It"** mentality, have players earn a **free pass** for their team, worth one lost possession, with a killer dribble.

64 Three Teams Game 2

sports-graphics.com

Create three teams, each in a different color scrimmage vest. Red and Blue play 3+3 v 3 (up to 6+6 v 6), within a square 20-by-20 or larger. The defending team, Gold, wins the ball by touching it, immediately joining the team that did not last touch the ball (Blue) to continue 3+3 v 3 against the team that lost it (Red). Attackers try to split defenders with a pass or dribble or to pass into the defenders' triangle. This activity is a staple of training in Spanish football. It is useful for developing movement of attackers without the ball, notably that where teammates create then fill space.

Variations: a) Limit (or mandate) the number of touches per player, b) limit the number of consecutive passes among three players in the same color, or c) add the Ronaldo Ball challenge (see chapter 15.4, activity 22) where players must use a move or foot skill before passing if taking more than one touch.

Keeping score: Play for three to five minutes. A team loses two points each time it becomes the defending group, two more if they are the defenders at game's end.

Scoring variations to earn points (mix and match) attackers must: a) complete five consecutive passes, b) complete a pass into and then to a different teammate and another back out of the center of the defense, c) complete a killer pass (a point to both attacking teams), d) do a killer dribble (at least two points, but only for that attacker's team), e) pass the steal: when a defender wins the ball, pass to a teammate with the same touch (worth at least two points.)

20.4 THE BEST GAME EVER

65 Breakout Game (★★★★★)

The ultimate possession game for training sessions would be one that could be adapted to every possible game-related scenario. This activity comes close. It can be used in numbers from 4v4 upwards, with or without neutral players, in a wide variety of spatial configurations.

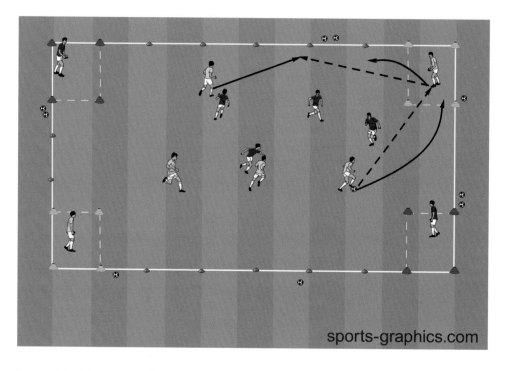

sports-graphics.com

In a 20-by-30 space (adjust as necessary), teams play 4v4 in the middle zone with supporting teammates as target players in boxes at both ends of the playing area. Pass to a target player and switch with that player. If playing with a neutral player, that player cannot play the ball into a target player.

Keeping score: A point is earned by working the ball from one target box into the other, then back into the middle zone *without the opponents touching the ball*. The target player has one touch to break the ball out of the back into the middle zone: (choose one) **a)** by a pass or dribble, **b)** only by a pass – completion of the pass scores the point, **c)** only when both the pass into *and* pass out of the target box are one-touch (so that there's an "assist" to every ball played to the target.) **Note:** The target player cannot return a pass to the one who played the ball in, nor play a ball to the team's target player at the opposite end.

Comment: The greatness of the Breakout Game is in its versatility. It works with numbers in the middle from 2v2 (*very* challenging) up. It is a game of fast combinations, ideal for working on wall passes, takeovers, overlaps, blind side runs, and three-player combinations. It is a game of quick transitions between attacking and defending, but also one to learn when an attack is **on** or **not on**, when to pressure defensively or back off. It presents lots of "back to pressure" situations. It requires great vision (those who fail to **look before receiving** are doomed!) and anticipation, especially on the part of the target players. It can be configured long or wide (the latter to train how to switch the field or to work on creating the easy goal; see chapter 21.5) That athletes will play the Breakout Game *forever* is just a little bonus.

21 CREATING THE EASY GOAL

Organizing attacking play in the penalty area turns every player into a goal scorer.

21.1 INTRODUCTION

Perhaps you've noticed how little attention so far has been given to the kind of tactical organization that will be needed on the field on Saturdays. This chapter addresses the one significant exception to a technically-focused training regimen. It's a way to produce enough goals to give a team a chance against all the teams that spend most of their practice time on team organization. (It also generates enough goals to keep parental pressures about wins and losses at bay until superior skills start to make the difference on game day.)

21.2 AN EXPERIMENT

Every team has a "least likely" goalkeeper, the player who is helpless and hopeless in that position. Put that player in the goal. No other defenders. In a manner similar to what is shown in the figure in activity 66, set three lines of finishing runners about 25 yards from the goal. Add a fourth line of players wide, each with a ball. These will be the servers.

The first player on the outside line dribbles a ball to the corner then serves it to the middle. The first runners from the three lines try to finish the cross. One touch only. Do 12 repetitions. Note how many goals are scored.

Now repeat the exercise with the team's best goalkeeper in the net. Only this time, the server **turns the corner** and **dribbles end line** to the **deep cross spot** (where the side of the goal area meets the end line) before crossing **on the ground** for the finishing runners. Ask the runners to bend their runs away from the play to come from the keeper's blind side. Do 12 repetitions. How many goals are scored this time?

Typically, the first scenario produces, at best, one or two goals. The second: five or more. This simple exercise makes an important point: You will score a lot more goals with some organization around the goal. With a little more organization and some repetition, it's possible to score goals by the bucket load.

This is called **Creating the Easy Goal**. It is based on two simple ideas: 1) Instead of serving a ball from the corner, the wing player beats the defender, turns the corner, dribbles along the end line to a specific spot, then crosses on the ground, while 2) teammates make finishing runs to the near post, far post, and penalty mark. There's some skill involved—you need strong 1v1 players on the wing—but it's mostly about organization: getting to the right place at the right time.

CoachNotes

What follows is how this works when teams are playing 11-a-side. Much of it can be applied in the 9v9 and 7v7 formats, and some of the most basic ideas will even work in 3v3, 4v4, and 5v5 games.

21.3 ORGANIZING THE BOX

Blue, Red, and Yellow

In an 11-a-side game format, there will three finishing runs coming from the **weak side**—the side of the penalty area away from the ball. All will go on the far side of the "D" (the penalty arc). This should draw defenders away from and create space in front of the goal. It will always make it difficult for defenders to track both the attackers and the ball.

The first finishing runner to reach the penalty area makes the **near post**, or *"blue,"* run. (We use the colors as **"sticky note"** verbal shortcuts.) Optimally, this runner is the far side wing player, making a sprint that goes across the corner of the penalty area, across the corner of the goal area, to the near (to the ball) post. This player's first responsibility is to make sure the keeper doesn't scoop up the cross. (Nothing freaks out a goalie more than having an attacker come from behind and nip in front as the ball arrives.)

The **far post**, or *"red,"* run is second and loops in behind the blue run to the back post, looking to find the back side of a gap between defenders that the cross can come through. Most goals come from this run. This player is also responsible for preventing any cross from going all the way through the goal area.

The **middle**, or *"yellow,"* run is third and looks to find an open spot in the vicinity of the penalty mark. In youth soccer, this player will almost always be unmarked.

A. 1. RESPECT THE "SHOOTING CONE".
no shots from outside its borders, especially on the flanks !!!

B. 2. OUTSIDE PLAYERS MUST "TURN THE CORNER" ...
beat the defender with a good move
leave her behind with an explosive change of pace then a touch inside,
   accelerating to *"FULL SPEED"*

no cutbacks !!! (these allow the defense extra time to get back,
   to think and to get organized)
serve balls from the corner only as a last choice

3. ... *"DRIBBLE FULL SPEED"* TO *"DEEP CROSS"* SPOT ...
"panic the defense" by going as hard as you can: allow no time to think
draw defenders to you and away from the front of the goal
take the extra touch if it's there (this will *really* make opponents panic)

4. ... "AND CROSS ON THE GROUND."
send a ball that's easy for the finishers to handle (like you'd want to get)
cross through the gaps (or seams) in the defense - you are crossing to
   <u>space</u> not to a person (**"Pass to Green"**); finishers must find the ball
big gap = softer crossing pass; small gap = firmer crossing pass
no crosses to the keeper !!!

C. 5. FINISHERS NEED *"GOOD POSITIONING,"* ...
three runners: **near** post (*"blue" – don't let keeper get the cross*),
far post (*"red" – don't let the ball go through*)
and middle (*"yellow" – the one who's always open*).
stay out of the "no-fly-zone" !!! Any shot off a cross here will be weak.
Also, you'll be in the way (and so will the person marking you!)

6. ... "WITH RUNS FROM BEHIND THE DEFENSE" ...
go around the "D" (watch for "Gators")

7. ..."REACHING THE GOAL MOUTH AS THE BALL DOES."
adjust to different styles & speed of your team's different outside players
"HOLD" outside the penalty area until it's time to make the finishing runs
a little late is better than a little early, then your run is *"FULL SPEED"*
listen for *"leave it"* if a finisher behind you has a better chance
if the cross is behind you, let it continue on for one of the other finishers
"Frame the Goal" on any shot

D. 8. FINISHERS MUST "RESET"...
if they get to goal too early
if the cross goes all the way through
never be standing in the penalty area, especially in front of the goal !!!

Two things are needed to set up the "Easy Goal" situation. First, the outside players must have *strong one-on-one skills* and the confidence to use them.

Next, the team must be able to *isolate the outside defender* in a 1v1 situation (or, better, get the ball behind the outside defender which isolates a sweeper or covering defender in a 1v1 situation.)

There are several ways to do this including:
- an attacking run - the outside forward takes on the defender
- an overlap by an outside midfielder or outside defender
- a diagonal run to the corner by a central forward
- a diagonal run to the corner by a central midfielder
- a diagonal pass to the corner behind the outside defender

In general, better chances are created when the ball goes through the area between the center circle and the top of the "shooting cone". (It's the best place for the "midfielder-to-midfielder" pass.) This gives some time for additional attacking players to race forward. It also keeps a defending holding midfielder or sweeper centered and less able to give support once the ball goes wide.

Finally, once the ball does go wide, attack at only one speed: **full speed !!!**

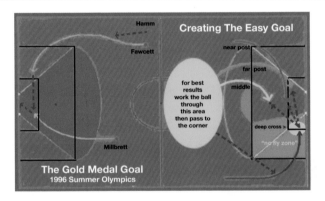

When training the Easy Goal situation, finishing runners should call out their colors as early as possible, first **"blue,"** then **"red,"** then **"yellow."** It doesn't hurt to do this in games as well. In any situation where the run of play results in just two finishing runners, the first makes the near post blue run, the other a blend of the red and yellow. Call it **"orange."** Where there's just one finishing runner, like in that Olympic goal, again it's an orange run.

The Cross

It's important to get as close as possible to the **"deep cross spot,"** where the goal area meets the end line. This makes the crossing pass easier. The cross needs to be angled back, not straight across where it will be easier for a keeper to snare. The cross must also be **"on the ground,"** making it an easy ball for the finishers. Finally, the cross must find a gap between defenders. It's a pass to space, not to a teammate; the teammate must find that space as well.

Timing Is Everything

Outside players can have different styles. One will power by the defender on the way to the deep cross spot. The other, more of a dancer using more elaborate ball moves to get by, will take a little longer. Finishing runners must be aware of these differences. Once the corner is turned, the *only* speed is **"full speed"** for the dribbler. That's the speed for finishing runs as well. The runners need to wait outside the penalty area if necessary in order to arrive at the right place at the right time, then make their runs at **"full speed"** as well. Finishing runners need to keep the space in front of the goal open as long as possible, pausing at the edge of the penalty area if necessary; it's actually much better to be a bit too late than to be too early.

21.4 PUTTING IT TOGETHER

66 Finishing Runs

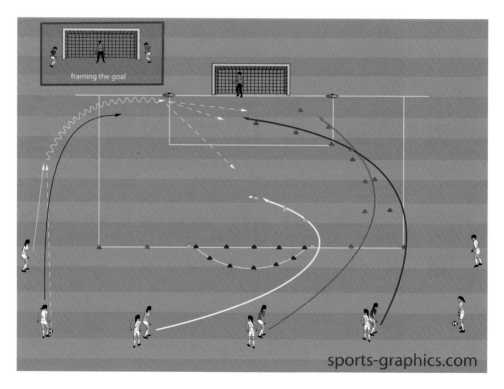

framing the goal

sports-graphics.com

This is just a variation on the introductory experiment. The second player on the outside line plays a ball down the line from 10 yards behind the first, then gives chase. The first player must *"turn the corner," "dribble end-line"* and *"cross"* before being tagged by the chaser. This develops the "at full speed" component of the winger's role. (Note: play still continues if the tag is made.)

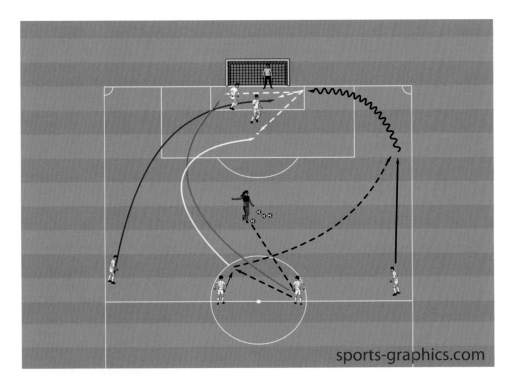

sports-graphics.com

Variation: With four lines at midfield, the coach serves a ball to the first player on one of the inside lines. As both wings streak down their sidelines, that player passes (1) to the first in the other inside line, who reverses the ball (pass 2) to the farther winger who will *"turn the corner"* (*"full speed"*), *"dribble end line,"* and *"cross."* The other winger makes the *"blue"* run. The player who made pass 1 follows that pass in an overlapping run to make the *"red"* run. Passer two loops away to make the *"yellow"* run. Have one or two defenders in the penalty area with the keeper so that the crosser must find a gap for the ball. **Note:** This activity is a good one to use as the last element of a pre-game warm-up (see chapter 17, activity 43).

21.5 EASY GOAL GAMES

67 5v3 to Goal

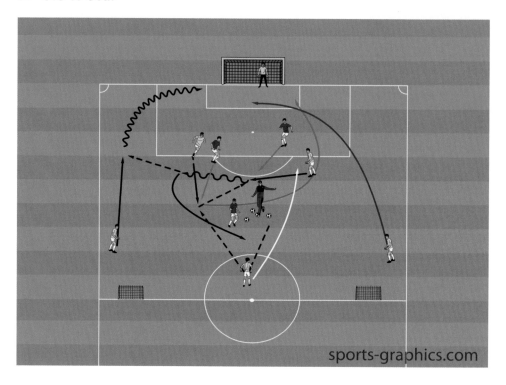

Using a half field with a goal, five players (configured as 3 attackers and 2 midfielders or 2 attackers and 3 midfielders) take on three defenders and a keeper.

To start, the coach plays a ball to any of the attackers. This group must combine, to **spring the wing** for an opportunity to get around one corner and an **Easy Goal**. Should the defenders win the ball, they counterattack to Pugg goals set wide on the halfway line. Attackers will need to use diagonal runs, wall passes, overlaps, blind side runs, and use their 1v1 skills in the buildup of the play. This will frequently mean that players are switching positions during the attack. But they must take care not to flatten out; there always needs to be at least one player who is in position to deal with a breakout by the defenders if possession is lost. When that happens, attackers who regain possession within six seconds can have a second chance to score. If they regain the ball after that time, play ends and the next five attack.

Variations: a) Use the offside rule or not, b) allow a defender beaten in the corner to chase or not, c) only allow one or two defenders inside the penalty area, or d) all passes other than the angled-back cross must go forward.

68 Alley Game (★★★★★)

sports-graphics.com

This uses a field 60 to 70 yards long and 60 to 65 wide, including the 8- to 10-yard alleys on either side. (It is similar to the field for the Mini-Alley Game, just bigger.) Use two full goals and keepers. Use discs to define a penalty area if necessary.

A team wins the ball by getting it to a team member in an alley. That team is *free to move the ball down the alley and all the way to the **deep cross spot** without opposition.* Meanwhile, attacking teammates are organizing the near, far, and middle runs (calling the **"Color"**). Emphasize ***"full speed"*** in turning the corner and in the finishing runs. *Any attacking run through the "D" is disqualified.*

Variations: a) At first limit the defenders in the penalty area to one or two plus the keeper; loosen the restrictions as the attacking players get better at the organization of their runs. b) The speed of this game can be increased by encouraging the first player with the ball in the alley to quickly pass down the line to a teammate, making a diagonal run into that space (as shown). That's much quicker than dribbling the length of that alley. c) With a more advanced team, have the attackers switch the field from the first alley to the second. Play through the middle can be contested: If the defenders win the ball they play it into an alley and can score without switching the play again.

WCPGW: Teams can get in the habit of playing only into the alley on one side (usually the one on the right).

69 Mini-Alley Game

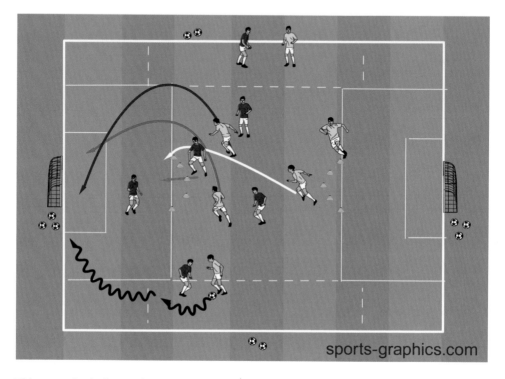

This game is similar to the previous one, but more difficult due to the smaller space—no more than 40-by-40 yards, including the 5- to 7-yard alleys on either side. Each team has a player in the middle half of the alley; play is 2v2 up to 4v4 in the central zone. When a ball is played into the alley, the receiver must beat the defender on the dribble before initiating the **Easy Goal** finishing sequence. If the outside defender wins the ball, a counterattack goes unopposed in the alley and turning the corner to the deep cross spot. Outside players may not chase after being beaten. Inside players must finish quickly. Emphasize the timing, direction, and spacing of the finishing runs. The 1v1 element of this activity in the alleys is very good training for a team's outside players.

Variations: a) Vary the number of defenders allowed back in the box. b) The 1v1 players are only allowed in the alleys after a possession change. c) Allow players to interchange between alleys and center area. d) Where numbers in the middle are 3v3 or more, allow a central player to combine 2v1 in the alley with a blind side run or overlap. e) The outside defender may chase if beaten.

70 Back-to-Back (★★★★★)

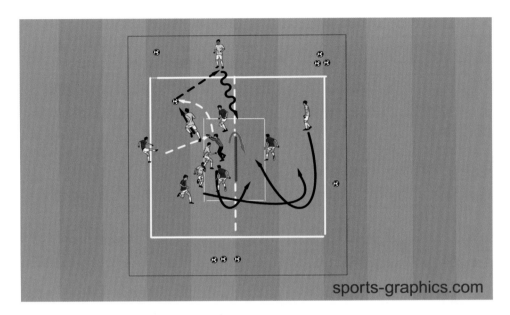

sports-graphics.com

This is a wonderful tactical game involving crossing, shooting, and quick combination play in the penalty area. It is particularly useful for working on organization around the goal and how attacking players can get themselves both into the right spots and out of the ones where they're only in the way.

There are two teams of five or more players, one or two goalkeepers (one goalkeeper can be required to defend both goals), and a Coerver Goal is set in the middle of a 36-by-44-yard space, dividing it into two zones, each the size of a penalty area. Team Gold will attack in one zone and shoot at one side of the goal, Team Blue at the other. (If there's just one keeper, as shown, he defends *both* sides.)

A team gains possession of the ball when they win it and get it outside the space. From there, the possessing team plays to the goal they're attacking. The other team is not allowed to defend outside the space, even when the attacking team makes a pass between two players out there. On balls at the flank, the attacking team should organize near post, far post, and trailing (middle) runs.

There are endless **variations**. Among them: a) Work on the **Easy Goal** by allowing a flank player to dribble to the deep cross spot and serve uncontested. b) Allow the other team's zone to be "contestable space," where a defender winning the ball team can serve "over the top" to teammates on their attacking side of the goal. c) Limit time, touches, or passes outside the space. d) Limit the number of defenders in their opponent's attacking zone.

71 5v5v5 (★★★★★)

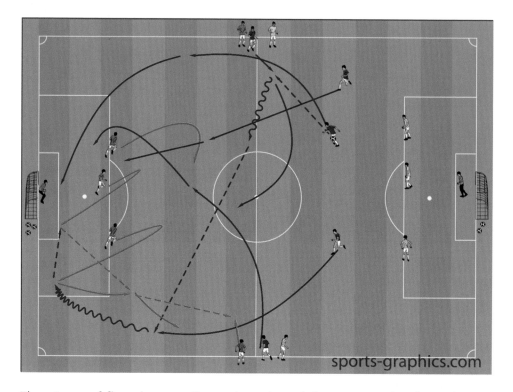

sports-graphics.com

Three teams of five, plus a goalkeeper in each goal. (WCPGW: Having fewer than 17 players.) Three of the five are on the field; the others wait as wingers where the halfway and touch lines meet. The field is full width and about 75 yards long. (This becomes mostly a fitness exercise if it's much longer.) The game is a continuous series of 5v3 attacks. The defending team wins the ball when a) the keeper gets control or b) defenders win the ball *and* complete a pass.

Team Gold's three defenders wait at their defensive 18 until the attack heads their way. Team Blue attacks Team Red 5v3. Play "winners: If Blue scores, they get the ball and attack team Gold.

Team Red wins the ball, a) when it is played out of bounds or to the keeper or b) when a defender wins the ball and completes a pass to any teammate, including the waiting wingers. They now attack team Gold 5v3.

This activity is used first to develop attacking patterns. **Examples:** Whoever passes to the winger then overlaps that player (shown in figure). Then: a) a pass wing-to-wing with a second overlap, b) winger dribbles square as the defenders move into the attack,

c) dribble square to a takeover with the other winger, d) winger must pass back to a supporting player who then switches the field. The idea is to use these patterns with the goal of isolating and then beating the widest defender to create an **Easy Goal**.

The exercise can also be used to develop a fast-break attack by giving the attacking team a time limit to shoot from the moment where possession is won. Unless part of a designated pattern, avoid negative passes (those that go away from the goal one's attacking).

Adapting Other Activities

Almost any activity 2v2 and larger can have an Easy Goal component. Just add a bonus point for any goal scored when one attacker turns the corner, dribbles the end line, then lays a ball across to a teammate, making a finishing run from the weak side.

21.6 BONUS TIME

Here are some advanced accessories to the Easy Goal model that should in time be worked into the above activities:

- Framing the Goal. (Shown in activity 66.) This is what the first two runners do if they don't get the ball. As the "blue" runner reaches the near post, he pivots to face back upfield, his body at a 45-degree angle to the end line. The "red" runner does the same at the far post. This has the effect of making the goal 2 to 4 yards wider, since either player can deflect into the goal a teammate's shot that is just wide. (WCPGW: offside position.)

- Resetting. Sometimes the cross does get all the way through the goal mouth and out the other side. Runners should quickly loop away and try to reset at least two of the finishing runs.

- The Early Cross. This is a ball bent in to the penalty mark from the corner of the penalty area. It can be a good change of pace, particularly if only one or two runners are going to get there.

⏎⏎⏎⏎⏎⏎⏎⏎⏎⏎⏎⏎⏎⏎⏎⏎⏎⏎⏎⏎⏎⏎⏎⏎⏎

22 SYSTEMS OF PLAY

"Attention to team play is limited to only what is necessary to avoid total chaos on game day."

22.1 INTRODUCTION

For nearly two decades the Coaching Forum (visit www.and-againsoccer.com) was a mecca where an experienced and passionate group of coaches posted, discussed, and often debated a wide variety of topics related to soccer coaching. An excessive number of those topics were about "formations" being used on the field. These tended to end up with contributors talking past each other because the formation under discussion (e.g., a 4-3-3— four defenders, three midfielders, and three forwards) could be configured in so many ways.

Far too much time is spent on "formations" with younger players, but that doesn't mean a team doesn't need some sort of organizational framework on the field. Some players must be assigned to roles that are primarily attacking, others to defending, and the remainder to providing linkage between the other two.

The first consideration in selecting a system centers on the attributes of the team's various players. Quite a few teams, and not just those at the younger ages, play the biggest, fastest, strongest players up front and have the others boot the ball to them. (Coaches of those teams will have never read this far.) Others will look to match competencies to certain roles. Commonly that will include having the players with the greatest poise and best "vision" in the center of things, the best 1v1 attackers outside in the front, those with the greatest tenacity as defenders or center attackers. It should also be noted that even within a group of six-year-olds, you'll find one or two whose sole purpose in life is to get the ball, attack, and score goals, while others delight in destroying attacks by their opponents.

Any system should provide balance on the field. In the 11-a-side game, there has been over time a change from systems with three attackers (e.g., 3-4-3 or 4-3-3), to two (e.g., 4-4-2 or 3-5-2), and now one (e.g., 4-5-1). While the roles in the latter system will include attacking responsibilities for midfielders (and possibly defenders), a system with a single designated forward typically lacks balance, especially where a guiding principle is to "get the ball as high (far up the field) as possible as quickly as possible."[1] With youth teams, a forward there might as well be on a desert island.

---

[1] "As high as possible." When you hear this being preached, it's a good sign that the team lacks the technical ability to play any other way.

Finally, the system needs to be simple. Especially with youth players, training time devoted to full-team organization will be time not spent on the primary purpose of developing the fundamental individual and small-group competencies of the athletes.

22.2 THE 2-3-2-3

In one of those forum discussions, a coach from South Dakota offered a system of play that meets those criteria.[2] He called it the **2-3-2-3 Double Sweeper**.

It may be the perfect starter formation for a team first playing 11v11. a) There's balance all over the field, and any player with the ball has support in two or more directions. b) It's easy to install (one coach introduced it at halftime of a U11 game, and it was presentable by game's end) and well suited to learning by doing (that same team only worked on the system during games). c) It promotes maintaining **width** (see chapter 18). d) For our purposes, it is well suited to a wing attack by skillful 1v1 players and **Easy Goal** finishing runs. e) It provides opportunities for players to try things they'll use later like attacks out of the back by outside players and overlapping and diagonal runs wide by central players. f) Lastly, it prepares well for other systems that will be used when players get older, whether with two frontrunners or three, whether in a stopper-sweeper or zonal defending scheme.

The **2-3-2-3** is outlined in the following figure. The basic attacking strategy is this: Win the ball. Get it to one of the central players. That player passes to another central player (allowing time for more teammates to transition into attacking mode) ideally with the ball going through the center circle. Play on from there. Note that by playing the ball through the middle, the opposition's defenders must respect the central position of the ball; going wide earlier makes it easier for them to provide defensive cover and balance. If playing 7v7 or 9v9, adapt ideas from the 2-3-2-3. Organizing the five field players in 6v6 play can use the idea of the pendulum from the following section.

CoachNotes
Nothing really changes in soccer. The 2-3-2-3 is similar in many ways to the W-M used decades ago in British soccer, while Barcelona's 4-3-3 when on the attack looks like the 2-3-2-3 in that end of the field.

---

[2] Hat tip: Bob Christensen, Mandan soccer. For more, visit www.eteamz.com/sawsl/files/2-3-2-3.pdf

The "2-3-2-3" is also called the "double sweeper" formation. It is very easy to learn and gives players great freedom to move about the field. Everyone attacks, everyone defends.

Even though this formation has FIVE defenders, it is designed for defenders to get forward into the attack. Defenders, especially wing backs, MUST attack out of the back, *"stay in the play"* all the way to the goal if possible. (Don't just pass the ball off and return to your spot on defense.) If this is happening, we are in good position to win balls back quickly if we lose possession.

SWEEPERS - THINK *"DEFENSE"*
1. Generally a defensive role. *"Push Up"* to halfway line when we attack.
2. Mostly stay on one side of the field, not beyond opposite side of goal area.
3. One must fill the position of any wing back who goes forward on the attack.
4. Be a backpass option for the wing and center backs (*"support behind the ball"*).
5. When you win the ball, try to pass to one of the midfielders. But you can also
   "eat up space" – dribbling forward if there's open field ahead of you.

WING BACKS - THINK *"ATTACK"*
1. ONE goes forward. EVERY TIME! Stay on the attack until the ball is totally lost,
   then get back quickly. (*Great fitness required!*)
2. Take advantage of open space every time. It's OK to dribble forward.
3. When you win the ball, try to pass to one of the midfielders, then *"stay in the
   play"* - getting forward for a return pass, or
   3b. *at least* be a backpass option for the midfielders.
4. If the wing forward has to come back for the ball OVERLAP, or
   4b. *at least* get in position for a backpass (*"s-b-t-b"*) from that wing forward.

CENTER BACK – THINK *"BALL LINE"*
1. ON DEFENSE: between the ball and the goal until ball is in the last 18 yards.
2. ON ATTACK: becomes 3rd midfielder in a triangle when we have possession.

MIDFIELDERS - THINK *"PARTNERS"*
1. ON DEFENSE slow the attack and *work together* to force the ball to the side
   of the field, out of the middle.
2. ON ATTACK, when we win the ball, BOTH must make themselves available
   (*"OPEN"*) for a pass from a teammate.
3. Then **we want a pass from one midfielder to the other.** *EVERY TIME!*
   At best, that pass should get the ball into or through the center circle.
4. From there, the ball can go to any of the forwards, to a teammate attacking
   out of the back, or back to the other midfielder.
5. Once the ball is forward, be a backpass option (but also look for the **"yellow"**
   {middle} "Easy Goal" run.)

WING FORWARDS (starting position: side of penalty area line extended)
1. Always be available (*"OPEN"*) for a pass up the line. Don't "hide".
2. **Think *"PASS"*** (backpass, to a midfielder, to center forward on diagonal run, to
   an overlapping defender) if you have to go back to get the ball. *"Play in the
   direction you're facing."* **Think *"DRIBBLE"*** when you get the ball going
   forward. *"Turn The Corner"* with your dribble to create the "Easy Goal"
3. The weak side wing forward makes the **"blue"** (near post) "Easy Goal" run.
4. Chase back hard to double team when possession is lost, especially if *you* lost it.

CENTER FORWARD
1. Start diagonal run behind the wing forward *every* time the WF goes back for the
   ball. Back off if a wing back's overlapping run can get to that space first.
2. **Think *"BACKPASS"*** to a midfielder if you have to go back to get the ball. **Think
   *"DRIBBLE"*** when you get the ball going forward.
3. Make the **"red"** (far post) "Easy" Goal run when ball comes down the flanks.
4. Chase back hard when possession is lost, especially if *you* lost it. Drop a little
   deeper, like a 3rd midfielder, when the ball goes into our penalty area.

*KEEP OUT OF ATTACKING PENALTY AREA UNTIL **a) PENETRATING WITH A
DRIBBLE OR FOR A PASS or b) MAKING A FINISHING RUN.***

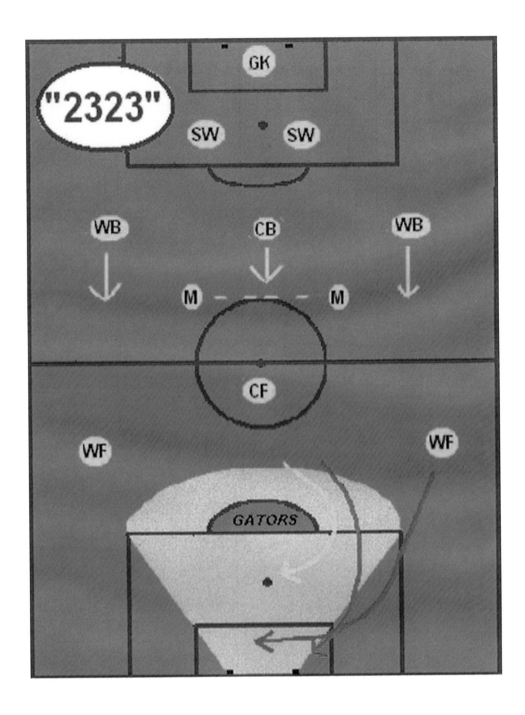

22.3 TWO SWEEPERS?

A sweeper was originally defined as a defender behind the defense who would a) stay on the **ball line** (between the ball and the goal) and b) clean up anything that got behind that line of players. While it is still used here and there, most teams will exploit the fact that the deeper defender makes it harder for attackers to be in an offside position. Rather than making it more difficult to get behind the defense, a sweeper can make it easier to play a through ball into a player making a run from the far side.

The double sweeper of the 2-3-2-3 is something of a misnomer. It's better to picture the back five as part of a **pendulum**. If the ball is wide, the defender on that side advances on the ball (or *with* the ball as part of an attack), the sweeper on that side fills that space, the second sweeper fills *that* space, and the weak side outside mid becomes the second player on the "sweeper line." Players will understand this quickly, and a pendulum is a good way to organize a back four for 7v7 play and the back five for 9v9.

22.4 WHO, WHEN, WHERE

Pigeonholing

There's a famous story that comes from a youth national team training camp. In a game, the last available defender was injured and had to come out. The coach pointed to a player and said, "You're in." "But I'm a forward," the player replied. "I'm in," said another forward and sprinted on to the field. Guess which one made the team and which one did not. What a disservice that player's youth coaches had done that athlete. Brandi Chastain was a forward with the 1991 WNT that won the first Women's World Cup but did not make the roster for the 1995 team. She made the team again in 1999 as a defender. The most famous goal (and goal celebration!) in women's soccer—taken with her weaker foot on instructions from the coach—was a result.

In the end players either can get it done on the field or they cannot. While better—usually significantly—at some position than others, they should understand and be capable at all of them. Coaches of younger players must begin to develop that wider competency. That means, at least through U12, playing all of them at various times in every position (with the possible exception of goalkeeper). Depending on age, players should be out of their "best" position between a third (U12) and half (younger) of the time in a team's weekly games.

Playing Time

Most youth sports organizations have rules about minimum playing times, often mandating that every player gets at least half a game. Those mandates tend to disappear once teams above the recreational level are selected by coaches. That should not change the basic half-a-game requirement. If the player the coach selected can't handle it, the coach needs to live with the consequences. (Sometimes coaches also get to learn how **"Mistakes are good; struggle makes you stronger."**)

It can be useful for a coach to script playing time and substitutions before the game. On teams at younger ages and where goalkeeping responsibilities are divided, a goalkeeper should play an entire half to experience the flow of a longer stretch of playing time. Then give that player full time as a field player in the other half. (Being guaranteed to play every minute might make trying the goalkeeping position more attractive to the other players.)

Where an older team has a roster exceeding 15 players, scripting becomes almost a necessity. As an example, let's consider a team of 17 players, including one goalkeeper, playing 70-minute games. That's seven 10-minute segments (or 70 chunks) of field player time. Assigning each player 4 (for 40 minutes of playing time) uses 64 of them. (Try to give players 20- or 30-minute segments so that they can develop some continuity in their play.) Use the remaining six chunks in the last 10 minutes for the most deserving players if the game is on the line or for players who need the extra work where things are in (or out of) hand.

Finally, being a starter is overrated. It's considered an honor, especially by parents and other spectators, but it's who's on the field at the end—when a game is on the line—that's more important. One good rule to have for a team, though, is that no player who has missed a training session during the week—for any reason—will start ahead of any player who was present and participating. Whether or not the missed training impacts actual playing time, however, is one of those places where hard-and-fast rules can become more of an issue than any case-by-case approach.

23 ESSENTIAL RESTARTS

"Be quick, but don't hurry."

–John Wooden

At the international level, up to 20% of a team's goals can come from restarts and set pieces. In youth soccer, such goals are far more rare. This is a part of the game that deserves some attention, but not so much that it takes too much time from more important topics in the player development process.

A guiding principle in what follows is based on the *"Change the Pressure"* soccer habit (see chapter 11). Most teams take a bit of a break before a throw-in or a free kick. The clever team will get the ball back in play as quickly as possible before the defenders have time to get organized. This is particularly useful early in the game, surprising opponents who have grown accustomed to that little break. And unless a free kick provides an opportunity to score in two touches or less, the goal should be to *"pass and play"* within five seconds of the referee's whistle.

72 The Throw-In

This is the most common restart in the Game and is one where quick play can often catch an opponent unprepared. The player serving the throw-in needs to see all the options as soon as the ball is picked up, not just when the taker has gotten back to the touch line, and get the ball back in play. The rest of the team must also continue to play, or the thrower is going to end up as a living statue.

In the defensive end of the field the throw-in is going to be down the line so that if the throw is intercepted there is little danger of a counterattack. The runners need to time the run so that they are passing the spot of the thrower as the server gets there.

See all your choices applies in that part of the field between the halfway line and the penalty area. The server should have three options: 1) down the line, 2) square to a player checking toward the ball, and 3) back to a defender. With option 2, the player might turn the ball and play it to the far side of the field, send a pass to the runner in option 1, or complete a wall pass by returning the ball to the server now on the field. With option 3, the receiving player will have several choices, with most of the best ones involving moving the ball toward the opposite side of the field. What's normally seen, though, is the ball booted up the field, which seems like something of a waste.

In the final 15 to 20 yards at the attacking end of the field, it is possible to create a scoring opportunity with a down-and-in run by the player making the down-line run past the server. The runner initially looks back over the shoulder as if expecting the ball between the run and the touch line. Instead, the server puts the throw-in to the other side of the defender (in the manner of a Foundation Move) as the receiver runs on to the ball and turns the corner to initiate the Easy Goal pattern of play (see chapter 21.3).

73 Corner Kicks

For over a decade, the US Women's National Team used the same corner kick play. The team also had a set formation for defending a corner. The examples used here are for 11v11 play, but the ideas can be adapted for 9v9, 7v7, and even 4v4.

On the Attack

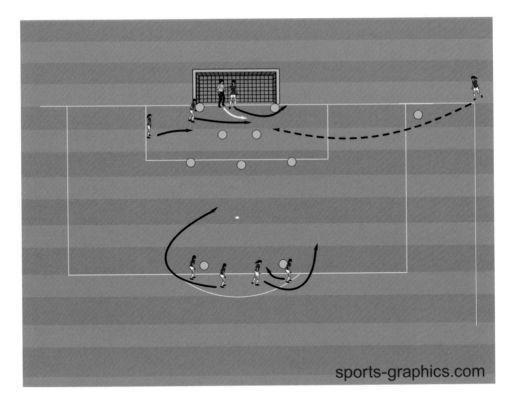

sports-graphics.com

Three attackers are in a line a yard or two off the end line. One is just in front of the goalkeeper, as if preparing to obstruct the keeper's ability to see and get to the ball. The second player is at the back post. The third is on the side boundary of the goal area.

At the server's signal, each moves one spot toward the incoming ball. The task of the first player is to battle the defender on the near post, win any ball that is not going to reach the goal mouth, and either play it back to the server or turn it out toward the "D" at the edge of the penalty area. The back post player, coming from behind, tries to get (and stay) between the keeper and the ball and close enough to win any ball the goalie might get. The farthest player must make sure that the ball does not go through the goal mouth and out the other side.

Four additional attackers lurk around the "D." One will loop away from the play and make a run toward the penalty mark. The others will stay outside the penalty area to gobble up and shoot balls that are "cleared but not out." WCPGW: They will tend to drift in toward the goal, leaving an opening for a counterattack

Defensively

Everybody's back. Eight players pack the goal mouth in a 3-2-3 formation (gold discs in previous figure). A ninth player guards against the "short corner" but will also take a sharp step sideways as the ball is served to slightly distract the server. The two remaining roam the top of the penalty area, with one always prepared to help defend a "short corner."

There is no sophistication to this. The defending team is packing the box with enough bodies to a) block any shot and b) clear the ball away. That said, bringing all 11 players back can lure the opposing defenders too far forward and expose them to a counterattack. That's why the two at the top of the penalty area should be among the team's fastest players; the keeper should always look for this option when getting the ball. Training corner kick situations, once or twice a season in depth with an occasional short refresher during a week's final training session, will pay off on game day.

CoachNotes

Can your keeper take a strong goal kick? If so, maybe that's who should take your corner kicks. It will drive your opponents insane. In the first half, the temptation of the wide-open goal is so great that they will make mistakes trying to clear the ball upfield. (Their parents going nuts on the sidelines only adds to the mayhem.) Then, at halftime, they will talk about nothing else. Finally, as they watch the keeper cross the halfway line, coming up to take the first corner of the second half, the player who fetched the ball puts it down in the corner and serves it in. WCPGW: A brief pre-game heads-up to the officials is a good idea to make certain all really understand the offside rule.

---

74 From the Goalkeeper

While technically not a restart, it should be treated like one when the keeper gets possession of the ball. The immediate opportunity to "change the pressure" in this situation is all but universally wasted. The keeper punt has been eliminated in the 7v7 game, and with heading banned—at least in theory—in 9v9 contests, the punt loses what usefulness it might still have had. (Not only does a keeper punt turn possession into a 50-50 ball, but more often than not possession is lost instead of retained.)

CoachNotes

Given the concerns about heading and concussions, it is just a matter of time until the keeper punt is removed from the youth game and maybe all of soccer. We will see a time when any ball controlled with a keeper's hands must be distributed from the hands. Teams will be forced to play out of that back and that will make for a more skillful game.

Goalkeepers should be taught to distribute the ball quickly before the defense has time to organize either from their hands (bowling the ball will often be more accurate than a throw or pass) or by putting the ball on the ground and playing from there. (The bold ones may even want to be encouraged to dribble the ball upfield.) Much like the Easy Goal, playing out of the back is a tactical situation where early training will bring both immediate and lasting benefits.

75 Penalties

Most players will never take a penalty kick in regulation time, and not many more will in a game-deciding shootout. Still, they will demand to take PKs in practice. Even if there's no shootout anywhere on the horizon, you'll have to do it.

So make the most of it. Use the games to refine shooting technique. Make them take PKs with the weaker foot. Get them to pick a target and shoot for it every time so that if it is needed in a game it will be there. (The easiest aiming point to target is the bottom back corner of the net.) Add pressure to the game, such as, "If you miss, you're out," or "We'll do this until somebody misses."

WCPGW: Goalkeeping is an issue. The team's goalie should only face as many shots as he or she can with the full effort and concentration that would be needed in a match. That's not going to be many. Having non-keepers in the net, especially once the Seven Words methodology has taken hold, is an invitation to sprained and broken wrists and arms. (It's happened to *coaches* of 8-year-olds!) If there will be a lot of shots, hang ropes 3 to 4 feet inside the uprights and only count shots that go in those corners.

Preparing for a potential shootout should start well ahead of the event.[1] Record each shot, where it went, and if it was successful. This will not only identify your best shooters but also allow you to set a shooting order that mixes up where the shots will go.

---

[1] There's no excuse for failing to prepare and then losing a Regional Cup Final in a shootout.

24 FITNESS

"If you won a competition, you were allowed to run, and if you lost, you did not get to run."

–Bruce Brown, *Teaching Character Through Sport*

For younger players, a program of dynamic practice activities with the ball should provide levels of fitness that meet their needs on game day. Nevertheless, most teams will still do some fitness activities. Properly selected and presented, these activities can have value to the athletes that can exceed the fitness benefits.

24.1 INJURY PREVENTION

As a specialty, Pediatric Sports Medicine dates only to 1975. It is now one of the fastest growing medical fields, with treatment for broken arms and sprained ankles being overtaken by a wave of serious soft-tissue injuries. The epidemic, for that is what it has become, is driven by a toxic mix of overtraining, early specialization in a single sport, diminished free time play, the downgrading of Physical Education programs in schools, inadequate provisions for rest and recovery, and the failure of youth sports organizations to provide meaningful injury prevention programs. You are not going to fix all of that, but there are some things you can address.

Let's consider knees. Female college athletes, notably those who played soccer and basketball, used to have a near monopoly on ACL and meniscus tears. Such injuries now are common in girls as young as 12, are widespread by 16, and the boys are catching up. In many instances (notably among people who are neither suffering the injury, nor financing its repair, nor dealing with a caged beast during months of recovery), these injuries are considered as just a "cost of doing business." However, these injuries are almost wholly preventable.

There are many programs designed to keep injury at bay. The Santa Monica Sports Injury Prevention Program, known as PEP, has led the way (you can search Youtube.com for informative videos from this program). FIFA, US Soccer, and others have since promoted similar regimens. Research has shown that sustained regular use of these programs significantly reduces the number of ACL tears and essentially eliminates the non-contact injuries that make up about 65% of the total.[1]

---

[1] *Warrior Girls* by James Sokolove offers a superb look at the sports injury and prevention landscape.

But First

Theories abound as to why female athletes are far more susceptible than males to knee and ankle injuries. But you can skip that debate because the solution seems to be tied to increasing stability around the knee joint, and there's a great activity that does just that.

We call it the **Vampire Bat**. Try it. Just stand on one leg, raise the other with bent knee (not bracing that leg against the standing one), and extend the arms like Dracula with his cape. Now close your eyes. If you lose your balance, touch the toe down and resume the pose. You will feel all the little adjustments around the knee and ankle that the body is making so that you can hold the pose and not lose your balance.

Have your players start this one at age 10. They should perform 30 seconds on each leg, then repeat. The goal over time is to be able to hold the pose, still as a statue, for 2 minutes or more. This should be done *every day*. (It's OK to "hold the cape" with one hand and combine the pose with brushing teeth or hair.) If you have a player who appears to be battling a gale when in the pose, double the daily regimen and give the parents a heads-up about why this is particularly important for their child.

Using PEP

The PEP program is a series of about 25 exercises. Completing the full set takes 30 to 40 minutes. The activities fall into six categories: warm-up, stretching, strength, plyometrics, agility, and cool-down. For even the youngest players, the three jogging exercises in the warm-up section are good to start the process of getting the muscles up and running.

At U12 athletes should be doing the plyometric hops, hopping over a disc at first since for now these exercises are more for developing stability than strength. Emphasize **"land once"** without any second bounce and **"over the foot/feet"** instead of tilted sideways. A **"quiet landing"** has absorbed the impact correctly. The full set is 100 hops and takes about 5 minutes. Players just starting will be sore the next day, so start at one-quarter or one-third of the full number. This needs to be done twice a week, every week, in season and out. By U14 the hops—now three times a week—should be over a ball; this adds a strength component. Add in different varieties of sit-ups; increased abdominal strength turns into more powerful shots.

Tournaments

While play in tournaments has benefits (see chapter 31), it remains common for their organizers to schedule teams for two games a day and up to five in 60 hours. Ten-year-olds, being essentially creatures made of rubber and still more self-protective than their older brothers and sisters, work at levels that allow quicker recovery. They can more easily survive this. But with each passing year the danger of injury associated with back-to-back games (i.e., within 24 hours of each other) grows. At three games in three days, the risk is exponentially higher. Five games in three days is just asking for trouble.

Soccer geezers remember **play days**. That's where four teams would get a pair of fields, a pair of referees, and play a round-robin of half-games over three to four hours. This was a great way to meet pre-season needs for competition and a lot less expensive. But if current cultural norms demand a winner, have each team pony up $20 to buy the "winning" team's pizza after the games.

Concussions

The game was 4v4 across a penalty area with full-size goals and goalkeepers. The objective was to shoot hard and shoot quickly, and one of the players was struck by a shot to the side of the head that was so hard and so sudden that it could not be avoided. The player was knocked silly, but after a few minutes on the side the coach inquired how the kid was doing and received the Warrior Girl response: "I'm fine." So the coach put her back into the game. Where she immediately scored a brilliant goal. At the wrong end. It was three weeks before that player was again cleared to play after this serious concussion. The only good news: The moron of a coach could not have chosen a worse player for this to happen when it came to the wrath of the athlete's parents.

Concussions are serious business, and any blow to the head is cause for concern. Coaches need to educate themselves about this—WebMD.com has a good article on traumatic brain injury[2]—and should consider any decision about a return to play to be "not my job, man." Inform the parents about what happened and let them handle the follow-up care.

When Injuries Occur

Safety first. Never move a player who does not want to move. You can carry off an ankle sprain, but when it comes to necks, backs, or maybe a broken leg, call the paramedics. And if a referee pressures you on this to restart the game (unbelievably this happens), a) refuse, b) take the name, and c) report it to the game authority and the referee association.

24.2 WARM-UP, STRETCHING, COOL-DOWN

Many people conflate warm-up and stretching. The first is the process of getting the muscles warm and ready for movement. Once the PEP jogs are done, working on foot skills and ball moves (see chapter 12) is ideal for turning up the heat while at the same time throttling up the intensity and moving players out of their comfort zones.

---

[2] www.webmd.com/brain/tc/traumatic-brain-injury-concussion-overview#4.

Stretching is used to increase flexibility. For that reason, is best done at the end of a training session as part of a cool-down, when the muscles are most thoroughly warmed up. Any stretching at the start of a session should be dynamic (parts are moving, e.g., "walking lunges" in the PEP series) with static stretching confined to cool-down. Note that muscle soreness is better dealt with by prevention—stretching during cool-down—than by stretching once the soreness has set in.

24.3 POSITIVE CONDITIONING

This is a wonderful concept promoted by Bruce Brown of Proactive Coaching. It is designed to turn work on fitness and conditioning from something athletes dread to a positive and constructive experience.[3]

One idea is foundational: *coaches must never—really, one slip-up can ruin this—never associate a physical consequence with failure or punishment.*

As players progress to higher levels of *the Game*, fitness demands move beyond what can be accomplished with the ball during practice. This requires athletes to work out on their own in pursuit of both their own goals and those of their team. That's a challenge in and of itself. But when physical activity has been repeatedly tied to a negative, summoning the emotional energy to get up and go is only made more difficult.

"Winners get 20 push-ups" is wildly counterintuitive. But the association that develops from these "gifts" is that *"fitness is a privilege."* Embracing that idea will make a huge difference when a player must complete sets of sprints all alone on a windy, rainy morning in order to prepare for a college sports season. Please don't be a youth coach that has imprinted a wrong message about fitness on this athlete.

24.4 RESPONSIBILITY

In the end, attaining and maintaining fitness will become almost wholly the responsibility of the athlete, so that idea is something that should be introduced at younger ages. The **Vampire Bat** can be a good start. Few can be "a statue" at first, but it quickly becomes apparent who's working on it and who is not.

One team started using the 12-minute version of the Cooper Run at the start of each season, beginning at U11. Preparing for that, usually with a parent on foot or a bicycle at first, produced levels of aerobic fitness more than sufficient for the endurance demands

---

[3] Brown, B. 2003. *Teaching Character Through Sport.* Coaches Choice Books, p.99.

of the game. At the same time, it required the players to assume greater ownership for their improvement and gave them the opportunity to demonstrate commitment to their teammates. (It also, on occasion, provided lessons in false confidence when players assumed they'd match previous performance—without matching the preparation—"because I did last time.") It was interesting that players on the team began to ask for a second test three to four weeks after the first, using the first to "beat my best" and the second in a **"Go-For-It"** attempt to crush it.

24.5 MENTALITY

Needless to say, those players developed a **confidence** in their game day endurance because they had prepared for it. Such confidence can be built in other ways. Maybe a team does, depending on the age, a set of 7 to 10 60- to 100-yard sprints at the end of practice once a week. The fitness benefits of this can be far outweighed by the *"I can do it"* mentality that develops as the number of sprints creeps up or the time between them decreases. *"We're into the sprints now"* on game-day says, *"we can finish strong"* (and might even imply that *"those guys don't prepare like we do"*).

Here again, some of the finer points of the positive conditioning concept can be applied. *"It's OK to take one off; I only want you to start a sprint if you commit to go full out all the way through the finish line"* adds **accountability** for producing full effort each time. This can be paired, occasionally, at age 13 or 14 with *"but I will stop you completely if you're not giving 100%."* And what a different message gets sent, both for the immediate and long-term benefit of the athlete, when *"You're not going hard enough, so you have to do more"* is replaced by *"You're not going hard enough, so that's all you get for today."*

24.6 HIGH PRESSURES

Fitness is a factor in two aspects of the adult game that are working their way down into youth soccer. One is high-pressure play. The other involves preparing players to play full games.

Playing high pressure offensively and defensively can win games at younger ages. This is the ultimate example of *"winning today at the cost of tomorrow,"* requiring ridiculous levels of athleticism or fitness that can only be achieved by severely short-changing practice time spent on technical and tactical fundamentals.

Some use hockey-like substitution to keep fresh players on the field in that scheme. Lately the flip side of this is found in the push to have players who can go the "full 90," most notably by limiting substitution with players as young as eighth and ninth graders.

The notion that you can prepare players to play a 90-minute game just by having them play every minute of those games is inaccurate. Players before their physical and athletic primes (generally in their mid-20s) will still by definition only be able to do somewhat less. Until that time, if the end goal is "full-on for the full 90," either teams must overemphasize the fitness component at a cost of continued player development or accept having players play longer shifts at lesser intensity. Neither of those outcomes makes sense. College substitution rules allowing limited reentry achieve the right balance. But recent attempts to impose the FIFA three-substitution rule for high school players is only going to produce players (and opponents) who have learned to play at less than their best.

25 FUTSAL

"As a little boy in Argentina, I played futsal on the streets and for my club. It was tremendous fun, and it really helped me become who I am today."

–Lionel Messi

"Whenever I played futsal I felt free."

–Christiano Ronaldo

The soccer club in a bedroom community in the Denver foothills fed a single high school whose soccer teams redefined what it meant to be a league doormat. The boys had never made the league playoffs, much less the state tournament. The girls had not even managed to *tie* a game in five years.

That was about to change.

The club hired a recently retired NASL/MISL player as its charismatic first club coach. He instituted training based on developing individual confidence on the ball and one-on-play. In a couple of years, the high school teams showed signs of life. The boys made the league playoffs. The girls tied a game, then won one in the same season.

By that time the club coach had also instituted a winter activity that he called *fulbito*. It was a 5-a-side game played with a smaller (size 3-4) ball that didn't bounce. With the support of the high school athletic director he managed to get the keys to the tiny gym at the local "alternative" high school—basketball had all the gym time everywhere else—and opened it up to middle and high school players, boys and girls, for pick-up *fulbito* games. There was some instruction, but it was all very informal. Quickly the venue became the place to be on winter week nights and weekends.

Three years later, in the state's last year of single classification soccer, the boys won the state championship. The following spring, the girls completed the double, the only time that had happened.[1] Some of them had been on the field as freshmen for that tie.

Fulbito is what's now known in the United Sates as **futsal**. Originating in Brazil, it became the game that outdoor players around the world played to maintain and refine their control, skills, and touch when they were forced indoors to play. Great soccer players such

---

[1] In the nearly three decades since, it has only happened three times in the four-classification system.

as Pele, Zico, and Ronaldo grew up playing futsal and credit the game for developing their skills. In recent years futsal has become a staple of training in Spain and it is widely recognized as a driving force in the success of Spain's national team.

Futsal has many advantages over walled soccer in terms of technical development. Normally played on a hard surface with boundary lines, the game requires precision passing that is made all the more difficult by the unforgiving nature of the low-bounce ball. (Without great technique, a poorly struck ball will still be at your feet.) In the more common wall-ball soccer, players regularly whack the ball (and sometimes each other) against the boards. This promotes improper technique, raises safety concerns, and too often rewards errant play. In futsal players are constantly reminded to play the same quality of controlled soccer that is required for sustained success in the outdoor game. The sport is a spectacular skill developer, demanding quick reflexes, fast thinking, pinpoint passing, and with a four-second limit on all play restarts, is an exciting game for kids and adults.

Even at the time, *fulbito* was recognized as the indispensable ingredient in the success of those high school teams and not just because of the skills developed. Note the degree that the entire process mirrored that which Matthew Syed[2] experienced becoming a world number 1 in table tennis, including the ramshackle facility that was always available and a person to provide ignition and coaching expertise. The low-key collaborative nature of the games allowed players to be totally spontaneous and daring. It was an athlete-driven environment where **failing well** was both common and uncommonly productive.

That program was well ahead of its time, and futsal has been a miniscule element of soccer in the United States. That is now changing, with US Soccer recognizing the tremendous potential of the game to improve the quality of players for the outdoor game. Money is being allocated for the development of leagues and facilities. The United Soccer Coaches has recently introduced a course for futsal coaches.

Find a way to get your team to play futsal. The impact will be astounding. If there's not a league, find an elementary school gym that you can use. It will be the right size. A tennis court (without the net, although it might be interesting to play a hybrid combining futsal and soccer tennis) works great, too.

---

[2] Syed, M. 2011. *Bounce*. Harper Perennial.

FINISHING TOUCHES

26 GOALS AND EVALUATIONS

"Goals are dreams with deadlines."

–Diana Scharf Hunt

26.1 SETTING GOALS

Players should be asked to set goals each season and then to examine what they've done to attain those goals at both mid-season and season's end.

A preliminary step in this process should happen at home. **Understanding expectations** is essential. Each season parents should consider the following questions: Why do I want my child playing? What will be a successful season for me as a parent? What are my goals for him? What do I hope she gains from the experience? What do I think his role will be on the team?

Once that's been done, it's time to ask the young athlete the same questions. Ideally, the child's answers will be in sync with the parents'. If they are not, a decision will have to be made about which set of expectations the athlete will pursue.

Goals should be specific, measurable, controllable (and in writing), and can be divided into several types. Outcome goals ("Did I score a goal?") are easiest to measure but they can be hard for the athlete to control. Effort goals, on the other hand, are controllable, but it's harder sometimes to make these specific and measurable. They include things like: "I will sprint after every ball going out of bounds" and "I will improve my juggling 75% of the time I'm tested."

For young players (U8 and younger), goal setting can be as simple as "This season, I want to 1. _____, 2. _____, and really get better at 3. _____." At U9, it can be time to start thinking about longer-term goals as well. By U11 or U12, goals should include long term (where players want to be in three to five years) mid-range (in the next two years), and for the season. Most players will also benefit from daily or weekly goals that can be instantly evaluated. There should be continuity to the goals so that daily or weekly goals contribute to the longer-term goals.

The process of individual goal setting has two parts. The first lays out the most immediate goals, usually three to five seasonal goals, each with two to four daily/weekly components. At least one of the seasonal goals should be related to the personal qualities and life skills that are prized in the team's culture (e.g., the **Qualities of a Great Athlete**; see chapter 4.2). Another should be related to the athlete's "soccer personality," the special on- or off-field quality that would set that player apart from others. The coach, in consultation with the athlete, may also want to contribute a seasonal goal with the athlete developing the daily/weekly components. Finally, add a stretch goal—one that appears only barely possible to attain.

The second part asks the athlete to paint a picture of the kind of player and person he or she wants to be. It begins with, "I want to be known as a player who ..." and includes the qualities the athlete wants to be known for both by teammates and opponents. Another good question is "At the end of the season, I will have had a good season if ..." All the above can and should be done as a team exercise as well. Here separate sets of team goals for training and competition can be useful.

26.2 EVALUATION

Each player's progress toward the goals needs to be formally evaluated twice a season. This will include a review of the things a team measures, such as juggling scores, shooting power, one-on-one ladders, and so on. It will also include a self-evaluation where the athlete reviews progress toward the goals set at the start of the season. Mid-season evaluations can be done in conversations (being sure to Check for Understanding about conclusions reached and next steps; see chapter 5.3).

End-of-season evaluations also need to have a written component. A way that works well is to discuss the player's self-evaluation and any testing or other objective results and then summarize the conversation in writing. The end-of-season evaluation then becomes the starting point for the next season's goal setting. Players should also be able to ask for intermediate updates at any time. Coaches may also want to provide updates more frequently for some of the players, particularly any who are struggling.

If performance is heading in the direction that could lead a player to lose a place in the program, the athlete should be notified immediately and given a timetable for turning things around before parents are notified. We believe strongly that matters of performance are best left between players and their coaches. If there's a need for parent notification, all should be aware that this is very much a last resort. Again, the same evaluation process is possible at the team level.

End-of-season evaluations are also an opportunity to get feedback about interpersonal dynamics. Athletes can be asked, for instance, to list in order teammates who best demonstrate the qualities that form the team's core values.

Finally, don't exclude yourself from an end-of-season evaluation. The membership of the and-again soccer forum put together a list of questions that can serve as a starter. **The Qualities of Great Coaching handout can be downloaded from www.PlayersFirst.com.**

27 THE MYTH OF EARLY SELECTION

Because you just don't know.

27.1 THE PROBLEM

It's always interesting to get word of upcoming tryouts for 8- and 9-year-olds. The clubs call them "clinics," but the obvious purpose is to evaluate players to put the "best" of them together on teams for the next season. That's a tryout. And that's certainly what parents are calling it. So what's wrong with that?

For openers, most State Youth Soccer Associations have rules prohibiting "stacking" teams of players at that age, whether by tryouts or more "creative" means. It's always troubling when youth sports organizations bend—or break—the rules. Kids aren't stupid, and they quickly figure out when this is happening. It then becomes a challenge for parents: How do you promote one set of standards around the dinner table while living a different set on the athletic field? The usual *aplologia* is, of course, "Everyone else is doing it." While sadly too true, it is a no more valid excuse here than when used as part of a child's plea to see *that* movie or buy the latest edition of *Grand Theft Auto*. Character issues aside, what everyone should know is this: *early identification and early selection (before puberty) just do not work*. If anything, it appears to be counterproductive in terms of the development of top-level players.

Early selection doesn't work at even older ages. A study conducted by the English FA is instructive. In 2002, England placed third in the U17 UEFA Championship. The following year 25 U17 players were graded by the FA as "certainties" for full England honors. Four (16%) achieved that status. By 2007, writes educational consultant Doug Lemov, "Members of the U17 national team (were) as likely to work for the gas company as a Premier League side. What to make of this? Even at the elite levels, present skill is easier to spot than 'talent' – i.e. future skill. We think we see the future but we don't. Learning curves, physiological growth curves, attitudes, health, commitment, psychology - they are all too unpredictable."[1]

In an issue of the NSCAA (now USC) *Soccer Journal*, Gary Allen of U.S. Youth Soccer took issue with the very premise of early selection:

---

[1] Lemov, D. 2014. Teach Like a Champion 2.0. Jossey-Bass, p. 24.

"The underlying rationale is flawed. It posits, erroneously, that we can spot future elite players (by age) 13, contrary to all research worldwide concerning athletes at these ages, as well as everything written by development experts."[2]

That research applies to most endeavors, not just to sport, and there are countless examples of "late bloomers" who in today's hurry-up culture would find far fewer opportunities. The bottom line is this: *you just don't know* at the younger ages, and anyone who tells you differently is either blowing smoke, woefully ignorant, or both.

Next, consider the flaws of the typical selection process in soccer. It's like trying to figure out who should be in a "King of the Hill" game in seven or eight years. The selectors think that in about two hours they are identifying superior "athletes" or (less commonly) above-average technique or tactical insight. Instead they are mostly selecting birthdays, especially so at the younger ages. (Rarely does the selection process focus on the personal qualities of the athlete, which are by far the best predictors of future success.)

Selection is followed by exclusion. Those not selected lose the challenges provided by those "moved up" and typically get progressively less and less in terms of coaching and other opportunities. Of course, they fall behind. Three years later the "best" teams are still heavily populated by the chosen players. The selectors see that as validation of their brilliant choices, but all they are really seeing is a self-fulfilling prophecy running its course.

Enrichment activities for younger players are fine, so long as there are opportunities for *any* interested player who is willing to make that extra effort. But that's not what we're seeing. We're seeing practices that promote exclusion. In the "King of the Hill" analogy, most of the potential players are being told to go home long before the contest is to start.

The best programs always seek to provide quality instruction for *all* players without regard to their current level of expertise or athletic ability. Through age 13 or 14 every effort must be made to encourage *inclusion*, providing the same quality instruction, coaching and curriculum to *all* players, raising the general level of play, letting, in Allen's words, "the cream of the crop rise above that level" as it surely will.

---

[2] assets.ngin.com/attachments/document/0112/0439/inclusion.pdf.

27.2 THE IMPACT ON PLAYER DEVELOPMENT

Unfortunately, the most visible outcome of early selection is how it seems to discourage effective player development programs and, consequently, good soccer. As one coach has lamented, "Once selection to teams starts, most player development stops."

That happens in settings where the scoreboard becomes the dominant measure of success. It's easiest (but superficial) to judge the quality of coaching by the win-loss record, and there are tremendous pressures on coaches to win at younger and younger ages. Much of that pressure is supplied by parents, but as least as much comes from organizational leaders seeking to tout winning percentages as a measure of "why you should play for us."

In those environments, there is little room for the patience and perseverance needed to cultivate skillful, fundamentally sound players. When the expectation is to win again in seven days, training a team will be very different than if the focus of training is to prepare players to be able to succeed consistently in seven years.

Game-to-game coaching easily leads to the trap of what North Carolina coach Anson Dorrance calls *"winning today (at the sacrifice of tomorrow)."* Here you see training that prioritizes team organization over player development, tactics over skill, play that emphasizes athleticism far more than (and sometimes to the exclusion of) game smarts. Players are pigeon-holed in prescribed roles on the field, thereby limiting their decision making, understanding, and control of *their* game. Team environments in this scenario often create a fear of mistakes—because "mistakes make you lose"—which stifles boldness and creativity. At its worst, an excessive concern about the scoreboard promotes overtraining scenarios, substituting quantity for quality in ways that too often put players' progress at risk, if not in reverse.

In the end, it's those "best" athletes who suffer most because it is precisely those situations that inhibit their becoming players who are not only skillful but creative, confident, and fearless—the very qualities that can take their play to higher levels and provide maximum enjoyment. While—in an ironic twist—*they* are now the ones being deprived of the challenges that "late bloomers" would have provided had they not been pushed aside at the earlier age. **This essay, The Myth of Early Selection, can be downloaded from www.PlayersFirst.com.**

28 ABC— THE 50-PLAYER TEAM

In much of the soccer world, all the teams in a club are united in the culture and style of play of the club's first team. That is rare in the United States, where clubs—even those with one or more layers of directors of coaching—are more often simply a collection of teams, each a reflection of the vision of the team's coach. When a team's coach changes, it's common for the resulting changes to make it seem like the team is starting over.

Even when a soccer club has its "way" of doing things, implementing that vision throughout the organization's teams is regularly hindered by a lack of qualified coaches. The most qualified coaches are normally tasked with responsibility for the oldest, most visible, and most accomplished teams. The remainder get something less. Having experienced specialists working with the younger players, the norm in the world's leading clubs, is a rarity on American fields.

The inefficiency of such a model is matched by its ineffectiveness. And it all but guarantees that those not named to the "A" teams at the earliest selection will remain on the lesser teams during their time with the organization (with the "A" teams scouting the top squads of opposing clubs in the search for potential replacements in the event of roster openings).

What if things were structured differently? Let's consider a model that can provide more players with the benefit of the coaching expertise that is available.

It's called the **50-Player Team**. Typically, it consists of three squads of 16 to 17 players (U12 and older), four of 12 players at U10-11 (where the game is 9v9), up to five of 10 players for teams playing 7v7. If the club is large, all the squads might be from one age group. In smaller clubs, squads from different age groups or boys' squads and girls' squads might be combined to make up the larger team.

Each squad has a coach who works under the direction and supervision of a head coach experienced in working with players at the age level. But the emphasis is on a "team" of coaches, with all working to provide the best possible program for every player on every squad.

In this model, the head coach has some nontraditional activities. Much time will be spent "teaching the teachers" and mentoring the development of the other squad coaches. It is a structure that will grow a staff that is consistent in both outlook and approach with coaches preparing for increasing positions of leadership. At the same time, the head coach will be the designated "point man" in matters relating to the parents of players in the team, allowing the other coaches to learn about this aspect of the "business of youth soccer" more as observer than participant, at least at the beginning.

Players will be assigned to squads in the normal manner of recreational teams until the time when league rules allow for ability grouping of teams. Each squad will train independently at times (with a fixed schedule of weekly sessions led by the head coach), side by side, or in combination with other squads regularly and once a week as part of a Team Training day where players are seen and known by a wider variety of coaches. The emphasis at first promotes a balance between membership in the larger program— teams of 50 players, if you will, that just play three (or four or five) different games on Saturdays—and belonging to the smaller group at the squad level.

CoachNotes

Many leagues have adopted a Club Pass rule. It allows any player to participate on any of a club's teams where he or she would be eligible. This can be useful in giving a player an opportunity to play a game at a higher level, and there are occasionally legitimate reasons for a player to compete on a lower-level squad (e.g., in a return from injury). But it should be used sparingly at U14 and below where players are still learning what it means to be a member of a team. Having weekly rosters that are like games of musical chairs defeat that important purpose (and guarantees unnecessary fun-and-games involving players' parents).

This 50-Player Team model also allows an academy-style approach to teaching the game. With the team's squads following a single curriculum under direction of the head coach, each player will receive essentially the same program of instruction and opportunity for competition (a higher-level squad will go deeper into each activity rather than faster through them), yet within a structure that is as challenging for the most talented athlete as it is for the less gifted one simply pursuing a love of the game. This structure should be considered as a basic outline.

29 BOYS AND GIRLS

"Coach us like men, treat us like women."

—Mia Hamm

As this is written, a local soccer program is under way that has as a specific goal of getting players to play with "spontaneity and daring." The 90-minute sessions for the girls are followed by sessions for the boys that are identical in time, curriculum, and coaching staff. Yet the difference in the sessions is obvious.

Boys, as a rule, love to *"go for it"* but often have their individualism suppressed, not only on the field but in the classroom and other venues. For that need to be met, the players need to be given free reign—like you would see in street soccer or pick-up basketball—particularly in their younger years. There's a restaurant in Paris, *Nos Ancestres Les Galois*, which has been described as "one step removed from a food fight." A freewheeling atmosphere of that sort has the potential to be a superior learning environment for boys to develop bold and creative play.

While girls also see individualism discouraged on the field ("We don't dribble here, Vanessa" was recently heard at a U10 tournament), for the most part the coaching challenge with them is to promote more of it. The boys' model won't do that. (Even though many girls might join in and even enjoy it, in the end they would be likely to describe it as somewhat barbaric.) Instead, the coaches should appeal to the more collaborative nature of the female athlete.[1] First to promote the other side of that coin: "When you go for it, you don't just make yourself better, you make everybody else better, too." Then, the coaches want to develop each athlete's expectation that others will play their best so that "they will make *me* better."

There are differences between coaching males and females, especially for a male coach coaching female athletes. (You really haven't lived until you experience the weekly encounter with the carpool of 14-year-olds whose trip to practice has featured the screaming match between the driver and her daughter.)

Rather than reinvent the wheel on this subject, a number of interesting (and entertaining) takes can be found on various websites. Visit socceramerica.com and search for articles on girls versus boys, or visit theartofcoaching.com and search for articles on coaching women versus coaching men for a few good examples.

---

[1] Anson Dorrance said, "Female athletes have superior understanding that relationships are more important than the game." One of the more interesting coaching challenges of that weekly program is this: to get the boys to appreciate the value of getting a good drubbing by a friend and to get the girls to appreciate the value of giving one to a friend.

30 PARTNERS IN THE ATHLETE'S DEVELOPMENT

"Next time, I'm going to coach orphans."

–Overheard at a gathering of coaches

That lament is not uncommon, but it should be. Both the player and personal development of an athlete are maximized when coaches and parents work in partnership, understanding their roles and supporting the roles of others.

30.1 TEACHING AND SELLING

Leadership, it is said, is teaching and selling. That is the primary task of a team's coach: creating a safe environment that inspires players to improve but is as enjoyable as it is challenging; developing technical and tactical abilities; setting and maintaining standards; and cultivating character and positive life skills.

Equally important is teaching and selling to the parents of the players about the team's and club's core values and philosophy of player development; about what is, and sometimes what is not, happening on the field; about ways that parents can be most helpful to the progress of their young athlete; and again, setting and maintaining standards. A coach cannot do this too much.

30.2 TEAM MANAGEMENT

There are many tasks involved in getting a team on the field. A well-run team will have several people managing those tasks, particularly those related to administrative matters. Done well, the coach can concentrate almost exclusively on what happens on the field.

Every team has a team manager. This person handles paperwork and team communications and can be a valuable set of eyes and ears on the sideline. Typically, the team manager will consult weekly with the coach then send out the team's upcoming schedule and any other news, following up during the week if there are any changes, weather cancellations, and so on. With a good team manager, "I didn't know" is never legitimate.

Clubs approach team finances in a variety of ways, but it is common to have a team treasurer, even if the team does not have a separate bank account. This person keeps the families informed about upcoming fees, fundraising activities, uniform purchases, for example, and should provide a comprehensive team statement at the end of each season. Teams that will be travelling often have a travel coordinator who makes all the arrangements, including airline, lodging, and restaurant reservations. Parents can also be enlisted to keep statistics and organize social events.

30.3 THE SUPER SOCCER PARENT

The First Task of a soccer parent is to provide unconditional love and support that is not based on performance. The definitive study in this respect is recounted in Dr. Benjamin Bloom's *Developing Talent in Young People*. Bloom identifies the most successful support systems as ones where athletes experience a "long and intensive process of encouragement, nurturance and support." In these systems, the message they (the parents) passed on to their children was "you can do anything you set your mind to, if you want to do it [... and] if you work at it."[1]

As part of this, it's important that parents recognize that "it's their thing" to be owned and managed as much by the athlete as his or her age will allow (see chapter 3.2). In particular, matters of performance belong to the athlete and the coach. (If parents really must make a suggestion to improve the child's play, they should tell the coach.) This does not mean that parents should disconnect. While some athletes could not care less whether their parents even attend games, others want an actively involved parent for the support and security that provides.

Game Day is a time for parents to keep it simple with just three things to say before the game: **"Give it your best. Have Fun! I love you."**

Athletes have strong feelings about parental involvement on game day. They appreciate it when their parents refrain from any comment to or about a referee at games, even more when they do not coach or provide instructions from the sidelines. (Games belong to the players, so it's best that any comments be limited to those with **no verbs**.) Parents should also be as unconditionally supportive of their athlete's teammates as they are of their own child. The referee standard pretty much applies with regard to opposing players and their supporters. It's fine to compliment good play, particularly at the end of the game. But there's no place for negative comments, no matter how barbarous the behavior directed at one's child, spouse, or self. The approach with the players is going to be *"you're better than that."* They must have that example on the sidelines.

---

[1] Thompson, J. 2003. *The Double-Goal Coach*. William Morrow Paperbacks, p. 249.

> **CoachNotes**
> The problem with parental instruction from the sideline is that it is always distracting, usually too late, and frequently wrong. (And sometimes risky; nothing silences a sideline more effectively than the player who turns to it and yells, "Mom! Shut up!") One novel solution to this problem happened when a coach took the child of an incessant instructor out of the game and sent the player around the field with "Your dad has a message he wants to give you." You can imagine how that 13-year-old handled that short, sweet conversation.

One area where players are all but unanimous relates to the PGA (post-game analysis) that happens during the car ride home. THEY! HATE! IT! Consider this. For most coaches, it takes at least all of that car ride to process a game. Is it reasonable to expect an 8- to 14-year-old to get it done faster? Parents should give their children the space and time they need to recover. The more competitive the athlete and the more competitive the sport, the more time and space a player needs. Parents should leave their children alone until they are receptive to interaction with them, and when they do come to them, parents should give them quiet understanding, be a reflective listener, and bring them back to their bigger perspective. Parents should keep their corrections and criticisms in check.[2]

Oh. And the three things to say after the game: **"Did you have a good time?"** **"I love watching you play!"** **"What would you like to eat?"**

The Positive Coaching Alliance (www.positivecoach.org) offers an online version of their "Second Goal Parent" workshop. The cost is $30, but if you can connect your computer to a TV, a gathering of parents can participate together. Just the information in the segment about empowering conversations between parent and athlete will be well worth the investment.

Empowering conversations are designed to help athletes process their sports experience. Here's where parents can be extraordinarily helpful to their child, but sometimes that won't be enough to help the athlete through the process. This happens most frequently in two areas. The first has to do with performance. Players should be happy with their efforts, with what they're learning, and with their improvement. When they're not, they need to be encouraged to talk to the coach about what's wrong. This is another way of asking young athletes to be the manager of their soccer experience.

There can also be times when the interpersonal relationships—particularly important on girls' teams—get out of sync. These can be player/player or player/coach. In both

---

[2] Brown, B. 2003. *Teaching Character Through Sport*. Coaches Choice Books, p. 130.

areas, a "heads-up" to the coach can be useful, particularly with relationship issues which can be happening off the coach's radar screen. It's amazing how opportunities can "coincidentally" arise during a training session for a coach and player to examine a topic of concern.

30.4 FINAL THOUGHT

A parent summarizes things from the standpoint of one whose son's days in youth sports are done:

"Here's the bottom line for parents. Your child's experience with youth sports will come to an end, and it may happen suddenly. If you are like me, you will look back and think, 'I wish I had enjoyed it more. I wish I hadn't obsessed so much about how well my child was performing, or the team's record, or whether he or she was playing as much as I wanted, or why the coach didn't play him or her in the right position. I wish I had just enjoyed the experience more.' Because the youth sports experience is so intense, we tend to forget how short it is and what a small amount of time parents and children get to spend together over the course of life. *These* are the good old days. Enjoy them."[3]

---

[3] Thompson, J. 2003. *The Double-Goal Coach*. William Morrow Paperbacks, p. 282.

31 SOCCER TRAVEL

The Game has much more to offer besides the games. Soccer travel can provide experiences and benefits that extend way beyond the field: encountering different competition; giving players opportunities to learn to function on and off the field in different environments; and broadening players' views of the world.

Teams must be clear about purpose when they travel. Unless otherwise stated, these are *soccer* trips. They are not, to dispel the most common misconceptions of parents and players respectively, family vacations or extended sleepovers. While off-field activities are an element of decisions about which tournament to attend, successful soccer travel puts **soccer decisions first**. No different from decisions about practice content and organization, these decisions are made with an eye on creating an environment where the team will perform at its best—despite the challenges of travel—both on the current trip and over the longer term.

Many teams will first travel to a tournament, usually one within a day's drive from home, at U10 or U11. For these younger teams, much of the soccer purpose involves stretching the comfort zone of the players so that they are better prepared to withstand the demands of the game back home. By U14 teams will travel in part to show their players and their program to college coaches around the country.

CoachNotes

Soccer travel is not inexpensive. If you must get on an airplane, the cost is going to be in the $1,000 range per player for a weekend tournament. So the first question should always be, "Is this trip necessary?"

Do newly formed U11 teams need to travel to a tournament out of state before they have ever played a game at home? Does another team of 10-year-olds need to fly to **three** tournaments—one at Thanksgiving where all costs are maximized and whole families go along—between the fall and spring seasons? What are these people thinking? How might families of athletes that age have better invested those monies in developing players? (Or in a 529 college savings plan?)

⚽ **PLAYERS 1ST**

31.1 THE BASICS

If you're going to travel, it makes sense to be the best on the field that you can be, and that priority needs to clearly be the focus both in the planning and execution of the trip. It starts with attention to three critical elements:

1. **Transportation.** If teams need to fly to their destination, they should fly together. Where some drive and some fly, establish a time when all are to be present. Travel from hotel to games should always be done as a group.

2. **Nutrition.** Similarly, with meals, the more that can be taken in common the better. This enables more direct supervision of the nutritional needs of the players and may be the best venue there is for team interaction. It takes some effort to do well—planning, making reservations (a must near many tournaments), settling the bill, and so forth. (For real fun, try to convince a Parisian head waiter that he wants to seat a group of twenty-four, *sans reservation*.) Often neglected are the immediate nutritional needs of athletes after a game. Players have a 30- to 45-minute post-exercise "Metabolic Window" in which they must eat (and drink) in order to protect muscles and keep metabolism up and steady.[1] Shoot for consuming 0.75 to 1.5 grams of carbohydrate per kilogram of body weight along with 7 to 20 grams of protein."[2]

3. **Rest.** By far the most important ingredient in successful soccer travel is adequate rest. Preparing to travel can be unsettling. Many players don't sleep well before trips, particularly if they haven't traveled much. Add to this the difficulty most people have the first night sleeping in a bed that's not their own (which explains why you see athletes on college sports teams in airports carrying their pillows) and a couple of games a day. And all the other things that are just "different" on the road.

CoachNotes

It takes much more rest than people think and much more than most teams provide. Some American teams playing in Sweden took grief from other teams at their Gothia Cup school lodgings as they were headed toward their bed (OK, air mattresses) most afternoons (every player slept) and many evenings before the sun set. They were also the only ones from that school who played (and in fact, won) on Finals Day at the week's end.

---

[1] www.spdhocke3y.org/news_article/show/262500?referrer_id=846478.
[2] www.purdue.edu/sportsnutrition/post-workout/index.html.

When staying in hotels, **players need to have their own rooms** (four players to a room is common). In this arrangement, there are no competing agendas. Players who must have "lights out" early will not be disturbed by adults coming in later or wanting to watch the late news. Similarly, players often need to get up very early for morning games to eat, digest, get ready, and be off to the fields on time. They should not feel the need to tiptoe around sleeping adults while doing this. Make no mistake, supervision is required (parents in adjacent or adjoining rooms are a good idea for U11 and U12 teams traveling the first few times), and some players inevitably require stronger measures to ensure their respect for others' needs for rest, if not their own. Still, no other arrangement provides as great a likelihood that this most basic of player needs will be met.

Many tournaments require visiting teams to use approved tournament hotels (gue$$ why[3]) where poorly supervised teams can create real problems for teams with early bedtimes due to early morning games. If you can't avoid such a tournament, it might make sense to choose lodgings farthest from the fields in the hope that other teams will choose the convenience of being closer to the soccer venue.

31.2 TRAVEL BY THE NUMBERS

1. Tournament Selection

This is primarily a soccer decision made by the coaching staff. Before all else, establish your purpose for playing tournaments—it will differ at different times—and select tournaments to meet those needs.

When considering tournaments, look for other activities or events nearby that might be available. Times Square or Jones Beach in New York, the Arch in St. Louis (with dinner on the Hill), Old Town Scottsdale, the M&Ms store and the sinking of the pirate ship at Treasure Island in Vegas, cable cars and Alcatraz in San Francisco, history museums, university tours. Try to find at least one local out-of-the-ordinary eatery for a team meal. It is often possible to create several options for your schedule of tournaments and then to put them to a parent meeting for a decision. "Here's what we need to do from a soccer standpoint. Here are three ways to do it. Which one works for you?"

2. Pre-Meeting Research

In advance of a final decision about the travel part of your tournament schedule, have the team manager and treasurer—or your team's travel coordinator if you have one— look into the potential tournaments in depth. Talk to those in the club who've been there. Obtain tournament brochures and prior years' programs. Get information about the

---

[3] One tournament allows you to opt out of their lodging policy for $160. The honesty is refreshing.

tournament's hotel program. Find out if there will be competing events that could drive up hotel prices.

Prepare a budget. Hotel expenses for players, including taxes and the full cost of the coach's room, are divided equally among the players attending—even those who might arrive late or leave early. (Hotels with continental breakfasts can save money but may not serve it before early tournament games.) The coach's airfare is also divided among the players. Van rental expenses should include an estimate for gas and extra insurance, again equally divided. Where a team rents vans to drive to a tournament, van drivers are usually given a discount on their child's portion. Estimate food costs to include meals, tips, and Metabolic Window feeding between games. Now add in expected costs for souvenirs, tournament T-shirts, entertainment like a team movie, and admission fees to museums (or theme parks). Some teams also make allowances for the expenses of those who will serve as chaperons or trip managers, splitting up to half their costs among the players. Finally, determine which portion of a guest player's tournament costs will be paid by the guest and which will be subsidized by the team.

3. Use a Travel Agency

It's a dying breed, but your club may have one, and there are still agents who specialize in finding group rates. Give them the tournament's hotel information, rooms requirements (with a list of names if possible), dates of arrival and departure, transportation needs, and so on. Parent rooms should be reserved in their own names with their own credit cards, as should airfares—although this is sometimes difficult with a group purchase.

If traveling by air, be sure to use an agent who has done a lot of group work. There can be deep discounts, free tickets, and time extensions on payments and the dates to put names on tickets. Fares vary greatly, but it's best to plan and buy as far ahead as possible. **But be sure of tournament acceptance before buying your tickets.** Also be aware that van drivers may be asked to leave a deposit or a credit card slip equal to the amount of the van's expected rental price and will need to make sure the credit limit on the card can handle this.

4. The Coach Develops the Rules

But the team manager or your team's travel coordinator can help. Decisions will need to be made, in advance, about travel to the tournament, provisions for meals together and rest, time that can be spent with parents, and limits on non-soccer activity. An extended trip to Europe for U14 players used the following guidelines to form a behavior contract:

Behavior Guidelines

All participants on the Tour are expected to be polite, positive, well-mannered, cooperative, good sports, and respectful and consider of others—those you encounter along the way as well as those with whom you are traveling. This will not always be easy. It will require your effort, your concentration, and, on occasion, your willing ness to "try, try again." *You will find that those who have the best time or trip are those who go out of their way to make the trip special for others.* It should be a goal of yours to be one of those who has the best time this way.

The few rules are for the health, safety, and happiness of us all.

Rooms: No member of our group belongs in rooms not assigned to us without the express permission of one of the Tour's adult leaders. Similarly, nobody other than those assigned to our rooms should be in them unless specifically permitted by one of these adults.

You will share a variety of "housekeeping" tasks along the way. Rooms need to be neat at least once a day and the vans will need regular cleaning. You can expect to give some of your free time to helping with laundry and marketing chores. Nothing major, but best accomplished promptly and with good cheer.

There will be times when you'll be without direct adult supervision. When this happens, one of the adults will expect to know where you are and when you'll be back. At the same time, it is always *your* responsibility a) to know how to find one of the adults, b) to know when and where to be next, and c) to be there on time. (Don't even think about using "I didn't know" as an excuse!) When you're off without adult supervision, we will insist on the "Rule of Three" (sometimes more, occasionally two, never one), that is, at least three players together. This rule has very little room for "another chance."

That covers most of the issues. Note that, at minimum, **a BUDDY SYSTEM should be in place whenever players are out of their rooms**, even for things like movies, tournament dances, and around the hotel.

Some teams designate room captains, the players who will be responsible for what goes on in their room. Know in advance how you will deal with serious violations of team rules and situations, especially those that might require a player to be sent home.

Room Captains

- Chosen by the coach, one player per room for the entire tournament who is responsible for leading his or her roommates.

- Establishes that everyone has a buddy every time they go out of the room.

- Designates who has room keys and keeps rooms locked at all times. Gets all roommates up on time for breakfast at the designated times. Gets roommates to respect players' pre-game rituals.

- Gets roommates ready to go to team meeting or game meeting sites on time. Establishes shower schedules and makes certain that roommates stay on schedule. Gets roommates to have uniforms ready for laundry at designated times.

- Gets roommates to dinner and other set activities on time.

- Makes sure all curfews are met and roommates in rooms at designated times.

- Gets roommates to keep rooms organized so personal items can be found.

- Communicates problems to the coach or other designated adult.

- If a problem occurs, the room captain is held as responsible as the player(s) involved and will face the same consequences.[4]

5. Meet With Parents

Set the tournament schedule. For a particular trip, establish the dates, discuss the budget and payment schedule, and set out the rules. Find out who will be traveling with the team and will need air and hotel arrangements. Assign parent duties: checkbook, laundry, meal reservations, van drivers, grocery duty, medical coordinator, and supervision of meals and curfews.

6. Tournament Application

Be aware of deadlines.

7. Packing List

A player's soccer bag must include all uniform items: shorts, shirts, socks, practice wear, cleats, and shin guards. Players must double check these bags before leaving home. **NEVER, NEVER, NEVER CHECK THESE ITEMS WITH THE AIRLINE.** Plan for unusual weather conditions—rain (umbrella), hot sun (sun screen), cold (gloves), wet fields (extra socks). The coach must let players know if they need to bring a ball or water bottle. Players

---

[4] Hat tip: Ed and Vicki Shaw, Lakewood Fury.

should be encouraged to travel light. That extended Europe tour placed outbound weight limits of 10.5 pounds for the carry-on bag, 23.5 pounds on the checked piece! Weight of bags included! For seven weeks! If there's room, players may want to bring their own pillow from home; it does help them to sleep better.

8. Travel Clothing

Players need to wear the same outfit for easy identification in airports and other places where there will be crowds. The club warm-up—at least the top—is recommended, as is the use of matching shirts (though not game uniform shirts.)

9. Final Documents

An itinerary with flight times, hotel information (name, address, phone), game times and field directions, team meals, planned activities, and other pertinent information should be distributed about a week before departure. Players and parents should have their own copies. At the same time **make sure that *you have at least* two copies of your Medical History Form (a sample Medical History Form can be downloaded from www.PlayersFirst.com)**, one for the coach, the other for the team or travel manager.

10. Finally

Seek out those who have traveled with teams to pick up their tricks of the trade.

31.3 TIPS FOR TRAVEL

Set a departure meeting time and place for all players, coaches, and parents to meet before group check-in. At airports, this should be at least two hours before departure. Gather the players to review the **Rule of Three**.

1. Have player passes at the airport for any photo ID required at check-in. (Note that the TSA does not require ID for those under 16 years old but check with your airline about their requirements, particularly for those who are not travelling with their parents.)

2. Triple check the carry-on bags for required uniform items.

3. Designate who has the team checkbook/credit card to register and pay for rooms and vans.

4. The coach plans the meeting place and departure time for all soccer events. The team manager, chaperons, and coach plan the schedule for eating and other activities around the game schedule.

5. At the first meeting after arrival, go over all the rules again and set the schedule for the coming day.

6. A three-step bedtime process works well. First, have a time when players must be in their rooms and end contact with other rooms. Next, a time for the room to be quiet (TV and phones off, quiet talk or silence so that teammates who want to sleep can do so) which is often called "Lights out with lights on." And finally, "Lights out."

7. Coaches control most of the schedule for players in order to have the best rested and mentally prepared team possible. Parents are not to take their children for activities without consulting the coach first. The coach may say no.

8. Designate someone to contact the parents who've stayed home to confirm arrival, report game results, and any other important information.

9. Players' names need to be on anything valuable. Better yet, leave all valuables at home.

10. Sending players to tournaments with large sums of cash is to be avoided. In any event, players will be responsible for their own money.

31.4 CUTTING THE CORD?

Communications have changed since that European Tour. Back then, newsletters were faxed back to a parent in the USA every few days and then distributed to the other families. Phone calls home were difficult to make and fabulously expensive.

What that primitive time provided, though, was a wonderful opportunity for those players to taste independence. One player spoke for others: *"I've never been away from home this long. **And I like it!**"*

The cell phone has changed all that, becoming for some kids (and parents) a permanent umbilical cord. And when not in use that way, it often becomes a tool for tuning out the interaction with teammates that is such a valuable part of travelling with one's team. This is something worth discussing with players and parents. (One sleep-away summer camp—cell phone free—tells campers that this is a way to help their parents to grow up.) If one of the team's goals is the development of *"stronger, more responsible, and confident individuals,"* some intentional cord cutting might be a valuable add-on to the players' travel experience.

32 FURTHER READING: A COACHING BOOKLIST

The following books are essentials for a coach's bookshelf.

Beswick, Bill. *Focused for Soccer*. Manchester United's first sports psychologist fills the largest lecture spaces at the United Soccer Coaches conventions. Here's why.

Beswick, Bill. *One Goal: The Mindset of Winning Soccer Teams*. Beswick's latest book examines the qualities and life skills that come together in the cultures of successful teams.

Bigelow, Bob. *Just Let the Kids Play: How to Stop Other Adults from Ruining Your Child's Fun and Success in Youth Sports*. Former NBA player, now a commentator on the youth sports experience. Key line: "What we are to do in youth sports is to build better children."

Bloom, Benjamin. *Developing Talent in Young People*. The definitive study of talent development, both in athletics and elsewhere. Demonstrates the folly of attempting to identify talent before puberty and identifies influences that maximize talent development. Out of print for a time, now available in paperback.

Brown, Bruce. *Teaching Character Through Sport: Developing a Positive Coaching Legacy*. (★★★★★) Great ideas for coaches about the role that youth sports can play in character development and how strength of character impacts teams. Highlights include "Spotlighting," "Positive Conditioning," "The Qualities of Great Athletes," and the chapter on "Great Teams." If you like the work of the Positive Coaching Alliance, go here for the graduate level study.

Brown, Bruce. *Empowering Messages for Parents*. This DVD contains three messages about how parents can enhance their child's experiences in sport. Available at www. proactivecoaching.info.

Colvin, Geoff. *Talent Is Overrated*. (★★★★★) Provides some of the best information about Deep (or Deliberate) Practice, the training methodology that's the key to developing optimal performance.

Coyle, Daniel. *The Talent Code: Talent Isn't Born. It's Grown. Here's How*. (★★★★★) The book delivers on the subtitle and explains how talent develops as the brain changes through practice.

Coyle, Daniel. *The Little Book of Talent*. (★★★★★) 52 tips related to talent development. For a time, Coyle would post more tips about twice a month on his blog. They are still available at www.thetalentcode.com.

Coyle, Daniel. *The Culture Code: The Hidden Language of Successful Groups*. This book unlocks the secrets of highly successful groups and provides readers with a toolkit for building a cohesive, innovative culture. It's based on a simple idea: Beneath the surface, all high-performing groups are fundamentally in the same place, following the same rules.

Damon, William. *Greater Expectations: Overcoming the Culture of Indulgence in Our Homes and Schools*. Exposes the low standards that children are confronted with in our homes, our schools, and throughout our culture. And the consequences. And how to fix it.

DiCicco, Tony, and Hacker, Coleen. *Catch Them Being Good: Everything You Need to Know to Successfully Coach Girls*. (★★★★★) Former Women's National Team head coach and the team's sports psychologist team up to discuss player and team development.

Dorrance, Anson. *Training Soccer Champions*. Player development at UNC Chapel Hill and a trailblazing book about coaching female athletes. Key line: "Female athletes have the superior understanding that relationships are more important than the game." Good descriptions of the early exercises in UNC's Competitive Cauldron training program. Available only on the used book market.

Dorrance, Anson, and Averbuch, Gloria. *The Vision of a Champion: Advice and Inspiration From the World's Most Successful Soccer Coach*. This is the UNC Chapel Hill program in depth, written in part for the high level U15-18 player. Chapter 11 ("Soccer Supporters – Players and Their Parents") is a must read for parents and players—boys and girls.

Duckworth, Angela. Grit: *The Power of Passion and Perseverance*. The researcher who has led the research into the "grit factor" describes her work and its implications. Filled with "sticky quote" ideas to use with players.

Dweck, Carol. Mindset: *The New Psychology of Success*. (★★★★★) Great companion book to *The Talent Code*. Explains the importance of one's beliefs about the limits of human potential and particularly how those beliefs impact personal qualities like perseverance, resilience, and "grit." Superb information about words that work when supporting a young athlete as well as some surprisingly to avoid.

Ericsson, Anders, and Pool, Robert. *Peak: Secrets from the New Science of Expertise*. Relates Ericsson's experiments that led to identifying the concept of Deliberate Practice. Fascinating section on how without ongoing effort to improve skills, competency in those skills will decline even if they are regularly used.

Farrey, Tom. *Game On: The All-American Race to Make Champions of Our Children*. A look at how some youth sports organizations really go over the top and how to deal with it.

Foudy, Julie. *Choose to Matter: Being Courageously and Fabulously YOU*. (★★★★★) The former captain of the world and Olympic champion US Women's National Team shares the lessons taught at her Sports Leadership Academy.

Galloway, Jeff. *Galloway's Book on Running*. Not soccer, but a good guide to assembling training regimens with the proper mix of activity, intensity, rest, and recovery.

Gladwell, Malcolm. *Outliers: The Story of Success*. (★★★★★) Looks at seemingly unusual circumstances that surround clusters of successful people in a variety of fields. Popularized the notion that 10,000 hours of preparation was a prerequisite to world-class achievement in any field. "No one has yet found a case in which true world-class expertise was accomplished in less time."

Gregg, Lauren. *The Champion Within*. A coaching manual for high-level player development by the long-time Women's National Team assistant coach. Good sections on nutrition and sports medicine.

Hogan, Frank. *Uncommon Goals*. A video with an insider's look at the Women's National Team 1991-1996 (Akers, Heinrichs, Hamm, Foudy, Lilly) The 12-year-old juggling through the opening segment did it in one take. Available from www.davebrett.com/Women.htm in the "Documentaries about women's soccer" section.

Holt, John. *How Children Learn* and *How Children Fail*. A pair of classics.

Hyman, Mark. Until It Hurts: *America's Obsession with Youth Sports and How It Harms Our Kids*. One of the best looks at the professionalization of youth sports. A good book for parents whose children are beginning the climb the ladder of play in their sports.

Lemov, Doug: *Teach Like a Champion 2.0*. (★★★★★) A collection of innovative teaching techniques. Things like *Check for Understanding*, *Cold Call*, and *Plan for Error* should be in the toolkit of every coach. Lemov is now working with US Soccer to teach them in the Federation's coaching courses (You can also get most of this information and much more by going to Lemov's twitter feed.)

Longman, Jere. *The Girls of Summer: The U.S. Women's Soccer Team and How It Changed the World*. The ultimate account of the US Women's National Team in the 1999 Women's World Cup.

McArdle, Megan. *The Up Side of Down: Why Failing Well Is the Key to Success*. What separates those who recover from failure from those who do not.

McGinniss, Joe. *The Miracle of Castel Di Sangro: A Tale of Passion and Folly in the Heart of Italy*. Nonfiction. A great read for a Soccer Dad.

Nater, Sven, and Gallimore, Ron. *You Haven't Taught Until They Have Learned: John Wooden's Teaching Principles and Practices*. (★★★★★) The place to start your study of legendary UCLA basketball coach John Wooden.

O'Sullivan, John. *Changing the Game: The Parent's Guide to Raising Happy, High Performing Athletes, and Giving Youth Sports Back to our Kids*. (An ongoing resource for parents and coaches is the Changing the Game Project's twitter feed.)

Rosenthal, Robert. *Pygmalion in the Classroom: Teacher Expectation and Pupils' Intellectual Development*. Believe you have a group of superstars and you will demand more, reward more, and create superstars. Expectations play a critical role in how we approach and develop players.

Saxena, Ashu. *Soccer Strategies for Sustained Coaching Success*. A syllabus for coaching high-level teams of 14- to 18-year-olds. Extraordinarily detailed from a coach who has led teams to National Youth Championships.

Silby, Caroline. *Games Girls Play*. Graduate school level sports psychology.

Smith, Kieran. *Rondos & Positional Games: How to Use Spain's Secret Weapon*. Only available in a Kindle edition.

Sokolove, Michael. *Warrior Girls: Protecting Our Daughters Against the Injury Epidemic in Women's Sports*. (★★★★★) Why? Early specialization in a single sport, lack of adequate recovery time, a focus on results over development at younger and younger ages, and a culture that urges girls to be strong and don't complain (not always a good thing). Here's an important guide to safety and sanity in sports for young female athletes.

Syed, Matthew. *Bounce: Mozart, Federer, Picasso, Beckham, and the Science of Success*. (★★★★★) Challenging the idea that greatness comes from innate talent rather than effort, practice, opportunity, solid coaching at younger ages and a healthy dose of "necessary failure."

Syed, Matthew. *Black Box Thinking: Why Most People Never Learn from Their Mistakes—But Some Do*. Syed argues that the most important determinant of success in any field is an acknowledgment of failure and a willingness to engage with it.

Thompson, Jim. *Shooting in the Dark*. A male coach's first experience coaching female athletes. Hilarious reading for those who've been there.

Thompson, Jim. *The Double-Goal Coach: Developing Winners in Sports and Life.* (★★★★★) The Positive Coaching Alliance founder's prescription for a mastery approach to youth sports (where the result on the scoreboard is viewed as less important than the effort, learning, and improvement of the athlete). A proactive approach without an emphasis on the horror stories found in Engh, Farrey, Hyman et al.

Thompson, Jim. *Positive Sports Parenting.* How to. Elegantly simple. The information on "Empowering Conversations" between parent and child is terrific.

Tough, Paul. *How Children Succeed – Grit, Curiosity, and the Hidden Power of Character.* Tough argues that the qualities that matter more in driving success are tied to personal character: skills like perseverance, curiosity, optimism, and self-control.

Tutko, Thomas, and Bruns, William. *Winning Is Everything (and Other American Myths).* Out of print, but available on the used book market. Tutko was the first to zero in on the trend toward "win-at-all-costs" in youth sports.

Vetter, Steve, and Antoniuk, Dan. *Soccer U.* A series of DVDs, including the "Blast the Ball" video about teaching soccer techniques. Very detailed with lots of little ideas that can make a big difference. Available at www.soccerwebsite.org.

Wooden, John with Jamison, Steve. *Wooden: A Lifetime of Reflections On and Off the Court.* Many consider the "Wizard of Westwood" to be the greatest coach of all time.

Wolff, Rick. *Good Sports. Sports Illustrated* columnist's "concerned parent's guide to competitive youth sports."

Zigarelli, Michael. *The Messiah Method: The Seven Disciplines of the Winningest College Soccer Program in America.* From 2000 to 2010, the Messiah College soccer program—the men's team and women's team combined—posted the best record in NCAA soccer: 472 wins, 31 losses, and 20 ties. Here's how an extraordinary culture married personal and athletic excellence.

Zimmerman, Jean, and Reavill, Gil. *Raising Our Athletic Daughters.* Gender equity and other issues in girls' and women's sports. The section on eating disorders is sobering.

EPILOGUE

"Too many years ago I shared coaching duties with a fellow teacher—let's call him Brian—at a small private school on the East Coast...We were the proverbial teachers one page in the textbook ahead of the students; except there was no textbook. In time, both of us moved on to other places and other responsibilities."

Shortly after the manuscript for *Players 1st* went to the publisher, a coaching opportunity as daunting as my first middle school team came along. It was to lead a group that was to attend the team camp of the North Carolina Girls Soccer Camp. The players, ages 13-15, came from a camp-like program. They knew each other to a certain degree but were usually opponents on Game Day rather than teammates.

I didn't know them at all, had no idea what made each one tick, yet went about the task of trying to prepare them for the challenges of that particular environment, both the soccer components and the cultural demands. I saw all of them play at least once. As expected, they had very strong individual skills. Still, the seven 90-minute prep sessions (late Sunday afternoons on weekends where most had played more than one game) were dreadfully clinical as they were introduced to some of the things they would see later, including training the back-to-goal situation and the underlying principles of UNC's system of play.

To their credit the athletes endured it, occasionally showing signs that the concepts being worked on during the prep sessions *might* be taking hold. But the trip to the airport was filled with WCPGW thoughts, and the conclusion that it could be "a lot."

The plane ride finally provided an opportunity for everyone to get better acquainted, and the next morning, a light pre-camp training session—the first time ever all had been on the field at the same time—was promising.

Camp began that afternoon with an "evaluation game," the group's first 11v11 match together. As planned, we used as best we could the UNC system, which was very different from what most were used to, and rotated all the players through the three lines of play—front, middle, and back. (Why make it easy?) Ragged at the start, things began to click as the match progressed, finally resulting in a rain of shots and goals on the other team in the final five minutes. At dinner, the girls were told that they'd been selected to be the players used in two of the five demonstrations the camp staff would present before the evening session. After that, they had their evening session with one of the most demanding coaches (whom, of course, we'd asked for), one known for bringing something "all the way back" if it wasn't just right. She did. Often. They loved it. This was getting interesting.

Things only got better from there. By the third day, when the hours, heat and humidity should have been taking a toll, the players were on fire, in full on **"Go-For-It"** mode, total sponges continuing to soak up everything being presented, on or off the field. (They would later say that the lectures with inspirational messages about self-belief, competitive fire, and "love for the ball" were their favorite things.) They finally even listened to the sage advice of their coach about the value of a brief nap after lunch. Clearly something very special was happening.

How special was revealed in the 1v1 debriefings after the camp had ended. Those were structured around four questions: 1. Did you ever find yourself thinking, "I've never worked this hard?" 2. The same but "I've never played this well?" 3. "Has this experience made you a different player?" 4. The Power Ball: "Has it made you a different person?" From the 14 respondents, "yes" was the answer all 56 times. The follow-up discussions (after the "how does that feel?" question you just had to ask; imagine those responses!) centered on how they planned not only to maintain that level of performance but seek to bring it out in their club teammates as well, which they seemed to be doing.

To be part of such a magnificent, transformative situation is a coach's dream. Oh to be able to bring that back to those teams from back in the day.

So many have contributed to the journey from then to now. Starting with the faculty at Saint Louis Priory School. The rigor of that classical secondary school education produces lifelong learners. It was my formal education, anything else was, to quote a classmate, "polish on the diamond." Of special note: Father Austin Rennick and Mr. Gerry Wilkes, who taught you to write, and the brilliant Mr. Ed Cook, who provided an enduring lesson about the value of using absurdity in an instructional setting.

There have been many soccer influences. Soccer America founder Clay Berling's editorial in *Soccer America* about the formation of a group to underwrite a bid for a World Cup in the USA changed my—and America's—relationship with the sport in ways I could never have anticipated. Decades later, that gift continues to give. There have been opportunities to work with master coaches like Franz von Balkom, Emilio Romero, and Tom Stone; to learn from the likes of Anson Dorrance, the late Tony DiCicco, and Jeff Tipping who always have time for your questions; to watch and learn from all the clinicians at the annual conventions of the NSCAA, now United Soccer Coaches. (If you've never attended, it's time.)

Charlie Cook of Coerver Coaching has been a wellspring of ideas, while Chelo Curi at Coerver Colorado (where every session begins with the words "Let's Get Better") provided and continues to provide a platform for test-driving inventive ideas and programs. The leaders of Coerver programs in the different states are an amazing group; much has been learned from Simon Whitehead, Tom Reilly, Roy Dunshee, and others. Ashu Saxena's wonderful book was an amazing inspiration for someone thinking about writing on preparing players for the sort of program he describes.

The ideas of Bruce Brown at Proactive Coaching about the role of character in sport are fascinating, especially those concepts like Positive Conditioning which are so counterintuitive. Jim Thompson, founder and executive director of the Positive Coaching Alliance, continues to do important work in trying to damp down the more insane characteristics found in the youth sports experience. To attend PCA's annual weekend workshop for the organization's trainers is mind-boggling for the wisdom and virtuosity found in that group (among them Rubin Nieves, the master of the comment disguised as a question," who trains the trainers?"). More recently, John O'Sullivan at the Changing the Game Project is doing just that.

Activities and ideas found in this book have come from, among others and apologies if I miss someone: Bob Christensen, Colleen Evans, Jill Mapes, Colin Schmidt, Deb Swan, Ed and Vicki Shaw, Ed Montojo, Jordan Crum, Mark Bahn, Mike Giuliano, Roby Stahl, Scott Raber, Theresa Echtermyer, Todd Gette, Tracey Bates Leone, Tyler Orzak, Vitor Bravo, the folks (present and past) at Adirondack Camp, and the members of the and-again soccer coaching forum. The forum, found at www.and-again.com is not as vibrant as it once was, but long-time members like AFB, Paulee, the inimitable CoachKev, and even Oldtimer still check in regularly. If you need a question about soccer coaching answered, they'll get it done.

And finally, in the adult end of things, an adage from my grandfather: "People are always potential allies until they die." So in that vein, props to those who have from time to time added value in the worst way: "Nobody is totally useless; they can always serve as a bad example."

When you do this for a while, you discover that you're often learning as much or more from your athletes as they are from you. Certain groups stand out in this respect, including that first middle school team and a varsity basketball team appropriately known as the Seven Dwarfs. A succession of such groups has picked up the collective title of The Crash Dummies as they've been subjected to first attempts at implementing any number of the activities found in this book. Those that stand out include the mighty Jaguars, the teams at EHS in the 1988-1989 school year, the European Tour teams notably those in 1995 (who inspired the collection of Great Soccer Habits) and 1998, the group of '95-'96 campers (eight of whom so far have collected All-American honors), the '98-'99 group now beginning to tear it up on college fields, and the Magnificents whose story is found above. Then there's the current work in progress, whose skills at a very young age are always described as "ridiculous." They could be very interesting.

And as for that Brian guy, he's done OK, too, recently picking up his 500th win as a coach.

PLAYERS 1ST

CREDITS

Design and Layout

Cover and Interior Design: Annika Naas

Typesetting: Guido Maetzing, www.mmedia-agentur.de

Editorial

Managing Editor: Elizabeth Evans

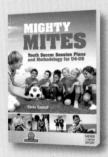
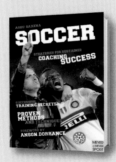